Closing the
Courthouse Door

Closing *the* Courthouse Door

*How Your Constitutional Rights
Became Unenforceable*

ERWIN CHEMERINSKY

Yale UNIVERSITY PRESS/NEW HAVEN & LONDON

Yale University Press books may be purchased in
quantity for educational, business, or promotional use.
For information, please e-mail sales.press@yale.edu
(U.S. office) or sales@yaleup.co.uk (U.K. office).

Set in Minion type by Newgen North America.
Printed in the United States of America.

ISBN 978-0-300-21158-0 (hardcover : alk. paper)

Library of Congress Control Number: 2016941955

A catalogue record for this book is available from the
British Library.

This paper meets the requirements of ANSI/NISO z39.48–1992
(Permanence of Paper).

10 9 8 7 6 5 4 3 2 1

For Catherine

Contents

Preface

I have been teaching constitutional law and federal courts for thirty-six years and have witnessed dramatic changes in the law. Many of these are familiar to lawyers and nonlawyers alike. The United States Supreme Court has held that corporations can spend unlimited amounts of money in election campaigns to get candidates elected or defeated. The Court has held that the Second Amendment protects a right of individuals to possess guns, at least in their homes for the sake of security. The Court has imposed limits on the application of the death penalty, preventing it from being used against the intellectually disabled or for crimes committed by juveniles or for crimes other than homicide. The Court has found that there is a constitutional right to marriage equality and that state laws prohibiting same-sex marriage are unconstitutional. Every year, in late June, the headlines are dominated by Supreme Court decisions that change the law and affect all of us.

But there are other Supreme Court decisions that significantly change the law and affect all of us that receive far less publicity. Over the decades since I became a law professor, the Supreme Court has made it far more difficult for those who are injured, even egregiously and horribly hurt, to have access to the federal courts. In case after case, year after year, the Supreme Court has closed the courthouse doors to those whose rights have been violated. The Court increasingly has held that state and local governments cannot be sued for their constitutional violations, that government officers who violate people's rights are immune from liability, that injured individuals lack "standing" to sue in federal court, that those convicted—even wrongly so—cannot be heard in federal court, that suits and especially class action suits are barred by language in form contracts requiring arbitration.

These, though, are decisions about procedural doctrines—sovereign immunity, *Bivens* suits, absolute and qualified immunity, standing, habeas corpus, abstention—that are unfamiliar to most nonlawyers and even many attorneys. These are not cases that gain the attention of the media. But rights are meaningless if they cannot be enforced. Closing the courthouse doors to those whose rights have been violated has the same effect as if the rights did not exist at all. The only difference is that the Court decisions rejecting rights get headlines, while rulings dismissing cases on these procedural grounds garner little attention.

My goal is to explain how the Supreme Court, through a series of doctrines and decisions, has closed the federal courthouse doors to those whose rights have been violated. I want readers to see how these rulings affect real people, and ultimately all of us. My vision, as explained in the first chapter, is that federal courts should be available to all who claim a violation of their constitutional rights. Above all, the federal courts exist to enforce the Constitution. In this book, I seek both to describe the Supreme Court's rulings that close the federal courthouse doors and to prescribe concrete solutions to ensure that those who have been injured are assured of their days in court.

My hope is that my analysis and proposals are ones that conservatives and liberals alike can embrace. Access to justice should be non-ideological in that all from every part of the political spectrum should be able to accept its importance. Yet, I also am aware that most of the decisions that I am criticizing in this book had the conservative justices in the majority. For decades, conservative justices have achieved their goal of narrowing rights by keeping federal courts from hearing cases and providing relief.

Perhaps I am unduly optimistic that liberals and conservatives can reconsider these cases and doctrines and reason from the same basic premise: The preeminent role of the federal courts is to enforce the Constitution, and doctrines which prevent this should be reexamined and changed.

As I wrote this book, I had in mind as a title, "Enforcing the Constitution: The Role of the Federal Courts." This expresses my central thesis, developed in the chapters that follow: the most important role of the federal courts is to enforce the Constitution; many doctrines created by the Supreme Court prevent the federal courts from fulfilling this mission; and these should be changed—by Court decision and legislative action. This book is a product of over three decades of frustration, as a professor and as a lawyer, with a Supreme Court that has lost sight of the basic reason for having federal courts and of the need to ensure that the Constitution is enforced. It is a book that is written in the fervent hope and belief that this can and must be changed to ensure that the Constitution's most important guarantees will have meaning in the years and decades ahead.

Why Do We Have Federal Courts?

I n 2014, the United States Court of Appeals for the District of
Columbia Circuit dismissed a lawsuit brought by a dozen current
and former sailors and Marines who had been severely sexually
harassed or raped while in military service.[1] The Court of Appeals
accepted that the plaintiffs had suffered great harms and egregious violations of their rights, but it concluded that the federal courts could provide no relief.[2] It described this resolution of the case as "easy."

Ariana Klay was one of the plaintiffs. While she was an active duty
lieutenant in the U.S. Marine Corps, her fellow Marines gang-raped her
at her home, a few blocks away from the Marine barracks in Washington, D.C. Apparently, one of Klay's colleagues felt that she had embar-
rassed him in front of a group of Junior Marines.[3] That Marine and a
friend, a former Marine, showed up at Klay's house one day around 5:00
in the morning and raped her in retaliation.

Klay testified that in the months before the rape, she was constantly sexually harassed. From her first day of military service, she said
that she and the other women in the barracks were treated with hostility by her fellow Marines. She described the culture in the barracks as
"vile."[4] When she reported the harassment to her superior, he told her
to "deal with it" and refused to take any action.

Not until Klay filed a restricted report—which gives the victim access to medical care or advocacy services—did the Marine Corps investigate the harassment. Although a restricted report is supposed to be confidential, Klay's rape was widely known soon after the report was filed and then leaked.[5] The Marine Corps investigation implied that because Klay wore skirts (which were regulation-length and part of her uniform) and makeup, and exercised in tank tops and running shorts, therefore she had invited and welcomed the harassment. During the pretrial hearing on the rape in the military court, Klay was questioned for sixteen hours, during which she repeatedly was asked inappropriate and humiliating questions. The prosecuting attorney made no objections on Klay's behalf. The court eventually ruled, mostly on the basis of the two perpetrators' testimony, that the sex was consensual and that there had been no rape. Afterward, because she had complained about the incident, the harassment grew so severe that Klay at one point attempted suicide.

Janet Galla was another plaintiff in the lawsuit. The Court of Appeals explained what happened to her:

> Galla served in the Navy from 1999 to 2005 as a Hospital Corpsman. On June 11, 2004, after having dinner with a group of friends, Galla returned to her ship. While she was checking her email in the ship's Medical Department, a fellow Corpsman asked if he could show her something in one of the Department's operating rooms. She followed him into an operating room, where he tried to kiss her. She resisted, asked him to stop, and tried to leave the room, but he prevented her from escaping and then raped her. Galla immediately reported the rape. Although her attacker was ultimately convicted and sent to prison, Galla faced retaliation from those within her chain of command. She was not allowed to work in enclosed spaces with male colleagues, a restriction her superiors claimed was for her own protection. This limitation not only made it difficult for her to do her job, but left her feeling ostracized from her shipmates. Galla began to receive negative performance evaluations and was

eventually told by her commander that it would be best for "morale" if she left the ship. She transferred to a duty station on land, but the retaliation continued when her new chain of command learned about the rape and the ongoing investigation. . . . One member of her new command told her that the rape was only "five minutes of her life" and she needed to "get over it already." In the face of such harassment and ostracism, Galla accepted her superiors' offer of immediate separation from the Navy in 2005.[6]

Galla and Klay were joined by ten other plaintiffs, all of whom had suffered sexual harassment or rape. When some of them reported "being raped by their colleagues, they were labeled as 'troublemakers,'"[7] a label that eventually got them discharged or forced them to resign from the military.[8] Some of the survivors "were directed to be silent, and refrain from telling anyone about the rapes and the subsequent mistreatment."[9] All of the plaintiffs "were on active duty when they suffered these sexual assaults and retaliatory actions at the hands of other service members."[10] Further, most of the sexual assaults detailed in the plaintiffs' complaint "took place on military bases, military ships, or during foreign deployment."[11] The rest "occurred at private residences that were located off-base or in connection with social events with other service members."[12]

Although the survivors faced immediate and lifelong consequences from their assaults, the rapists suffered few repercussions. "The vast majority," the women's complaint noted, "were not prosecuted or punished in any meaningful way."[13] Those who felt any consequences at all were permitted by their superiors to "receive nonjudicial punishment and to be honorably discharged."[14]

In 2012, Klay, Galla, and the other plaintiffs filed suit in federal district court against nine defendants: the three most recent Secretaries of Defense, Secretaries of the Navy, and Commandants of the Marine Corps. They alleged that the defendants were responsible for what they suffered and for the violations of their constitutional rights. The complaint explained that the defendants were fully aware of the prevalence of sexual misconduct and retaliation in the Navy and Marine Corps and had the power to eliminate it, yet they had taken no effective steps to do so.

But the United States Court of Appeals for the District of Columbia Circuit ordered the plaintiffs' suit dismissed, saying that military officials cannot be sued in federal court for constitutional violations. The Court declared: "Their appeal is both difficult and easy. Difficult, because it involves shocking allegations that members of this nation's armed forces who put themselves at risk to protect our liberties were abused in such a vile and callous manner. Easy, because plaintiffs seek relief under a legal theory that is patently deficient." The Court did not question the plaintiffs' allegations or their assertion that the defendants, top government officials, were ultimately responsible for what occurred. But it held that the federal courts cannot provide relief to those who have suffered violations of even their most basic rights while in military service. It concluded: "In affirming the district court's dismissal, we do not take lightly the severity of plaintiffs' suffering or the harm done by sexual assault and retaliation in our military. But the existence of grievous wrongs does not free the judiciary to authorize any and all suits that might seem just."[15]

The Court of Appeals accepted (as it had to at that stage of the litigation) that the women had been raped, sexually harassed, and retaliated against. But the women had absolutely no remedy. They could not sue the United States because it has sovereign immunity; that is, the United States government is completely immune from being sued unless there is a federal statute authorizing it. No such statute existed here. The victims could not sue their rapists and harassers, or anyone else in the military, because the Supreme Court has ruled that people cannot sue others in the military or its chain of command.[16] Although it agreed that female service members have a right to be free from sexual assaults and harassment, the Court concluded that federal courts cannot enforce that right or provide a remedy when it is violated.

This case is not an anomaly. Many legal doctrines fashioned by the Supreme Court over the last several decades prevent the federal courts from providing any remedy to those whose constitutional rights have been violated. The Court has expanded the immunity of government and government officials, making it difficult to sue even when there are egregious constitutional violations. The Court has restricted who has standing to sue in federal courts and limited the constitutional claims that can be adjudicated. Congress and the Supreme Court have greatly restricted the ability of federal courts to grant a writ of habeas corpus in favor of those convicted of crimes, meaning that wrongly convicted individuals are often left without recourse. In recent decisions, the Court has changed procedural doctrines to make it harder for injured plaintiffs to get into federal courts, especially with class action suits.

My purpose in this book is to describe these doctrines and prescribe changes. Because they involve technical doctrines that are often about legal procedure—matters like sovereign immunity, absolute and qualified immunity for individual officers, justiciability principles such as standing and the political question doctrine, habeas corpus, and pleading—they do not make headlines. But they mean that people whose rights have been violated and who have suffered great injuries, including even fatal ones, are left without recourse. They have rights under the Constitution, but the federal courts cannot enforce them.

If the Supreme Court were to hold that the government can give unlimited amounts of money to religious schools, the decision would make the front-page headline of every newspaper in the country. But if the Court were to hold that no one has standing to challenge the government when it gives money to parochial schools, that would get far less attention. Yet the effect is exactly the same: if no one can challenge a government action in court, the government can do what it wants. If the Secretary of Defense announced that men are permitted to rape and sexually harass women in the Army, Navy, Air Force, and Marines, the country would be justifiably outraged. But the Court of Appeals got almost no attention when it ruled that women in military service who are raped and harassed have no remedy.

Why Do We Have Federal Courts?

This is an obvious injustice, and if the situation of Klay, Galla, and their co-plaintiffs makes you feel angry, you are not alone. It is a situation that cries out for remedy. To understand how to correct it, in a manner consistent with our constitutional values, we must start with a question at the very foundation of our judicial system: why do we have federal courts at all?

The preeminent purpose of the federal courts is to enforce the United States Constitution. Legal doctrines should be directed toward allowing the federal courts to fulfill this mission.

This position should not be controversial, yet it is so at odds with many legal doctrines that it needs to be justified. The first justification comes from *Marbury v. Madison,* the 1803 Supreme Court decision which held that federal courts have the power to review the constitutionality of federal laws and executive actions.[17] The Constitution does not expressly give the federal judiciary the authority to do this; it is silent on the subject. In *Marbury v. Madison,* the Supreme Court found this authority in the Constitution, and the power of judicial review has existed ever since.

The facts of *Marbury v. Madison* are familiar. On February 27, 1801, less than a week before the end of President John Adams's term, Congress adopted the Organic Act of the District of Columbia, which authorized the President to appoint forty-two justices of the peace. Adams had lost his reelection bid, and his and George Washington's Federalist Party was about to leave power. Adams announced his nominations on March 2. On March 3, the day before Thomas Jefferson's inauguration as President, the Senate confirmed the nominees. Immediately, the departing Secretary of State, John Marshall (who was also Chief Justice of the Supreme Court), put the seal of the United States on these commissions and set out to deliver them. A few commissions, including one for William Marbury, were not delivered before Jefferson's inauguration. President Jefferson instructed his incoming Secretary of State, James Madison, to withhold the undelivered commissions.

Marbury filed suit in the United States Supreme Court seeking a writ of mandamus—a court order—to compel Madison to deliver his commission. He claimed that the Judiciary Act of 1789 authorized the Supreme Court to grant mandamus in a proceeding filed initially in the Supreme Court. Although Marbury's petition was filed in December 1801, the Supreme Court did not hear the case until 1803 because Congress had abolished the Court's June and December 1802 terms.

Near the beginning of his opinion, Chief Justice Marshall declared a basic principle of American government: "The very essence of civil liberty certainly consists in the right of every individual to claim the protection of the laws, whenever he receives an injury."[18] It follows that the preeminent role of the judiciary is to provide remedies to those whose rights have been violated.

The specific issue in *Marbury v. Madison* was whether the Court could give Marbury a remedy against the executive branch of government. The Court answered this by declaring that "the government of the United States has been emphatically termed a government of laws, and not of men."[19] In other words, no person—not even the President—is above the law.

Marbury's problem was that he filed his lawsuit initially in the Supreme Court under a provision of the Judiciary Act of 1789 that purportedly authorized this.[20] The Court concluded that the federal statute was unconstitutional because it expanded the Supreme Court's jurisdiction beyond what was authorized by Article III of the Constitution. Having decided that Congress had passed a law that was beyond its authority, the Court then considered the most important question: Did it nonetheless have to follow the law, or could it declare that provision unconstitutional? Marshall's decision began by stating: "The question, whether an act, repugnant to the Constitution, can become the law of the land, is a question deeply interesting to the United States; but, happily, not of an intricacy proportioned to its interest."[21] He then offered several reasons why the Court could declare federal laws unconstitutional.

Most important, he explained that the Constitution exists to impose limits on government powers, and these limits are meaningless unless subject to judicial enforcement. Borrowing from Alexander Hamilton's Federalist No. 78, Marshall wrote: "The powers of the legislature are defined and limited; and that those limits may not be mistaken or forgotten, the constitution is written."[22] And he went on, in perhaps the most frequently quoted words of the opinion: "It is emphatically the province and duty of the judicial department to say what the law is."[23] In other words, the Constitution depends on having judges with the power to enforce it.

I believe Marshall got it exactly right—and that is why *Marbury v. Madison* has been a cornerstone of American government for almost its entire history. The Constitution exists to limit government, and the limits are meaningful only if they are enforced. Enforcement often will not happen without the judiciary. Therefore, the most important role of the federal courts should be seen as enforcing the Constitution.

Of course, federal courts are not the only institution that enforces the Constitution. State courts also exist and can and do enforce the Constitution. But this in no way diminishes the importance of the federal courts doing so. State courts often have no authority over federal officers or the federal government. For example, it is firmly established that state courts cannot grant habeas corpus to federal prisoners.[24] Nor would it make sense to have state courts resolve issues of federal separation of powers, such as when there is a dispute between Congress and the President. To pick a recent example, it would not have been desirable to have a state court decide the constitutionality of a federal law requiring that the State Department allow the parents of children born in Jerusalem to have the passport indicate "Israel" as the birthplace.[25] In situations like this, when there is a constitutional impasse between the other branches of the federal government, the federal courts must act as the umpire. Also, many of the doctrines that keep federal courts from enforcing the Constitution—such as the limits on suing government entities and government officers—apply just the same way in the state courts.[26]

More generally, the very existence of federal courts reflects a particular view of how the Constitution should be enforced.[27] Under the Articles of Confederation, there were neither federal courts nor a federal judicial power. Article III of the Constitution created the Supreme Court and authorized the creation of the lower federal court because of a belief that the enforcement of federal law could not be left exclusively to the state judiciaries. Congress created the lower federal courts in 1789, and they have existed ever since, because the Supreme Court by itself does not have the capacity to review all state court decisions. Federal courts exist, above all, and have since their creation, to enforce federal law, and the most important federal law is the Constitution.

Nor can we rely on voluntary compliance from the other branches and levels of government.[28] Far too often, legislators and officials have a strong incentive not to comply with the Constitution. These situations, which often involve the most vulnerable in society, are where the federal judiciary is most needed.

Most dramatically, those without political power have nowhere to turn except the judiciary for the protection of their constitutional rights. The reality is that participants in the political process have little reason to be responsive to the constitutional rights of prisoners or criminal defendants or those who are not citizens. These individuals lack political power—they do not give money to political candidates, they generally are prohibited from voting, they are unpopular and often unsympathetic. When was the last time a legislature acted to expand the rights of prisoners or criminal defendants? In the competition for scarce dollars, legislatures have every political incentive to spend as little as possible on prisoners. Politicians compete to sound tough on crime, not to expand defendants' rights. Yet how much worse might it be if politicians and prison officials knew that no court would review the constitutionality of their actions? Admittedly, the Supreme Court has a less than stellar record of protecting these individuals' rights, but there is no doubt that judicial review has provided protections for criminal defendants and dramatically improved conditions for countless prison inmates abandoned by the political process. Although these are obvious examples, the nature of democracy is that the elected branches of government are often insensitive to the rights of those who lack political influence.

More generally, if not for the federal courts, what is to stop the Congress or the President from enacting a law that is unconstitutional but politically expedient? What, other than the drastic remedy of impeachment, is to stop the President from pursuing unconstitutional policies when they are politically popular? Often there is no one, other than the courts, to deter wrongdoing and compensate those injured by constitutional violations.

This view of the federal judiciary inevitably is derived from the purpose of the Constitution itself. My agreement with *Marbury v. Madison* ultimately is based on my belief that the written Constitution exists

to be the supreme law of the land and to limit what everyone in government, at all levels, can do.

Harvard Law Professor Laurence Tribe powerfully asked: "Why
would a nation that rests legality on the consent of the governed choose
to constitute its political life in terms of commitments to an original
agreement—made by the people, binding on their children, and deliberately structured so as to be difficult to change?" It is hardly original or
profound to answer this question by observing that the framers deliberately made the Constitution very difficult to change as a way of preventing tyranny of the majority and protecting the rights of the minority
from oppression by social majorities. If the structure of government
were placed in a statute, the urge to create dictatorial powers in times of
crisis might be irresistible. If individual liberties were protected only by
statutes, a tyrannical government could overrule them. If terms of office were specified in a statute rather than in the Constitution, those in
power could alter the rules to remain in power.

Thus the Constitution represents society's attempt to tie its own
hands, to limit its ability to fall prey to weaknesses that might harm or
undermine its most cherished values. History teaches that under the pas-
sions of the moment, people may sacrifice even the most basic principles
of liberty and justice. The Constitution is society's attempt to protect
itself from itself. It enumerates basic values—regular elections, separation of powers, individual rights, equality—and makes departure very
difficult. In large part, the decision to be governed by the Constitution
is animated by fear that a political majority could gain control of government and disenfranchise and perhaps persecute the minority. Compared to all other laws, the Constitution is uniquely difficult to amend or
alter, precisely to ensure that the limits it sets are not easily changed.

Accordingly, in deciding who should be the authoritative interpreter of the Constitution, the answer is the branch of government that
can best enforce the Constitution's limits against the desires of political
majorities. By this criterion, the federal judiciary is the obvious choice.
It is the institution most insulated from political pressures. Article III
of the Constitution provides that federal court judges have life tenure
unless impeached, and that their salary may not be decreased during

their terms of office. Unlike legislators or the President, they never face reelection.

Furthermore, the method of federal judicial selection reinforces its antimajoritarian character. Unlike the House of Representatives, whose members are elected at the same time, or the Senate, where one third of the members are chosen in each election, the Court's members are appointed one at a time, as vacancies arise. No single administration is generally able to appoint a majority of the Court or the federal judiciary. The result is that the Court reflects many political views, not just the one that dominates at a particular time.

Thus the primary reason for having federal courts—the Supreme Court and the lower federal courts—is to enforce the Constitution against the will of the majority. I do not mean to suggest that this is their only role. Twenty-five years ago, I co-authored with Professor (and later Dean) Larry Kramer an article entitled "Defining the Role of the Federal Courts," in which we identified the federal courts' functions.[29] First on the list was "enforcing the Constitution."[30] We also identified five other important functions:[31]

- protecting the interests of the federal government as a sovereign, including by providing a forum for enforcement of federal criminal law;
- serving as an umpire in interstate disputes;
- assuring uniform interpretation and application of federal law;
- developing federal common law, a body of judge-made law in the absence of statutes; and
- hearing appeals.

These categories are not mutually exclusive. There is no tension between saying that federal courts exist preeminently to enforce the Constitution and also identifying these other functions. I, of course, accept all of these as important tasks for the federal judiciary. But my focus in this book is on the task we intentionally put first: enforcing the Constitution.

Why the Judiciary?

There are other reasons, too, why the judiciary is the branch of government that is best suited to enforce the Constitution.

First, the judiciary is the only institution obligated to hear the complaints of a single person. For the most part, the federal judiciary's jurisdiction is mandatory. Although the Supreme Court can choose which cases to hear, a lower federal court must (with relatively rare exceptions) rule on every case properly filed with it. Long ago, Chief Justice Marshall wrote, "It is most true that this Court will not take jurisdiction if it should not but it is equally true that it must take jurisdiction if it should. . . . We have no more right to decline the exercise of jurisdiction which is given, than to usurp that which is not given."[32]

The legislature and the executive, on the other hand, are under no duty to hear any single person's complaints. An individual or small group complaining of an injustice to a legislator or the president could be easily ignored. If only a few constituents care about something, and if acting to help them would consume too much time for the number of votes it will yield, they often will be ignored. Moreover, if helping the few will hurt more constituents, the few are likely to be disregarded no matter how just their cause. To use the example mentioned above, prisoners are a constituency with little political power. In many states, felons are permanently disenfranchised from voting, meaning that elected officials need not worry about meeting their demands.[33] Providing adequate resources for prisoners—for their shelter, food, medical care, and training—requires expenditures unlikely to be popular with taxpayers, and certainly less popular than if the money were spent on almost anything else. With no constituency to pressure for their humane treatment, prisoners' rights and needs are likely to be ignored.

The courts, however, are obligated to rule on any properly filed complaint, no matter whether the litigant is rich or poor, powerful or powerless, incarcerated or not. The judiciary is much more likely than the legislature to listen to criminal defendants' claims that their rights were violated or to poor individuals' objections that they are denied equal justice—because they must at least give such claims a hearing. The Constitution's purpose of protecting the minority from the tyranny of the majority is best fulfilled by an institution obligated to listen to the minority.

Second, the judiciary is not only the branch most likely to listen to complaints, it is also most likely to respond to them. The judiciary is supposed to decide each case on its own merits, subject to the accepted norm that like cases should be treated alike. In every case where there is an allegation of a constitutional violation, the judiciary is obligated, if it has jurisdiction and if there is no way to decide the case on nonconstitutional grounds, to issue a constitutional ruling. The legislature, by contrast, need not decide each matter before it on its merits—or at all. Logrolling, vote trading, and the tabling of bills are accepted parts of the legislative process. Procedural devices like the filibuster and holds often let a minority prevent legislative action; for decades Southerners in the Senate used them to block civil rights legislation. Although legislators are forbidden by their oath of office to enact laws they believe to be unconstitutional, they are not required to provide a remedy every time someone complains that government is violating the Constitution. Only the judiciary is obligated to respond to such complaints—and this makes the courts an ideal forum for ensuring that the Constitution is upheld.

Third, as the branch most insulated from day-to-day politics, the judiciary is the branch most willing to enforce the Constitution in the face of strong pressures from political majorities. Even if the legislature and executive were to listen to all claims and respond on the merits, they are still less likely to uphold the Constitution against the intense opposition of their constituents. It is this insulation that moved Alexis de Tocqueville to remark that "the power vested in the American courts of justice of pronouncing a statute unconstitutional forms one of the most powerful barriers that have been devised against the tyranny of political assemblies."[34]

The argument is not that legislators act in bad faith and disregard their oath to uphold the Constitution, although this sometimes happens. Rather, it is that constitutional interpretation inherently requires choices as to what the Constitution should mean: how its abstract values should be applied in specific situations. These choices are best made by an institution whose primary commitment is to the Constitution, not to gaining reelection. Professor Owen Fiss observed that "legislatures are not ideologically committed or institutionally suited to search for the meaning of constitutional values, but instead see their primary function in terms of registering the actual, current preferences of the people."[35] The judiciary is much more to be trusted in deciding, for instance, whether the Constitution should protect the speech activities of a politically unpopular group like the Nazi Party. Being committed to upholding the First Amendment and not faced with intense pressure from constituents, it is in a better position to decide whether school prayer violates the Constitution or whether the right of privacy includes the right of a woman to decide whether to have an abortion.

The best institution for interpreting the Constitution is thus not the one that most reflects the majority's current preferences. Constitutional interpretation is best done by a relatively politically insulated body. Harry Wellington explains:

> If society were to design an institution which had the job of finding society's set of moral principles and determining how they bear on concrete situations, that institution would be sharply different from one charged with proposing policies. The latter institution would be constructed with the understanding that it was to respond to the people's exercise of political power. . . . The former would be insulated from pressure. It would provide an environment conducive to rumination, reflection and analysis.[36]

Constitutional interpretation is a process of deciding what values are so fundamental that they should be safeguarded from political majorities. It makes little sense to entrust these decisions to those same political majorities. The judiciary's insulation and commitment to decisions based on the merits make it far better suited for this task. Alexander Bickel remarked that "courts have certain capacities for dealing with matters of principle that legislatures and the executive do not possess. Judges have, or should have, the leisure, the training, and the insulation to follow the ways of the scholar in pursuing the ends of government. This is crucial in sorting out the enduring values of a society."[37] Constitutional interpretation requires an institution to serve as the nation's moral conscience—an institution responsible for identifying values so important that they should not be sacrificed, and reminding the country when its own most cherished values are being violated. The Supreme Court, at times, has functioned in exactly this way: as a moral conscience holding the nation to its highest values.

The legislature is to be trusted least when the question is the constitutionality of a statute it has enacted. Allowing the same body to both enact laws and determine their constitutionality is no way to protect constitutional values. Review by another branch of government creates a necessary check on the majority. The executive veto provides something of a check, but Congress can override a veto. Moreover, the President is electorally accountable, at least in his first term, and may feel the same pressures as Congress. The judiciary is most detached from both the enactment of laws and the implementation of policies.

The Court's self-interest is in enhancing its long-term powers. Certainly, the judiciary's institutional self-interest justifies fear of its deciding cases to aggrandize its own powers. I would argue, however, that in resolving specific controversies it is better to trust an institution with only long-term interests than one with immediate interests in the outcome of the matter.

In sum, once it is decided that society should be governed by a constitution in order to make certain matters less amenable to majoritarian control, judicial review is an essential mechanism for interpreting and enforcing the document's limits on majority action.

The methods of judicial decision-making also make it the best institution for constitutional interpretation. The judiciary is the only institution committed to arriving at decisions based entirely on arguments and reasoning. Executive and legislative officials frequently offer no formal explanations for their decisions, and the statements they provide usually do not purport to be comprehensive. The judicial method is a process of hearing arguments from the parties, reaching decisions based on those arguments, and justifying the results with a written opinion. Although neither the Constitution nor any statute compels a court to write and publish opinions, publicly stated reasons for these decisions are embedded in the American legal system. It has long been recognized that the "traditional means of protecting the public from judicial fiat . . . [are] that judges give reasons for their results."[38]

For each ruling it hands down, the Court must write an opinion demonstrating that its decision was not arbitrary. It must explain why the values it is protecting are worthy of constitutional status, how those values are embodied in legal principles, and how they are to be applied in a specific case. It must also explain why its decision is consistent with prior holdings, is legitimately distinguishable from precedents, or justifies overruling conflicting cases.

In contrast, the legislature and the executive need not follow any particular decision-making process. Neither Congress nor the President is required, by law or tradition, to state reasons for their decisions. Although Congress produces legislative histories and the President issues executive proclamations, only the judiciary is committed to reaching its decisions through logical reasoning from principles rather than via political considerations. A legislature is allowed to make arbitrary choices unsupported by a guiding principle. Even though inevitably the Supreme Court's constitutional decisions are a product of the justices' ideology and values, the Court still must justify them in legally acceptable terms. Moreover, only the judiciary is committed to following precedent.

For all of these reasons, I believe the judiciary's essential role is to enforce the Constitution, and legal doctrines must facilitate its performing this task. There are alternative conceptions of the judicial role, but I reject them.

One such alternative is that the federal courts' primary role should be to resolve disputes between litigants, and that resolving constitutional issues is a secondary function that comes into play only when they are presented in litigation. The so-called traditional model described adjudication as a process for resolving disputes among private parties that have not been privately settled.[39]

This is not an accurate depiction of the role of the federal courts; nor should it be. Almost thirty years ago, Professor Abram Chayes wrote in a famous article: "Whatever its historical validity, the traditional model is clearly invalid as a description of much current civil litigation in the federal district courts. Perhaps the dominating characteristic of modern federal litigation is that lawsuits do not arise out of disputes between private parties about private rights. Instead, the object of litigation is the vindication of constitutional or statutory policies. The shift in the legal basis of the lawsuit explains many, but not all, facets of what is going on 'in fact' in federal trial courts."[40] The traditional model focuses only on private civil litigation and does not account for all of the criminal prosecutions in federal court that are brought by the federal government, or the civil cases where a government entity or officer is a party.

Moreover, the distinction between "private" and "public" adjudication is largely false. Most of the cases I describe in this book involve individuals who have suffered harm, often great harm, at the hands of the government and seek a remedy. Ariana Klay and Janet Galla sought redress for the violation of their rights that they suffered while in the military. In later chapters I will discuss other people who were injured and could not get into federal court because of the immunity of government entities and officers or because of restrictive procedural requirements. If any of these people have a desire to vindicate the Constitution, it is secondary to their personal interests. But the public's interest in these cases is different: it has to do with the rights we all should possess. Every decision is a precedent that controls lower courts in subsequent cases and even, more or less, the Supreme Court. Every Supreme Court decision is making law that affects all of us and not simply resolving individual disputes.

Finally, if there is a choice to be made between the "private rights" and the "public law" models of adjudication, the latter should be followed to the extent that it better facilitates enforcement of the Constitution. The choice of a model for adjudication, if one needs to be made, should follow from the reasons for having federal courts. My argument is that the most important role of the federal courts should be to enforce the Constitution and thus legal doctrines should facilitate that.

A second alternative vision says that the role of the federal courts needs to be constrained by the separation of powers. In a dissenting opinion urging a narrow view of who has standing to bring a case to federal court, Justice Antonin Scalia wrote in 2015: "That doctrine of standing, that jurisdictional limitation upon our powers, does not have as its purpose (as the majority assumes) merely to assure that we will decide disputes in concrete factual contexts that enable 'realistic appreciation of the consequences of judicial action.' To the contrary. '[T]he law of Art. III standing is built on a single basic idea—the idea of separation of powers.' It keeps us minding our own business."[41] This restrictive view has been expressed many times, in regard to several doctrines that limit federal court jurisdiction that are examined throughout this book.[42]

But such an argument begs the question of the appropriate role of the federal courts. Courts, of course, should "mind their own business." But that requires defining what their business is. The proper role of the federal courts has to be determined based on the purposes the federal judiciary should serve. If the business of the federal courts is enforcing the Constitution, that is what the doctrines defining federal court jurisdiction should facilitate. It cannot be assumed, as Justice Scalia did, that separation of powers is best served by restricting the courts' role. Less judicial review is not inherently better. Doctrines that facilitate the courts' function of enforcing the Constitution advance the courts' proper role in the system of separation of powers. Doctrines that limit its authority undermine separation of powers.

Finally, there are those who argue for a more limited role for the federal judiciary based on their concern that the courts must conserve their scarce institutional capital. This position is most frequently associated with Justice Felix Frankfurter and Professor Alexander Bickel.[43] Their view rests on several assumptions: that the judiciary's credibility is fragile; that unpopular, controversial decisions will undermine the Court's legitimacy; that if the Court comes to lack legitimacy it will be disobeyed and rendered less powerful; and that the risk of this outweighs the costs of not enforcing particular constitutional provisions.

All of these assumptions are highly questionable. History shows that judicial credibility and legitimacy are not fragile. Some of the Court's most controversial rulings—such as those desegregating schools and reapportioning state legislatures—ultimately enhanced the judiciary's stature. As John Hart Ely wrote: "The possibility of judicial emasculation by way of popular reaction against constitutional review by the courts has not in fact materialized in more than a century and a half of American experience. The warnings probably reached their peak during the Warren years; they were not heeded; yet nothing resembling destruction materialized. In fact, the Court's power continued to grow and probably never has been greater than it has been over the past two decades."[44]

There is no reason to believe that greater enforcement of the Constitution by the federal courts will undermine their credibility, lead to disobedience of judicial orders, or decrease the judiciary's power. Quite the contrary, additional enforcement of the Constitution could well enhance the Court's public esteem and credibility. At the very least, it is entirely speculative whether greater enforcement of the Constitution would have any ill effects.

Most important, even if there were such a risk, it is worth bearing in order to ensure constitutional enforcement. The Court's very reason for accumulating institutional capital is to enforce the Constitution. As Professor Laurence Tribe remarked, "The highest mission of the Supreme Court, in my view, is not to conserve judicial credibility, but in the Constitution's own phrase, 'to form a more perfect Union,' between right and rights."[45]

Enforcing the Constitution

When I teach constitutional law and federal jurisdiction to law students, I always encourage them to focus not just on the legal rules, but also on what they mean for people's lives. Ariana Klay, Janet Galla, and the other plaintiffs in their lawsuit were sexually harassed and raped. Their constitutional rights were violated, but the federal judiciary ruled that it could not hear their case or give them any remedy. In fact, no court could. This cannot be reconciled with John Marshall's words in *Marbury v. Madison:* "The very essence of civil liberty certainly consists in the right of every individual to claim the protection of the laws, whenever he receives an injury."[46] The Court of Appeals decision in their case cannot be reconciled with *Marbury*'s declaration that no one is above the law. It cannot be reconciled with the most important reason we have federal courts: to enforce the United States Constitution.

Suing the Government
The King Can Do Wrong

P atricia Garrett began working for the University of Alabama at Birmingham Hospital in 1977.[1] In 1992, after a series of promotions and upon obtaining her master's degree in nursing, she was appointed Director of Nursing, Women's Services/ Neonatology at the university.[2] In August 1994, after working at the university for seventeen years, she was diagnosed with breast cancer.[3] She underwent two surgeries as well as chemotherapy and radiation treatment.[4]

In one surgery, Garrett had twenty-eight lymph nodes removed from under one arm, which left only the other arm functional for a time.[5] Three weeks later, she returned to work and continued to work while undergoing radiation and chemotherapy.[6] She received thirty-seven radiation treatments, causing radiation burns to her upper body,[7] as well as six months of chemotherapy.[8]

Garrett said that when she returned to work after her surgery, she was harassed by her supervisor, Sabrina Shannon,[9] who pressed her to take leave and threatened she'd be transferred to a lesser job if she did not.[10] Shannon also solicited one of Garrett's subordinates to assume her duties.[11] On one occasion, Garrett's co-worker told her that Shannon "didn't like 'sick people'" and "had a history of getting rid of them."[12] Another time, Garrett found herself locked out of the hospital's computer system.[13] During this time, she continued to perform satisfac-torily in her job despite taking intermittent time off for treatments and sometimes working from home when she was fatigued.[14]

A few months into her chemotherapy, in March 1995, Garrett was hospitalized for an infection.[15] On the advice of her physician, she de-cided to take full medical leave, to which she was entitled according to the University of Alabama's employee handbook.[16] She remained on leave for the rest of her chemotherapy treatment, a total of four months.[17]

When Garrett returned from leave in July 1995, she said that Shan-non "announced UAB did not want [her] back."[18] The hospital's person-nel department allowed her to return to work.[19] But two weeks after her return, Shannon declared "there was no way Garrett could be successful in her job," and gave her a choice of quitting, accepting a demotion to the nursing pool, or being let go.[20] Garrett eventually took a position as a nurse manager at a convalescent home, which paid $13,000 per year less than her previous position.[21]

Garrett sued the University of Alabama for discriminating against her in violation of the Americans with Disabilities Act,[22] a landmark civil rights statute adopted in 1990. Title I of the ADA prohibits employ-ment discrimination against people with disabilities and requires that employers make reasonable efforts to accommodate disabilities. Garrett presented a strong claim.[23] The statute explicitly authorizes suits against state governments as well as other employers. Additionally, she had a claim against the state of Alabama for denying her equal protection un-der the United States Constitution.

Nonetheless, the Supreme Court, in a 5–4 decision, ruled against her.[24] Chief Justice Rehnquist wrote the majority opinion, joined by Jus-tices O'Connor, Scalia, Kennedy, and Thomas, in which the Court held that state governments have sovereign immunity and cannot be sued, even for violating a federal statute that expressly authorizes suits against state governments. The Court ruled that congressional authorization of the suit was unconstitutional and that Garrett could bring neither an ADA claim nor a constitutional claim against Alabama.

The idea that a state can violate the law and nowhere be held ac-countable is inconsistent with the most basic notions of justice and with the view that federal courts exist to enforce the Constitution and laws of the United States. Nonetheless, both the federal and state governments, but not local governments, are deemed to have sovereign immunity and cannot be sued in any court without their consent. Sovereign immunity is an anachronism, and the entire doctrine should be eliminated from American law. The principle is derived from English law, which assumed that "the King can do no wrong."[25] Since the time of Edward I, it has not been possible to sue the Crown of England unless it specifically consents to the suit.[26] United States courts have applied this principle throughout American history, despite often admitting that its justification in this country is unclear.[27]

A doctrine derived from the premise that "the King can do no wrong" deserves no place in American law. The United States was founded on a rejection of a monarchy and of royal prerogatives.[28] American government is based on the fundamental recognition that the government and government officials must be held accountable for their actions. Sovereign immunity violates that basic notion.

It is also inconsistent with the Constitution, which does not mention or even imply that governments have complete immunity to suit. Quite the contrary: Article VI states that the Constitution and laws made pursuant to it are the supreme law of the land. As such, they should prevail over government claims of sovereign immunity.[29] Yet the Supreme Court has deemed that sovereign immunity, a common law doctrine, trumps the Constitution. It has barred suits against government entities when they violate the Constitution or the federal laws made pursuant to it.

Sovereign immunity is inconsistent with a central maxim of American government: no one, not even the government, is above the law. Sovereign immunity effectively places the government above the law and ensures that some individuals who have suffered egregious harms cannot receive redress for their injuries.[30] It also undermines the basic principle announced in *Marbury v. Madison,* that "the very essence of civil liberty certainly consists in the right of every individual to claim the protection of the laws, whenever he receives an injury."[31] The judicial role of enforcing and upholding the Constitution is rendered illusory when the government has complete immunity to suit.

All of this seems clear and obvious, yet sovereign immunity refuses to fade from American jurisprudence. The Supreme Court over the past two decades has dramatically expanded its scope. In *Alden v. Maine,* the Court held that sovereign immunity broadly protects state governments from being sued in *state* courts without their consent, even to enforce federal laws.[32] Probation officers employed by the state of Maine sued, claiming that they were owed overtime by the state under the federal Fair Labor Standards Act. Initially they sued in federal court, but their suit was dismissed because of sovereign immunity and the Eleventh Amendment (which says that a state cannot be sued in federal court by a citizen of another state or of a foreign country). They then sued in Maine state court for the money they were owed. But the Supreme Court, in a 5–4 decision split along ideological lines, held that the principle of sovereign immunity, albeit nowhere stated in the Constitution, means that a state cannot be sued in state court even when it violates federal law and even when no other forum exists where the injured individuals can gain redress.

In a 1996 case, *Seminole Tribe v. Florida,* the Court greatly limited the ability of Congress to authorize suits against state governments or to override sovereign immunity.[33] The Court subsequently applied this principle to bar suits against states for patent infringement[34] and for age discrimination in violation of federal law.[35] Although all of these cases involve suits against state governments, the Court has indicated no willingness to relax the sovereign immunity of the United States government.

This entire body of law is wrong. Sovereign immunity restricts the federal courts' ability to enforce the Constitution and laws of the United States, and should be banished from American law. No government—federal, state, or local—should have sovereign immunity in any court.

In this chapter I will focus on the ability to sue governments in federal court. I will begin by making two arguments about sovereign immunity: first, it is not a doctrine based on the United States Constitution; and second, that it is inconsistent with the Constitution. Finally, I will argue that as a practical matter, it undermines both government accountability and compensation for injured individuals. I also will look at the justifications for sovereign immunity: protecting government treasuries, separation of powers, the lack of authority for suits against government entities, the existence of adequate alternatives to suits against the government, and tradition. None of them justifies the doctrine.

I then consider suits against local governments—cities and counties. Although they are not protected by sovereign immunity, the Supreme Court has made them very difficult to sue. Virtually all other entities are liable when their employees injure others, but local governments can be held liable only when their own policies violate the Constitution. The Court has compounded the difficulty by making it very hard to prove that there is a municipal policy. The result is that federal courts are greatly limited in their ability to enforce the Constitution and hold local governments liable when their employees inflict injuries.

I conclude the chapter, like all of the chapters, by offering concrete ways of dealing with this problem. Obviously, I do not foresee the Supreme Court eliminating sovereign immunity any time soon. The trend is in the opposite direction. Yet I am confident that in time some future Supreme Court will abolish sovereign immunity. The doctrine conflicts with too many basic constitutional principles to survive. In the meantime, there are ways in which Congress—and state governments—can greatly lessen the effects of sovereign immunity and increase government accountability.

The Unconstitutional Status of Sovereign Immunity

The Supreme Court has repeatedly found that sovereign immunity, particularly for state governments, is a constitutional requirement. In *Alden v. Maine,* the Court declared: "We hold that the powers delegated to Congress under Article I of the United States Constitution do not include the power to subject nonconsenting States to private suits for damages in state courts."[36] In *Seminole Tribe v. Florida,* the Court was explicit that the Eleventh Amendment (which says that states cannot be sued by citizens of another state or those of a foreign country, but which also has been interpreted to bar a state from being sued by its own citizens) is a constitutional limit on federal courts, and that Congress can override it only to enforce the Fourteenth Amendment.[37] In other words, the Court has found state sovereign immunity to be part of the Constitution and that this prevents Congress from overriding it with a statute. In the eyes of the Court, sovereign immunity operates just like an individual right, limiting Congress's legislative power and trumping all other claims.

Moreover, the sovereign immunity of the United States government is firmly established. Long ago, Chief Justice John Marshall declared, "the universally received opinion is, that no suit can be commenced or prosecuted against the United States."[38] The Supreme Court has reiterated this principle many times, holding for instance in *United States v. Lee* (1886) that "the United States cannot be lawfully sued without its consent in any case."[39]

In considering the constitutional status of sovereign immunity, I make two distinct arguments. First, sovereign immunity is not a constitutional doctrine; it should not be seen as created or required by the Constitution. Second, sovereign immunity should be regarded as *unconstitutional* because it conflicts with many aspects of the Constitution. It is important to separate these two points. The former explains why the doctrine should not be found in the United States Constitution. By itself, this would not justify abolishing it, though if this conclusion were accepted, Congress would be able to authorize suits against state governments. The latter argument, however, goes further: the doctrine should be deemed unconstitutional and therefore must be eliminated.

Is There a Constitutional Basis for Sovereign Immunity?

For several decades, discussions about constitutional interpretation have been dominated by a debate between "originalist" and "nonoriginalist" views. Originalism, as John Hart Ely defined it in 1980, is the idea that "judges deciding constitutional issues should confine themselves to enforcing norms that are stated or clearly implicit in the written Constitution."[40] Nonoriginalism is the "contrary view that courts should go beyond that set of references and enforce norms that cannot be discovered within the four corners of the document."[41] Originalists believe that the Supreme Court should find a right under the Constitution only if it is expressly stated in the text or was clearly intended by its framers. If the Constitution is silent, originalists say, it is for the legislature, not the courts, to decide the law. Nonoriginalists consider it permissible for the Court to interpret the Constitution in order to protect rights that are not expressly stated or clearly intended but that are part of the system of values embodied in the Constitution. The right to privacy, for instance, is probably the most hotly contested example; it underlies the Court's decision in *Roe v. Wade* and many other rulings. Originalists decry the decisions protecting privacy as illegitimate; non-originalists defend the rulings as an essential aspect of a living Constitution. Sovereign immunity cannot be found in the Constitution under either of these theories of constitutional interpretation.

The many cases expanding the scope of sovereign immunity— *Seminole Tribe v. Florida, Alden v. Maine, Florida Prepaid v. College Savings Bank, College Savings Bank v. Florida Prepaid, Kimel v. Florida Board of Regents, Coleman v. Maryland Court of Appeals,* and, of course, *University of Alabama v. Garrett*[42]—were all decided in the past twenty years, and all by 5–4 margins. In each case, the majority was comprised of the five most conservative justices on the Court. Before 2005, that majority consisted of Chief Justice Rehnquist and Justices O'Connor, Scalia, Kennedy, and Thomas. After 2005, it was Chief Justice Roberts and Justices Scalia, Thomas, Kennedy, and Alito. These groups include all of the justices who profess an originalist philosophy.[43]

Yet, sovereign immunity cannot be justified by originalism. Originalists maintain that rights should be found in the Constitution only if they are stated in the text or clearly intended by its framers. The right of governments to be free from suit without their consent cannot be found in the text of the Constitution, nor the framers' intent. The text itself is silent on the subject. Not one line of the first seven articles even remotely hints at the idea of governmental immunity from suits, and no amendment has bestowed such immunity on the federal government.

One might claim that the Eleventh Amendment provides sovereign immunity to state governments. Yet a careful reading of the text does not support this. The Eleventh Amendment reads, "The Judicial power of the United States shall not be construed to extend to any suit in law or equity, commenced or prosecuted against one of the United

States by Citizens of another State, or by Citizens or Subjects of any foreign state." First, by its terms, this amendment applies only to suits filed in the federal courts; it is a restriction on "the judicial power of the United States." The Court recognized this in *Alden v. Maine.* Justice Kennedy wrote for the majority that "Sovereign immunity derives not from the Eleventh Amendment but from the structure of the original Constitution itself," which he said contained a broad principle of state sovereign immunity.[44]

Moreover, the text of the Eleventh Amendment only restricts suits against states coming from outside the states themselves; it says that the federal judicial power does not extend to a suit against a state by a citizen of another state or of a foreign country. Nothing in its text bars a suit against a state by its own citizens. Yet in *Hans v. Louisiana,*[45] more than a century ago, the Court said that the Eleventh Amendment also prevented states from being sued by their own citizens in federal court. The Court in *Hans* said that it would be "anomalous" to allow a state to be sued by its own citizens when it could not be sued by citizens of other states. This argument, though, is not based on the language or the original meaning of the Eleventh Amendment.

In *Alden v. Maine,* Justice Kennedy makes a textual argument for sovereign immunity by stating that the existence of states is mandated by the Constitution. He writes: "The founding document 'specifically recognizes the States as sovereign entities.' Various textual provisions of the Constitution assume the States' continued existence and active participation in the fundamental processes of governance."[46] Yet the fact that the Constitution preserved the states as entities says absolutely nothing about whether they should have immunity in state court, or sovereign immunity more generally.

Nor can sovereign immunity be justified by the framers' intent. It is important to remember that where the text is silent, originalists believe a right is protected under the Constitution only if the framers showed a clear intent to protect it.[47] If the intent is unclear, the right is not constitutionally protected. With sovereign immunity, the framers' intent is at best completely ambiguous.

There was no recorded discussion of sovereign immunity at the Constitutional Convention in Philadelphia in 1787. As Justice Souter observed, "The 1787 draft in fact said nothing on the subject, and it was this very silence that occasioned some, though apparently not widespread, dispute among the Framers and others over whether ratification of the Constitution would preclude a State sued in federal court from asserting sovereign immunity as it could have done on any matter of nonfederal law litigated in its own courts."[48]

This "dispute among the Framers" erupted with full force at the state ratification conventions, where the prospect of suits against state governments in federal court caused much worry. States had incurred substantial debts, especially during the Revolutionary War, and there was a fear that creditors might sue them in federal court to collect on these debts.

The debate revolved around the language in Article III, which created the Supreme Court and authorized Congress to create the lower courts. Two of this article's clauses specifically deal with suits involving states: they permit suits "between a State and Citizens of another state" and "between a State . . . and foreign . . . Citizens." But it was not clear whether this language was meant to override the sovereign immunity.

Could states be sued in federal court without their consent? The question arose in ratifying conventions in state after state.[49] One group argued that Article III clearly made states subject to such suits. In Virginia, George Mason, who opposed ratification, thundered: "Claims respecting those lands, every liquidated account, or other claim against this state, will be tried before the federal court. Is not this disgraceful? Is this state to be brought to the bar of justice like a delinquent individual? Is the sovereignty of the state to be arraigned like a culprit, or private offender?"[50] Mason believed that Article III "would have the effect of abrogating the states' sovereign immunity defense."[51]

Patrick Henry also opposed the Constitution at the Virginia convention, in part based on the same belief. As for the claim that Article III allowed states to be plaintiffs but not defendants, he called it "incomprehensible."[52] "There is nothing to warrant such an assertion," he said. "What says the paper? That it shall have cognizance of controversies between a state and citizens of another state, without discriminating between plaintiff and defendant."[53] In Pennsylvania, North

Carolina, and New York as well, opponents of ratification raised major objections to this part of the Constitution.[54]

Nor was the idea that Article III overrides state sovereignty limited to opponents. Many of the Constitution's supporters took the same view. They argued that this lack of immunity was desirable to ensure that states could not escape their liabilities or avoid litigation necessary to hold them properly accountable. Edmund Randolph, a member of the Committee of Detail at the Constitutional Convention, argued: "I ask the Convention of the free people of Virginia if there can be honesty in rejecting the government because justice is to be done by it? . . . Are we to say that we shall discard this government because it would make us all honest?"[55] In Pennsylvania, Timothy Pickering argued that it was important for federal courts to be able to give relief to citizens of other states or nations who might be unable to receive fair treatment in a state's own courts.[56]

Other supporters of the Constitution argued that Article III did not override state sovereignty at all, and that, the text's apparent meaning notwithstanding, states could be sued in federal court only if they consented to the litigation. Alexander Hamilton wrote in *The Federalist*: "It is inherent in the nature of sovereignty not to be amenable to the suit of an individual without its consent. This is the general sense and the general practice of mankind; and the exemption, as one of the attributes of sovereignty, is now enjoyed by the government of every State in the Union. Unless, therefore, there is a surrender of this immunity . . . it will remain with the States."[57]

James Madison likewise argued that states have sovereign immunity and that Article III serves only to allow states to come to federal court as plaintiffs, not to be sued as defendants without consent.[58] He wrote that "jurisdiction in controversies between a state and citizens of another state is much objected to, and perhaps without reason. It is not in the power of individuals to call any state into court."[59]

The ratification debates reveal that there was no consensus, even among the Constitution's supporters, about whether state sovereign immunity survived Article III. Justice Souter, recounting this history in his dissent in *Seminole Tribe v. Florida,* observed that "the Framers and their contemporaries did not agree about the place of common-law state sovereign immunity even as to federal jurisdiction resting on the Citizen-State Diversity Clauses."[60] He went on:

> There is almost no evidence that the generation of the Framers thought sovereign immunity was fundamental in the sense of being unalterable. Whether one looks at the period before the framing, to the ratification controversies, or to the early republican era, the evidence is the same. Some Framers thought sovereign immunity was an obsolete royal prerogative inapplicable in a republic; some thought sovereign immunity was a common-law power defeasible, like other common-law rights, by statute; and perhaps a few thought, in keeping with a natural law view distinct from the common-law conception, that immunity was inherent in a sovereign because the body that made a law could not logically be bound by it. Natural law thinking on the part of a doubtful few will not, however, support the Court's position.[61]

Nor do common practices at the time support sovereign immunity.[62] Prior to independence, the American colonies did not enjoy sovereign immunity because that was a privilege understood in English law to be reserved for the Crown. None of the colonies was, or pretended to be, a sovereign state. In fact, as Justice Souter noted, "several colonial charters, including those of Massachusetts, Connecticut, Rhode Island, and Georgia, expressly specified that the corporate body established thereunder could sue and be sued."[63]

One might say in response that the ratification of the Eleventh Amendment shows that the framers wanted to protect sovereign immunity. Yet as scholars (and judges) like John Gibbons and William Fletcher have persuasively argued, the Eleventh Amendment was intended only to preclude suits against the states where jurisdiction was based solely on diversity of citizenship.[64] It was enacted to overrule *Chisholm v. Georgia*,[65] in which a resident of South Carolina brought a suit against the state of Georgia for breach of contract, in order to collect on Revolutionary War debts. Gibbons and Fletcher both demonstrate that the Eleventh Amendment was meant only to amend the provisions of Article III that allowed so-called diversity suits—those in which state governments were sued by citizens of other states. Nothing in its history suggests that the Eleventh Amendment was designed to prevent claims involving federal questions, such as constitutional claims or those based on federal statutes.

As a result, Justice Kennedy in *Alden v. Maine* can defend sovereign immunity only as being implicit in the framers' silence. He invokes this silence as key evidence of the framers' intent:

> We believe, however, that the founders' silence is best explained by the simple fact that no one, not even the Constitution's most ardent opponents, suggested the document might strip the States of the immunity. In light of the overriding concern regarding the States' war-time debts, together with the well known creativity, foresight, and vivid imagination of the Constitution's opponents, the silence is most instructive. It suggests the sovereign's right to assert immunity from suit in its own courts was a principle so well established that no one conceived it would be altered by the new Constitution.[66]

The problem with this argument is that silence is inherently ambiguous. Perhaps Justice Kennedy is correct that the framers were silent because they thought it obvious that states could not be sued in state court. But it could also mean they thought it clear that states could be sued in state court. Most likely, the framers were silent because the issue did not come up and they never focused on it. Silence is inherently uncertain and a highly questionable basis for knowing intent. For example, I am highly skeptical that originalists such as Justices Scalia and Thomas would accept the argument that the framers' silence about the right to privacy indicates that they considered it a right so obvious that it did not need to be enumerated.

If there is a flimsy basis for finding that state governments are protected by sovereign immunity, there is even less justification for extending that immunity to the United States government. At least for states there is the Eleventh Amendment. Nothing in the Constitution says or implies anything about immunity for the federal government. The only argument for federal sovereign immunity is that the framers were so certain of it that they saw no need to mention it in the Constitution. But this is difficult to sustain. The drafters of the Constitution sought to reject royal prerogatives and ensure limits on federal power. Sovereign immunity, based on the notion that the King can do no wrong, is at odds with the very reasons for drafting the United States Constitution.

Simply put, sovereign immunity cannot be found in the Constitution from an originalist perspective.[67] This is a powerful argument because, ironically, it is the originalists on the Supreme Court who champion sovereign immunity. A nonoriginalist like me would argue that the framers' intent as to sovereign immunity, even if it could be known, should not be controlling. Since the Constitution's text neither mandates nor prohibits sovereign immunity, the Court's decisions about it should be based on contemporary functional considerations, not the framers' intent. In any case, the framers' conception of government is radically different from how government operates in the twenty-first century, so their views on sovereign immunity should not be binding upon us today.

Does Sovereign Immunity Violate Basic Constitutional Principles?

Since originalism gives little guidance on sovereign immunity, consider it from a nonoriginalist viewpoint. Should it be seen as a value embodied in the Constitution? Sovereign immunity is inconsistent with three fundamental constitutional principles: the supremacy of the Constitution and federal laws; the accountability of government; and due process of law. Each of these doctrines, by itself, is sufficient to justify declaring sovereign immunity unconstitutional.

THE SUPREMACY OF THE CONSTITUTION AND FEDERAL LAWS

Article VI of the Constitution states: "This Constitution, and the Laws of the United States which shall be made in Pursuance thereof; and all treaties made, or which shall be made under the Authority of the United States, shall be the Supreme Law of the Land; and the Judges in every State shall be bound thereby, anything in the Constitution or Laws of any State to the Contrary Notwithstanding."[68]

This is one of the most important provisions in the entire Constitution. It ensures that the document is not merely aspirational but that it trumps all other law. In *Marbury v. Madison,* Chief Justice John Marshall relied, in part, on the Supremacy Clause to justify judicial review.[69] Without judicial review, he argued, there is no way to ensure that the Constitution and federal laws are supreme.

Marshall addressed the importance of the Supremacy Clause again in *McCulloch v. Maryland:* "This great principle is, that the constitution and the laws made in pursuance thereof are supreme; that they control the constitution and laws of the respective states, and cannot be controlled by them."[70] He went on:

> If any one proposition could command the universal assent of mankind, we might expect it would be this—that the government of the Union, though limited in its powers, is supreme within its sphere of action. This would seem to result, necessarily, from its nature. It is the government of all; its powers are delegated by all; it represents all, and acts for all. . . . The nation, on those subjects on which it can act, must necessarily bind its component parts. But this question is not left to mere reason: the people have, in express terms, decided it, by saying, "this constitution, and the laws of the United States, which shall be made in pursuance thereof," "shall be the supreme law of the land," and by requiring that the members of the state legislatures, and the officers of the executive and judicial departments of the states, shall take the oath of fidelity to it. The government of the United States, then, though limited in its powers, is supreme; and its laws, when made in pursuance of the constitution, form the supreme law of the land, "anything in the constitution or laws of any state to the contrary notwithstanding." [71]

The doctrine of sovereign immunity is inconsistent with this. Most simply, it allows a common-law doctrine to reign supreme over the Constitution and federal law. A plaintiff asserting a constitutional or statutory claim against the federal or a state government will automatically lose because the defendant can invoke sovereign immunity.

Sovereign immunity also frustrates the supremacy of federal law by preventing the enforcement of the Constitution and federal statutes. How can federal law be supreme if states can violate the Constitution or federal laws without consequence? The probation officers in *Alden* had a federal statutory right to overtime pay, but because of sovereign immunity, they had no recourse for ensuring that the states would meet this federal obligation. In *Florida Prepaid v. College Savings Bank* in 1999, College Savings Bank had a federal patent right that it claimed was infringed by the state of Florida, but there was no way to hold the state liable. In *Kimel v. Florida Board of Regents* in 2000, a suit involving age discrimination claims by state government employees, the Supreme Court did not declare that the Age Discrimination Act could not be applied to state governments. Instead, it said that states cannot be sued for violating the Act. The deeply disturbing result of these decisions is that states are subject to federal law, but no court can hold them accountable.

In his oral argument in *Alden v. Maine,* the Solicitor General of the United States, Seth Waxman, quoted from the Supremacy Clause and contended that suits against states are essential to assure the supremacy of federal law. The Court's response to this argument in its decision is astounding:

> The constitutional privilege of a State to assert its sovereign immunity in its own courts does not confer upon the State a concomitant right to disregard the Constitution or valid federal law. The States and their officers are bound by obligations imposed by the Constitution and by federal statutes that comport with the constitutional design. We are unwilling to assume the States will refuse to honor the Constitution or obey the binding laws of the United States. The good faith of the States thus provides an important assurance that "[t]his Constitution, and the Laws of the United States which

shall be made in Pursuance thereof . . . shall be the supreme
Law of the Land. U.S. Const., Art. VI." [72]

What assurance do we have that state governments will comply
with federal law? According to the Court, we must rely on the good faith
of state governments. A half century ago, at the height of the civil rights
movement, would the Supreme Court have assured us that state governments could be trusted to voluntarily comply with federal law? James
Madison said that if people were angels, there would be no need for a
Constitution, but there would be no need for a government either. [73]
The reality is that state governments, intentionally or not, at times will
violate federal law. Reliance on their good faith gives no assurance at all
of the supremacy of federal law.

The Supreme Court should declare that claims of sovereign immunity by federal and state governments are inconsistent with the
Supremacy Clause of the Constitution, and that sovereign immunity
therefore cannot be used as a defense to a federal constitutional or statutory claim.

GOVERNMENT ACCOUNTABILITY

The principle of government accountability is inherent in the Constitution's structure and embodied in many of its provisions. As described
in Chapter 1, Chief Justice Marshall explained in *Marbury v. Madison*
that the central purpose of the Constitution is to limit the actions of
government and government officers. [74] In other words, the government
should be accountable for its actions. Marshall's opinion in *Marbury*
emphasized the need for accountability and redress by declaring that
every individual has "a right to a remedy when he or she receives an
injury." [75]

Sovereign immunity violates every element of this principle. It
allows the government to violate citizens' constitutional and statutory
rights and leave them with no recourse. The probation officers in *Alden*,
the company with the patent in *Florida Prepaid*, and the state employees
in *Kimel* and *Garrett* all sued governments that violated their rights, but
because of sovereign immunity they had no remedies. This makes the

laws of the United States subordinate to the will of the men and women making government decisions.

Consider another simple and tragic example. James B. Stanley sued the U.S. government because of severe injuries he allegedly sustained as a result of having been given LSD, without his knowledge or consent, in an army experiment in 1958. In *United States v. Stanley*,[76] the Supreme Court held that the United States government was immune from his suit. Moreover, the government officers who subjected Stanley to medical experimentation were also immune. In an opinion by Justice Scalia, the Court flatly declared that in suits against military officers, no remedy was "available for injuries that 'arise out of or are in the course of activity incident to service.'"[77]

Thus no recourse whatsoever existed for a person subjected to treatment that Justice O'Connor described in her dissent as "so far beyond the bounds of human decency that as a matter of law it simply cannot be considered a part of the military mission."[78] Justice Brennan drew parallels to the Nazis' medical experimentation and argued that victims like Stanley must have a remedy for violations of their constitutional rights.[79]

The principle that the government must be held accountable can be found in many parts of the Constitution. Professor Akhil Amar has argued that it is embodied in the document's very first words, "We the People," a phrase that makes the people sovereign.[80]

Moreover, if the United States Constitution rests on any universally agreed upon understanding, it is that it rejects a monarchy and royal prerogatives.[81] By itself, Article II's simple declaration that the "executive Power shall be vested in a President of the United States," who serves for a limited four-year term, is an emphatic rejection of royalty in the United States. Article I, Section 9, prohibits any title of nobility being granted by the United States. Scholars have shown that sovereign immunity in the United States is very much based on English law and particularly the idea that "the King can do no wrong." But the Constitution rejects, implicitly and explicitly, all royal prerogatives including this one.

The principle of accountability can be found elsewhere in the Constitution as well. Professor James Pfander has persuasively argued that the First Amendment's right-to-petition clause is inconsistent with the notion of sovereign immunity.[82] In a lengthy and carefully researched article, Pfander demonstrates that "the Petition Clause guarantees the right of individuals to pursue judicial remedies for government misconduct"[83] and that it "affirms the right of the individual to seek redress from government wrongdoing in court, a right historically calculated to overcome any threshold government immunity from suit."[84]

Damages are often essential to ensuring accountability. The real prospect of damages can be crucial in creating the incentive for the government to comply with the law. I have certainly witnessed this in examining the Los Angeles Police Department; it is damage awards, and concern over them, that give governments the incentive to implement controls when they otherwise would not. Without damage awards, often no relief is available to a plaintiff, and there is no incentive for states to comply with the law. Sovereign immunity prevents this basic precept of accountability, even when the government egregiously violates the Constitution and federal laws.

DUE PROCESS OF LAW

Even if it were accepted (without basis) that some such principle of sovereign immunity exists in the structure of the original Constitution, two constitutional amendments should be seen as eliminating sovereign immunity: the assurance in the Fifth and Fourteenth Amendments that no person will be deprived of life, liberty, or property without due process of law. The Due Process Clause certainly strengthens the argument for government accountability. Even more specifically, however, it imposes a constitutional mandate that those who suffer a loss of life, liberty, or property at the hands of the government are entitled to redress.

The Supreme Court has recognized many times that the absence of any court to provide redress for a plaintiff, whether state or federal, raises a serious due process issue.[85] In a long line of cases, the Court has said that because due process requires a judicial forum, federal laws that appear to preclude all jurisdictions violate the right of due process.[86] The prohibition against depriving a person of life, liberty, or property, the Court has emphasized, depends on courts being available to provide redress.[87]

But the Court's sovereign immunity decisions mean that there will be many times when individuals will be injured and yet deprived of any judicial forum to seek redress. The probation officers in *Alden* have a federal property right to overtime pay[88] but there is no way for them to get due process. College Savings Bank has a federal property right in its patent, but it cannot get due process because federal and state courts are both closed to it. The state employees in *Kimel* have liberty and property interests under federal law in being free from age discrimination, but again they are denied due process because there is no forum in which they can have these rights enforced. The Americans with Disabilities Act gives Patricia Garrett a right to be free from employment discrimination on account of her disability, but the Court's decision left her without any remedy.

Thus, sovereign immunity is inconsistent with the supremacy of the Constitution and federal laws of the United States, the basic principle of government accountability, and the central requirements of due process of law. On all of these grounds, the Supreme Court should banish the doctrine from American law.

Can Sovereign Immunity Be Justified?

Conceptions of tort law have changed dramatically from the time that the United States Constitution was written and ratified. Today, liability is justified primarily based on two rationales: the need to provide compensation to injured individuals and the desire to deter future wrongdoing.[89] In fact, the Supreme Court has recognized the importance of these rationales in the context of suits against the government. In *Owen v. City of Independence,* the Supreme Court held that local governments are liable even when their constitutional violations are a result of actions taken in good faith.[90] The Court stressed that allowing cities to have good faith immunity would frustrate the underlying purposes of deterrence and risk-spreading.[91]

Sovereign immunity frustrates compensation and deterrence. Individuals injured by government wrongdoing are left without a remedy. Stanley received no compensation for the human experimentation inflicted on him; nor were the probation officers in *Alden,* or the company in *College Savings Bank,* or the state employees in *Kimel* and *Garrett* compensated for their losses. Moreover, sovereign immunity frustrates deterrence, as the government knows that it can violate federal law without risking liability.

What, then, are the justifications for sovereign immunity, and do they warrant its continued existence? The current doctrine is based on five primary rationales: the importance of protecting government treasuries, separation of powers, the absence of authority for suits against the government, the existence of adequate alternative remedies, and tradition. None of them, I will argue, justifies the continued existence of sovereign immunity.

PROTECTING GOVERNMENT TREASURIES

Without question, sovereign immunity has the virtue of protecting government treasuries from the costs of damage suits.[92] Indeed, that is its main effect. Doctrines exist that facilitate injunctive relief against the government through the ability to sue individual government officers.[93] But sovereign immunity protects government treasuries from liability for damage judgments.

In *Alden,* Justice Kennedy expressly mentioned this justification: "Not only must a State defend or default but also it must face the prospect of being thrust, by federal fiat and against its will, into the disfavored status of a debtor, subject to the power of private citizens to levy on its treasury or perhaps even government buildings or property which the State administers on the public's behalf."[94] This concern underlies all of the Supreme Court's sovereign immunity decisions. If the government can be sued for money damages, the cost of this liability will ultimately fall to the taxpayers.

But this argument for sovereign immunity rests on an unsupported, and I believe unsupportable, assumption: that protecting the government treasury is more important than deterring government wrongdoing. Immunity, in other words, is seen as more important than accountability. Yet in none of the sovereign immunity cases has the Supreme Court ever justified this value choice. Statements like Justice Kennedy's, that sovereign immunity protects government treasuries, are descriptive, not normative. Of course sovereign immunity protects treasuries. But that does not explain whether this benefit outweighs the costs of leaving people uncompensated for their injuries, or of having the government undeterred from future wrongdoing.

Moreover, this is the wrong value priority under the Constitution. Basic constitutional principles such as ensuring the supremacy of federal law, holding the government accountable, and providing due process all should outweigh the virtue of protecting the public purse. Ultimately, it is the question of who should bear the cost of the government's wrongdoing. Although abolishing sovereign immunity would impose financial burdens on the government, it is better to spread the costs of injuries from illegal government actions among the entire citizenry than to make the wronged individual bear the entire loss. Unlike wronged individuals under sovereign immunity, the public at large does have a recourse: if it sufficiently dislikes the costs of damage awards (as well as the conduct that caused them), it can vote the responsible officials out of office.

SEPARATION OF POWERS

A separate, though related case for sovereign immunity is based on separation of powers. The operation of government, goes the argument, would be hindered if the United States or state governments were liable for every injury it inflicted.[95] Sovereign immunity is therefore necessary to protect the government from undue interference by the judiciary.[96] It preserves unhampered discretion and limits the time the government must spend responding to lawsuits. The Supreme Court declared in a 1949 case, *Larson v. Domestic & Foreign Commerce Corp.,* that the "government, as representative of the community as a whole, cannot be stopped in its tracks by any plaintiff who presents a disputed question of property or contract right."[97]

Separation of powers is often advanced as a reason for limiting federal judicial power. By definition, every restriction on the authority of federal courts limits the judiciary's role relative to the other branches of government and to state governments.

But this particular separation of powers argument rests on un-justified assumptions. No evidence is offered to support the assertion that suits against the government would prevent effective governance. In fact, the evidence is to the contrary. The Supreme Court has held that local governments are not protected by sovereign immunity[98] and that they can be sued under Section 1983 of the Civil Rights Act of 1871.[99] The Civil Rights Act was passed at President Grant's request to help the federal government fight the Ku Klux Klan; its most important provision, Section 1983, authorized lawsuits against government officials who violated citizens' constitutional rights. Yet there is no evidence that this liability has significantly hamstrung local governments. Perhaps this is because of the limits on municipal liability I will discuss below, but these governments' experience offers no evidence that allowing suits against the states for their violations of the Constitution and federal statutes would harm governance.

Moreover, it is unclear why suits for money damages will disrupt government more than suits for injunctive relief against government officers, which are allowed. As Professor Pamela Karlan observed, injunctive relief is often more intrusive than damages remedies.[100] The likely answer is that suits for monetary compensation might take away funds that could be used for other government activities. This argument, though, collapses the separation of powers argument into the prior claim concerning the need to protect the government fisc.

Separation of powers never has been understood to insulate the other branches of government from judicial review. Quite the contrary, ever since *Marbury v. Madison,* it has been accepted that the separation of powers created by the Constitution is judicially enforceable. As Chief Justice Marshall emphasized, enforcing the Constitution's limits requires judicial review and government accountability.

Moreover, sovereign immunity forces plaintiffs seeking redress for government wrongdoing to sue individual government officers[101] for money damages that will be paid from their own pockets.[102] Many consider this result undesirable and would prefer that government entities be sued rather than individual officers.[103] It has been argued that officers' discretion is more likely to be chilled if they are exposed to personal liability than if the government entity is held responsible. But since the government usually defends such suits against officers and indemnifies the officers if they are held liable, the difference in terms of separation of powers is negligible.[104]

Most important, the separation of powers argument is incomplete. It depicts separation of powers being enhanced by limiting the role of the judiciary, but this relies on unstated assumptions about the appropriate judicial role. If the courts' preeminent role is to enforce the Constitution, then separation of powers calls for eliminating sovereign immunity because it prevents courts from fulfilling that function.

LACK OF AUTHORITY FOR SUITS AGAINST THE GOVERNMENT

A third justification for sovereign immunity is that there is no authority in the Constitution or federal laws for suits against the government. Justice Oliver Wendell Holmes argued that liability cannot exist unless the law provides for it.[105] Claiming a right to sue the government, he wrote, is "like shaking one's fist at the sky, when the sky furnishes the energy that enables one to raise the fist."[106] From this viewpoint, rights do not exist independent of positive law. To exist, the right to sue must be grounded in a statute.

But this argument would mean that any statute could override sovereign immunity. Holmes's claim is simply that there must be authority for suits. Congress, if it is acting pursuant to any congressional power, could override sovereign immunity and authorize suits. The Supreme Court took this approach that Congress could authorize suits against states in *Pennsylvania v. Union Gas* in 1989,[107] but rejected it seven years later in *Seminole Tribe v. Florida*. More important, Holmes's argument means that state governments may be sued pursuant to Section 1983 of the Civil Rights Act of 1871. During the 1960s and early 1970s, the Supreme Court often said that this statute was meant to ensure state and local compliance with the Constitution.[108] But in 1979, in *Quern v. Jordan*,[109] it held that Section 1983 does not override sovereign immunity, and in *Will v. Michigan Department of State Police*[110] a decade later, it ruled that state governments are not persons and therefore cannot be sued at all under the law. The Court based this conclusion on the doctrine of sovereign immunity. Without that doctrine, Section 1983 can and should be read to allow suits against state governments that violate the Constitution or federal laws.

Moreover, the positive argument for sovereign immunity ignores the fact that suits against the government do have a basis in law: the Constitution itself. The Constitution mandates the supremacy of federal law, government accountability, and due process. As I will argue in Chapter 3, it should be interpreted to give rise to a cause of action for money damages or injunctions against those who violate it, including government entities.

EXISTENCE OF ADEQUATE ALTERNATIVES

The fourth claim, that government liability is unnecessary because there are adequate alternatives, is implicit in many defenses of sovereign immunity. Most notably, individual government officers can be sued, particularly for injunctive relief, and the argument is that this renders suits against government entities unnecessary.

Although suits against individual officials are important, they are no substitute for damage suits against governments themselves. Injunctive relief—court orders to comply with the law—obviously can prevent future violations, but it does nothing to provide redress for past infringements; this, as I argue above, is a constitutional mandate. The probation officers in *Alden* can sue for an injunction to ensure that they are paid overtime in the future, but that would not give them the money that they are owed for past violations of their rights under the federal Fair Labor Standards Act. College Savings Bank might get an injunction against state officers to prevent the State of Florida from infringing its patents in the future, but that gives them no remedy for past infringements. For all of the states' violations of federal law that occurred prior to the injunction, which could be extensive and have caused great harm, federal law is powerless.

Nor are suits against government officers a reliable substitute for litigation against government entities. Sometimes, as discussed in the next chapter, the Court has ruled that these officers cannot be sued. For instance, in *United States v. Stanley,* the Court held that military personnel cannot sue their superior officers even when they engage in egregious violation of rights.[111] Ariana Klay and Janet Galla, the women discussed in Chapter 1 who were raped while in the military, could sue no one. And often, even when a cause of action exists, some government officers, such as judges, prosecutors, and legislators, have absolute immunity to suits for money damages.[112] Consider, for example, a claim that state court judges are systematically violating criminal defendants' rights by setting higher bail amounts for racial minorities or paying public defenders too little to protect defendants' Sixth Amendment rights.[113] Who can be sued? The state government cannot be a defendant. State judges cannot be sued for damages or injunctive relief because a federal law expressly bars such suits.[114] It seems that no suit could be brought, even in response to a serious violation of a basic constitutional right.

Government officials who do not have absolute immunity still have qualified immunity, which often makes recovery for violations of federal law impossible. The Supreme Court has held that government officials can be held liable only if they violate a clearly established right that every reasonable officer should know.[115] This standard often leaves injured individuals no recourse except to sue the government entity. Without such litigation, the supremacy of federal law often cannot be protected. Again, *McCulloch* is instructive: "It is of the very essence of supremacy, to remove all obstacles to its action within its own sphere. . . . This effect need not be stated in terms. It is so involved in the declaration of supremacy, so necessarily implied in it, that the expression of it could not make it more certain."[116]

TRADITION

The strongest argument for sovereign immunity is tradition: The United States government has been accorded some form of sovereign immunity for most of American history. State governments have been immune from suits by their own citizens in federal court at least since *Hans v. Louisiana* in 1890. But other aspects of sovereign immunity are more recent. It was not until 1996, for example, in *Seminole Tribe v. Florida,* that the Supreme Court greatly limited the ability of Congress to authorize suits against state governments. And it was not until 1999, in *Alden,* that the Court held that sovereign immunity barred suits against state governments in state courts.

The nature and extent of this tradition might be questioned. As Justice Souter showed in his dissent in *Alden*, the early American states did not have a clear tradition of sovereign immunity.[117]

Still, sovereign immunity has long been a part of American law. The argument from tradition, though, begs the central question: Is this a tradition that should continue? As Justice Blackmun remarked in another context: "Like Justice Holmes, I believe that '[i]t is revolting to have no better reason for a rule of law than that so it was laid down in the time of Henry IV.'"[118] That sovereign immunity has long been part of American law says nothing about whether it should continue. Slavery, enforced racial segregation, and the subjugation of women also were, at one time, deeply embedded traditions. Like them, sovereign immunity is at odds with the most basic precepts of the American Constitution.

Suing Local Governments

Although the federal and state governments can rarely be sued, the Supreme Court has held that local governments—cities and counties—do not have sovereign immunity.[119] Yet it has made suing these governments very difficult: it has ruled that a local government can be held liable only if its own policies violate the Constitution, not on the grounds that its employees acted unconstitutionally. This is different from almost all other areas of law. A nongovernment employer is always liable if its employees injure someone while performing their duties. This principle is termed "respondeat superior" liability and it means that employers are liable for harms inflicted by their employees who were acting within the scope of their duties. If a UPS driver gets into a car accident while on the job and is at fault, UPS is liable to those injured in the accident. This ensures that the victim gets compensation and the employer has an incentive to do all it can to prevent harm. But the Supreme Court has been emphatic that local governments cannot be held responsible on this basis, rather only if their own policies violate the Constitution.

How did the Court reach this conclusion? In 1961, in *Monroe v. Pape*, the Supreme Court held that municipal governments may not be sued under Section 1983.[120] In *Monroe,* the plaintiffs sought damages for unconstitutional police conduct from both individual officers and from their employer, the city of Chicago. Although the Court upheld the officers' potential liability, it concluded that "Congress did not undertake to bring municipal corporations within the ambit" of the law.[121]

The *Monroe* Court based this conclusion on its reading of the legislative history. When the Civil Rights Law of 1871 was debated in the Senate, Senator John Sherman of Ohio proposed an amendment that would have created municipal liability for certain acts of violence occurring within a county's or town's borders. Essentially, the amendment would have imposed strict liability on cities for specified violent acts, even if the city and its officials did not participate and were not directly responsible. Sherman's apparent goal was to deter municipal inaction in the face of widespread Ku Klux Klan activity by giving cities a powerful monetary incentive to prevent violence. Although the Senate approved the amendment, the House rejected it and it was deleted in a conference committee.[122]

Justice Douglas, writing for the majority in *Monroe,* concluded that the rejection of the Sherman Amendment reflected a desire to immunize cities from liability. He also rejected the argument that the Dictionary Act (a federal statute that defines how words in federal laws should be understood), which defined "person" to include "bodies politic and corporate," was a basis for holding cities liable.[123] Douglas concluded that the definition found in the Dictionary Act was "merely an allowable, not a mandatory one."[124] Thus the *Monroe* Court precluded all municipal liability under Section 1983, whether for damages or injunctive relief.[125]

Douglas's review of Section 1983's legislative history later came under sharp criticism.[126] Lower courts, meanwhile, developed techniques for circumventing the *Monroe* decision and creating municipal liability for constitutional violations. They permitted liability based on other civil rights laws,[127] and some allowed suits against cities based on causes of action inferred directly from the Constitution.[128]

In 1978, in the landmark decision *Monell v. Department of Social Services,* the Supreme Court expressly overruled *Monroe*'s limitation on municipal liability.[129] *Monell* involved a suit against the city of New York challenging a policy requiring pregnant teachers to take unpaid leaves of absence. The Supreme Court again reviewed the legislative history of Section 1983 and this time concluded that Congress had never intended to preclude municipal liability. Justice William Brennan, writing for the majority, stated that the rejection of the Sherman Amendment was meant to prevent local governments from being held liable for the wrongful acts of others—not to protect them from liability for their own violations of the Fourteenth Amendment.[130] Furthermore, the Court emphasized that the Dictionary Act of 1871, enacted only months before the Civil Rights Act, defined "persons" to include "bodies politic and corporate."[131]

Thus the *Monell* Court declared that "Congress *did* intend municipalities and other local government units to be included among those persons to whom §1983 applies."[132] But it imposed a substantial limitation: municipal governments may be sued only for their own unconstitutional or illegal policies, not for the acts of their employees. Section 1983, the Court noted, refers to "every person who . . . subjects or causes to be subjected, any citizen . . . to the deprivation of any rights, privileges, or immunities." In the Court's eyes, this language meant that cities could be held responsible only for the actions they caused. "A local government may not be sued under §1983 for an injury inflicted solely by its employees or agents. Instead, it is when execution of a government's policy or custom, whether made by its lawmakers or by those whose edicts or acts may fairly be said to represent official policy, inflicts the injury that the government as an entity is responsible."[133] Since that decision, the Court has held that the requirement for proof of municipal policy applies in all suits against local governments, whether for money or for injunctive or declaratory relief.

Monell was wrong in holding that local governments can be held liable only when their own policies violate the Constitution.[134] In interpreting the meaning of "under color of law," the Court in *Monell* employed exactly the same distinction it had rejected in *Monroe*: the difference between unauthorized acts and official policies. In *Monroe*, the Court was clear that Section 1983 was meant to have a broad reach and create liability for constitutional violations, whether authorized by the government or not.

Furthermore, the Court's rejection of the deterrence and risk-spreading arguments for broader liability is unjustified. In *Monell,* the Court concluded that although deterrence and risk-spreading would be served by allowing respondeat superior liability, the defeat of the Sherman Amendment evidences a rejection of these policies. But the defeat of the Sherman Amendment, as the *Monell* Court noted, only was a refusal to create an affirmative duty for cities to keep the peace by making them monetarily liable for the actions of *private citizens.* Just because deterrence and risk-spreading were not accepted as sufficient to justify municipal liability for private actions, does not mean that deterrence and risk-spreading were completely repudiated as the underlying objectives of Section 1983. In fact, two years after *Monell,* the Court held that municipalities do not have good faith immunity in suits brought under Section 1983 because such immunity would frustrate the objectives of deterrence and risk-spreading.[135]

In a subsequent case, Justice Breyer, in a dissenting opinion joined by Justices Stevens and Ginsburg, sharply criticized *Monell* and declared that the "case for reexamination is a strong one."[136] Justice Breyer argued that neither the language of Section 1983 nor its legislative history supports *Monell's* preclusion of respondeat superior liability.[137] Moreover, Justice Breyer stated that "*Monell's* basic effort to distinguish between vicarious liability and liability derived from 'policy or custom' has produced a body of liability and liability derived from 'policy or custom' that is neither readily understandable nor easy to apply."[138] Justice Breyer also argued that "relevant legal and factual circumstances may have changed in a way that affects likely reliance upon *Monell's* liability limitation. The legal complexity . . . makes it difficult for municipalities to predict just when they will be held liable for policy or custom."[139]

Yet the Court has greatly compounded the problem by making it very difficult to prove the existence of a municipal policy. No city ever will have an officially stated policy that its police officers should use excessive force, even if the culture in the police departments condones it. Yet absent such an express policy, the Court has created obstacles to proving municipal liability that are often insurmountable.

Consider, for example, the Court's decision in *Board of the County Commissioners, Bryan County, Oklahoma v. Brown.*[140] The Bryan County

Sheriff, B. J. Moore, hired his nephew's son, Stacy Burns, as a deputy even though Burns had a long criminal record that included guilty pleas for assault and battery, resisting arrest, and public drunkenness. Moore obviously did not completely trust Burns: he authorized him to make arrests, but not to carry a weapon or operate a patrol car. Despite this, Burns became involved in a high-speed car chase. Once the fleeing car finally stopped, Burns ordered the driver and passenger out of the car. When the passenger, Jill Brown, did not immediately comply, Burns pulled her from the automobile so violently that he caused permanent damage to both of her knees. As the Supreme Court noted, Burns "used an 'arm bar' technique, grabbing [Brown's] arm at the wrist and elbow, pulling her from the vehicle, and spinning her to the ground. Respondent's knees were severely injured, and she later underwent corrective surgery. Ultimately, she may need knee replacements."[141]

This should have been an easy case. The jury found that the sheriff, Moore, was "deliberately indifferent" in his hiring and supervision of Burns. But in a 5–4 decision, the Supreme Court ruled that there was not sufficient proof that the local government had caused Jill Brown's injuries. "A finding of culpability," Justice O'Connor wrote for the majority, "simply cannot depend on the mere probability that any officer inadequately screened will inflict constitutional injury. Rather, it must depend on a finding that this officer was highly likely to inflict the particular injury suffered by the plaintiff. The connection between the background of the particular applicant and the specific constitutional violation must be strong."[142] In other words, Brown would have had to show that it was "highly likely" that Burns would inflict that "particular injury"—put that way, it would seem that it would need to be shown that he would break her knees and not, presumably, dislocate a shoulder instead. This is, needless to say, often an insurmountable burden.

The Court's decision is especially troubling because the jury had found that the sheriff's deliberate indifference in hiring Burns had caused Brown's injuries. This decision was supported by the record: Sheriff Moore had deputized a close relative whose criminal record he surely knew, with the full awareness that such a person, empowered to perform police duties, could cause great harm. It is unclear how much worse the criminal record would have had to be for the Supreme Court to allow the verdict of liability to stand. It should have been obvious that Burns would injure people as a deputy, but it is an impossible obstacle to liability to say that it had to be foreseeable that he would cause any "particular injury."

Another, more recent decision underlines how difficult it now is to prove municipal liability.[143] In 1987, John Thompson was convicted of murdering a man and spent eighteen years in a Louisiana prison, fourteen of them on death row, because of egregious prosecutorial misconduct. One month before he was to be executed, Thompson's defense lawyers found blood evidence that prosecutors possessed, but had never disclosed, that exonerated him for an armed robbery for which he had been convicted and that greatly affected his murder trial.

Two days before Thompson's murder trial in New Orleans, the assistant district attorney received the crime lab's report, which stated that the perpetrator had blood type B and that Thompson has type O blood. The defense was not told of this at the trial. The assistant district attorney who had the blood report simply hid it. Many years later, when he was dying of cancer, he told another assistant district attorney about it. That person, too, told no one, and in fact was later disciplined by the Louisiana State Bar for not informing Thompson and his lawyers immediately.[144]

All the while, Thompson remained on death row with his execution date approaching. It was only through a series of coincidences that his lawyer discovered the blood evidence with a month to go before Thompson was to be executed. New testing was done on blood that came from the perpetrator of the murders, and it didn't match Thompson's DNA or even his blood type. His conviction was overturned and he was retried for the murders. This time he was acquitted of all charges.

The New Orleans District Attorney's office conceded that by not turning over the blood evidence, it had violated its obligations under *Brady v. Maryland*[145]—the landmark 1963 case in which the Court ruled that withholding exculpatory evidence violates the Due Process Clause of the Fourteenth Amendment. There was no way to argue otherwise. Thompson's lawyers, though, knew that they could not sue the District Attorney or the prosecutors themselves because the Supreme Court had ruled that they had absolute immunity to civil suits for money damages. So Thompson sued the local government that employed them. The New Orleans District Attorney's office has a notorious history of not disclosing exculpatory information to defendants. The jury ruled in Thompson's favor and awarded him $14 million.

But the Supreme Court reversed, in a 5–4 decision, and held that the local government could not be held liable for the prosecutorial misconduct. Justice Thomas, writing for the Court, said that a single instance of prosecutorial misconduct was not enough to show sufficient deliberate indifference or establish liability of the city government.

But as Justice Ginsburg pointed out in her dissenting opinion, this was not a single instance: "Throughout the pretrial and trial proceedings against Thompson," she wrote, "the team of four engaged in prosecuting him for armed robbery and murder hid from the defense and the court exculpatory information Thompson requested and had a constitutional right to receive. The prosecutors did so despite multiple opportunities, spanning nearly two decades, to set the record straight. . . . What happened here, the Court's opinion obscures, was no momentary oversight, no single incident of a lone officer's misconduct. Instead, the evidence demonstrated that misperception and disregard of *Brady*'s disclosure requirements were pervasive in Orleans Parish."[146]

This was not even the only serious *Brady* violation prosecutors committed in the case. Police interviewed an eyewitness to the murder who described the assailant as having short hair. At that time, Thompson had a large Afro. That, too, never was disclosed to the defense. Thompson suffered one of the worst harms a government can inflict on a person, and the Court once more refused to allow any remedy.

The Supreme Court's decision has made it very difficult to hold local governments, or anyone, accountable for prosecutorial misconduct. I recently filed a petition for Supreme Court review, which was denied, on behalf of two men, Earl Truvia and Gregory Bright, who spent twenty-eight years in prison for a murder they did not commit.[147] They were convicted in 1976. In 2002, the Orleans Parish Criminal District Court found that the Orleans Parish District Attorney—the same office that had prosecuted John Thompson—had also suppressed crucial evidence in Truvia and Bright's case. The Orleans Parish Criminal District Court vacated the convictions, and the Louisiana Supreme Court subsequently denied review. In 2004, twenty-eight years after being wrongfully convicted, Truvia and Bright were released from prison.

After their convictions were vacated, Truvia and Bright filed a complaint against the local government, asserting claims under Section 1983 of the Civil Rights Act of 1871 for constitutional violations. They submitted substantial evidence to the federal district court that the Orleans Parish District Attorney's office had a policy and custom of withholding exculpatory evidence, including that it failed to train its prosecutors of their obligations under the *Brady* decision. The evidence consisted of: (a) discovery responses from forty-four different Orleans Parish assistant district attorneys in ninety cases, in which they told the criminal defendants that they were not entitled to materials they were in fact entitled to under *Brady*; (b) the admission by Henry Julien, the prosecutor in Truvia and Bright's case, that he withheld evidence from them; (c) Julien's testimony that he believed that he had no duty under *Brady* to obtain critical exculpatory materials such as witness statements; (d) testimony from Truvia and Bright's 2002 postconviction proceeding that the Orleans Parish District Attorney did not allow defense counsel to examine the prosecution file; (e) the affidavit of former assistant district attorney Bill Campbell, showing that the Orleans Parish District Attorney's office not only did not train him on *Brady* violations but actually instructed him to provide "not entitled" responses to *Brady* requests. Truvia and Bright pointed to twelve other instances since 1990 of individuals whose convictions were overturned because of *Brady* violations committed by the Orleans Parish District Attorney's office.[148]

But the federal district court and the federal court of appeals ruled against them, saying that even this weight of evidence did not establish a municipal policy. The Supreme Court declined to review the case.

Local governments are not protected by sovereign immunity, but under current law they might as well be. The requirement for proving municipal liability and the difficulty of establishing it make it almost impossible to enforce the Constitution and federal laws against cities and counties.

Holding Governments Accountable

Criticism of sovereign immunity is not new. President Abraham Lincoln declared: "It is as much the duty of Government to render prompt justice against itself in favor of citizens as it is to administer the same between private individuals."[149] How can this injustice be fixed? The easiest way would be for the Supreme Court to hold that sovereign immunity is not a bar to suing the United States or state governments. This is not implausible. For the last quarter-century, the four most liberal justices on the Supreme Court—previously Stevens, Souter, Ginsburg, and Breyer, now Ginsburg, Breyer, Sotomayor, and Kagan—have taken the position that the Eleventh Amendment does not bar suits against state governments under the Constitution or federal statutes. Four justices—Stevens, Souter, Ginsburg, and Breyer—have indicated a desire to reconsider (and likely overrule) *Monell* and hold local governments liable for the actions of their employees.

It is conceivable that future vacancies could create a majority to limit or even eliminate sovereign immunity and expand the ability to hold local governments liable. But even if the Court does not do this, Congress could solve the problem. The law is clear that Congress can waive sovereign immunity for the United States. It did so in the Tucker Act, which allows the United States to be sued for breach of contract, and in the Federal Tort Claims Act for some actions by federal employees. Congress could pass a statute more broadly waiving sovereign immunity for any constitutional violations by the United States or its employees.

Also, Congress can amend Section 1983 to allow for liability of local and state governments. For local governments, the statute only needs to be changed to make clear that local governments are liable for constitutional violations by their employees. *Monell* was premised entirely on an interpretation of the statute, which means Congress can effectively reverse the decision by revising the statute. As for state governments, the Court held in *Quern v. Jordan* that Congress was not sufficiently explicit in stating that it meant to allow state governments to be sued under Section 1983.[150] Congress could revise the statute to explicitly authorize suits against state governments. The powers granted by Section 5 of the Fourteenth Amendment clearly give it this authority.[151]

People whose rights have been violated by state or local governments should have a remedy in federal court. Eliminating sovereign immunity for the federal and state governments, and allowing cities to be held liable for the wrongs of their officers—whether by judicial decision or statute—would enable the federal courts to fulfill their constitutional role of enforcing the Constitution and federal laws.

Suing Government Officers

On July 9, 1971, Ora Spitler McFarlin requested a court order to have her fifteen-year-old daughter, Linda Spitler, surgically sterilized. McFarlin's petition, prepared by her attorney and titled "Petition to Have Tubal Ligation Performed on a Minor and Indemnity Agreement," was an unusual document. It contained only an affidavit by McFarlin and did not even have a case caption identifying the parties to the case or saying in which court it was filed. The affidavit asserted that McFarlin's fifteen-year-old daughter, Linda, was "somewhat retarded," although it conceded that Linda attended public school and had passed each grade "along with other children in her age level."[1] It stated that Linda was dating and spending the night with "older youth or young men" without her mother's knowledge or consent. Because McFarlin believed she could not look after Linda well enough to "prevent unfortunate circumstances," she felt the appropriate solution was to have her permanently sterilized.

The petition was submitted to Judge Harold D. Stump of the Circuit Court of DeKalb County, Indiana, and approved the same day. Stump did so without giving notice to Linda, without a hearing to receive evidence, and without appointing a guardian or lawyer to protect Linda's interests. His order was a sentence long and neither offered any reason for his approval of the petition nor cited any statutes or common law in support of the decision. It simply stated that Judge Stump approved the petition on behalf of McFarlin to have Linda surgically sterilized.

Indiana did have statutory procedures for sterilization in specific circumstances, but only if the individuals were institutionalized. Moreover, these statutes required that notice, administrative proceedings before a board, and an evidentiary hearing all be completed before there could be review in an Indiana state court.[2] Judge Stump followed none of these requirements. The petition had not been given a docket number and had not been placed on file with the clerk's office. Years later, the *Indianapolis News* commented that "the paper [petition] never was filed in court" and that "Judge Stump approved the sterilization without disclosing his actions to anyone."[3] The decision seems to have been made as quickly and as secretly as possible.

Other than her affidavit, there is no evidence showing why McFarlin wanted her daughter sterilized. But Linda's life before the procedure may help us understand the circumstances of her mother's petition. Linda grew up in a small rust belt town in northern Indiana with her mother, two sisters, brother, and a series of stepfathers. Ora McFarlin worked two jobs and was usually absent from the household. During Linda's childhood, she was beaten by her older sister, by an alcoholic brother, and by her stepfather, and she was often sent away to live with another older sister or with foster parents.[4] She recalls that she "was never wanted or loved" during her childhood.[5] When she sought more autonomy through socializing with young men, her mother and sister called her a "whore" for letting "dirty old men climb" on her.[6]

Ora's behavior toward Linda likely stemmed from her own history. McFarlin married her first husband, Pete Spitler, at age seventeen and had four children by her mid-twenties. One of Linda's older sisters, Kathy, became pregnant during her senior year of high school, when Linda was fifteen. This is when Ora McFarlin sought a court order to sterilize Linda. Teen pregnancy and unwed motherhood in a small Midwestern town in the 1970s were viewed with little sympathy.

On July 15, 1971, Linda entered DeKalb Memorial Hospital under the impression that she was to have her appendix removed. The next day, doctors at the hospital performed the irreversible procedure of surgically sterilizing her. Linda recalled hearing one of the nurses say, right before she received anesthesia, "make sure she is really out. If she finds out what's really going on, she will run."[7] "They laid me on the table," she later wrote in a memoir. "I was cryin' for my mom but she wasn't there. I saw this door that had two windows and I looked up to yell again, and when I did, a man in a green gown put a black mask on my face and told me to count backwards. Everything went black."

Linda left the hospital thinking she had only had her appendix removed. In 1973, at the age of seventeen, she married Leo Sparkman but was unable to become pregnant. It was only after she sought medical help for her infertility that she learned from one of the doctors who performed the procedure that she had been surgically sterilized. With this newfound knowledge, Linda brought federal civil rights claims against McFarlin, McFarlin's attorney, the doctors who sterilized her, the hospital, and Judge Stump.

The case against Judge Stump should have been easy. A compelling argument can be made that he acted without jurisdiction. He had no authority to hear such a case or issue such an order. No case was filed with the court, there were no pleadings, no docket number was assigned, and neither the girl nor any representative for her was present or allowed to respond.

Nonetheless, the Supreme Court ruled that the judge had absolute immunity to a suit for money damages. Because he sat in a court of general jurisdiction, the Court emphasized, he was acting in excess of jurisdiction but not in the absence of it.[8] In other words, even though he irreparably harmed Linda and violated one of her most basic rights— the right to procreate—he was completely shielded from liability.

Linda had no remedy at all. She could not sue the state of Indiana because, as explained in the last chapter, it was protected by sovereign immunity. But neither could she sue the judge who violated her rights. He was protected by absolute immunity. She could not sue the hospital or the doctors—at least not successfully—because they believed they were acting under a legitimate court order.

This is not an exceptional circumstance. The Supreme Court has made it increasingly difficult to recover from government officers when they violate the Constitution. Because the federal and state governments are protected by sovereign immunity and because local governments can be held liable only if their own policies or customs violate the Constitution, which is difficult to prove, often the only chance to enforce the Constitution is through suits against individual officers.

If a state or local officer violates the Constitution or laws of the United States, he or she can be sued under Section 1983 of the Civil Rights Act of 1871, which creates a cause of action against persons acting under state authority who violate the Constitution and laws of the United States. But in the past thirty years, the Supreme Court has made it increasingly difficult to bring such suits.

Moreover, whenever a government official—federal, state, or local—is sued for money damages, he or she always can assert an "immunity defense." The Supreme Court has held that some government officers have absolute immunity and cannot be sued at all for money damages, no matter how egregious their constitutional violations. Absolute immunity exists for judges for their judicial acts, for prosecutors for their prosecutorial acts, for legislators for their legislative acts, for law enforcement personnel testifying as witnesses, and for the President for presidential acts. *All* other government officers are protected by qualified immunity and are liable only if they violate clearly established law that every reasonable officer should know, and only if the right they violate is established beyond dispute. In recent years, the Supreme Court has expanded the scope of both absolute and qualified immunity, making it much harder for those whose rights have been violated to obtain any remedy.

These doctrines present enormous obstacles to enforcing the Constitution. Because government entities generally cannot be sued, usually the only possibility of recovery is from the individual officer. In this chapter, I first discuss how the Court has limited suits against federal officers and then consider the expansion of absolute and qualified immunity in suits against local, state, and federal officers.

The Rise and Fall of *Bivens* Suits

No federal statute authorizes federal courts to hear suits or give relief against federal officers who violate the Constitution of the United States. Although Section 1983 authorizes suits against state and local officers, it has no application to the federal government or its officers.[9] Nor are suits against federal officers allowed under any analogous statute.

Yet the Supreme Court long has held that federal officers may be sued for injunctive relief to prevent future infringements of federal laws.[10] In fact, Congress amended the Administrative Procedures Act to provide that suits against federal agencies, officers, or employees "seeking relief other than money damages" shall not be dismissed on account of the United States being a necessary party.[11] The statute even allows the United States to be named as the defendant in a suit for prospective relief. In short, when the federal government acts unconstitutionally, assuming all other jurisdictional requirements are met, the plaintiff generally may sue the officer or the United States for an injunction.

The federal courts' ability to entertain suits seeking money damages against federal officers, however, is both more controversial and far more limited. In the landmark 1971 decision of *Bivens v. Six Unknown Named Agents of Federal Bureau of Narcotics,*[12] the Supreme Court ruled that federal officers who violate constitutional rights can be sued for money damages directly under the Constitution. Such lawsuits are named for that decision: "*Bivens* suits." They are a necessary way to enforce the Constitution and hold federal officers liable—especially since the United States government has sovereign immunity and generally cannot be sued for money damages. But over the past thirty-five years, the Supreme Court has backed away from the *Bivens* decision and made it increasingly difficult to sue federal officers, even when they commit egregious constitutional violations.

For the first decade after the decision, the Court expanded citizens' ability to file *Bivens* suits.[13] But beginning in the 1980s, *every* Supreme Court decision about *Bivens* suits has narrowed their availability.[14] In fact, in a recent opinion, Justice Scalia, joined by Justice Thomas, indicated a clear desire to overrule *Bivens:* "I would not extend *Bivens* even if its reasoning logically applied to this case. *Bivens* is a relic of the heady days in which the Court assumed common-law powers to create causes of action. . . . *Bivens* and its progeny should be limited to the precise circumstances involved."[15]

People continue to file *Bivens* suits against federal officers for money damages and occasionally succeed. But there is no doubt that the Supreme Court has tremendously narrowed their availability, and lower courts generally follow this lead.[16]

THE DECISION

The original case, *Bivens v. Six Unknown Named Agents of the Federal Bureau of Narcotics,* ended with the Supreme Court allowing a plaintiff to seek money damages from individual federal officers for their alleged violation of his rights under the Fourth Amendment.[17] Before this decision, courts had protected constitutional rights through injunctive relief and doctrines such as the exclusionary rule, but plaintiffs could not sue federal officers for monetary remedies in federal court. They could only pursue state tort claims, which almost always had to be litigated in state courts.

The Court's holding in *Bivens* was foreshadowed in the 1947 decision in *Bell v. Hood.*[18] Bell claimed that he was falsely imprisoned by FBI agents and he sought damages of $3,000 for the violation of his Fourth and Fifth Amendment rights. The federal district court dismissed the case, saying it lacked jurisdiction because the action did not arise under the Constitution or laws of the United States. The Supreme Court reversed that decision, holding that there was jurisdiction because the case arose under the Constitution, and remanded the case back to the district court to determine whether he could bring a suit for money damages. The Court did not resolve this question, but certainly intimated a positive view toward causes of action inferred directly from the Constitution. It stated that although it had never decided whether money damages could be awarded for violations of the Fourth and Fifth Amendments, "where federally protected rights have been invaded, it has been the rule from the beginning that courts will be alert to adjust their remedies so as to grant the necessary relief."[19]

The Court did not address the issue again until *Bivens,* twenty-five years later. The plaintiff, Wesley Bivens, alleged that he had been subjected to an illegal and humiliating search by agents of the Federal Bureau of Narcotics, and sought money damages as compensation. The district court dismissed the case saying that the law provided no basis for relief, and the Court of Appeals for the Second Circuit affirmed, holding "that the Fourth Amendment does not provide a basis for a federal cause of action for damages arising out of an unreasonable search and seizure."[20] Bivens's only remedy against the federal officers, according to the Second Circuit, was under state tort law in state court.

The United States Supreme Court reversed this ruling. It held that Bivens did not need to rely on a federal statute to sue, but could sue for damages based on the Fourth Amendment alone. The majority opinion, by Justice Brennan, emphasized that individuals whose rights have been violated should not have to resort to state remedies, which might be inadequate or hostile to the federal constitutional interest.[21] The Fourth Amendment, Brennan wrote, "operates as a limitation upon the exercise of federal power regardless of whether the State in whose jurisdiction that power is exercised would prohibit or penalize the identical act if engaged in by a private citizen."[22] Furthermore, the judiciary has the authority and the duty to provide remedies to ensure the necessary relief for violations of federal rights.[23]

Brennan's opinion suggested two situations in which the Court would not recognize causes of action for constitutional violations; neither exception applied in *Bivens*. First, there could be no suit if there were "special factors"—which the opinion did not specify—"counselling hesitation in the absence of affirmative action by Congress."[24] Brennan found no such special factors in *Bivens*. Second, he suggested that the Court would not allow a federal suit for damages if Congress had created an alternative mechanism that provides an equally effective substitute.[25] Again, the Court found no such alternative mechanism available for Bivens and did not say what would be such a mechanism.

In an important and often-cited concurring opinion, Justice John Harlan explained that the federal courts long have devised remedies for violations of federal law.[26] It does not make sense, he wrote, that "the fact that the interest is protected by the Constitution rather than statute or common law justifies the assertion that federal courts are powerless to grant damages."[27] Furthermore, he explained, it is essential that federal courts be able to provide such relief: "It is apparent that some form of damages is the only possible remedy for someone in Bivens' alleged position. . . . For people in Bivens' shoes it is damages or nothing."[28]

Harlan rejected the argument that the Court violates separation of powers when it creates such a cause of action and remedy. In his view, the Court is responsible for upholding and enforcing the Bill of Rights and thus need not wait for the legislature in order to act.[29]

Justices Warren Burger, Hugo Black, and Harry Blackmun dissented, in three separate opinions. Chief Justice Burger contended that separation of powers meant that Congress, not the Court, should create a cause of action for damages against federal officers.[30] He also used his dissent to mount a lengthy attack on the exclusionary rule, a judicially created rule making illegally obtained evidence inadmissible at trial. Black and Blackmun also argued that it is for Congress alone to authorize suits against federal officers for money damages.[31] Black wrote that "should the time come when Congress desires such lawsuits, it has before it a model of valid legislation, 42 U.S.C. §1983, to create a damage remedy against federal officers."[32] Until then, in his view, no such cause of action should exist. Blackmun also argued that "it is the Congress and not this Court that should act."[33]

Bivens is a vital decision in ensuring the enforcement of the Constitution. As I explained in Chapter 1, it is the judiciary's role to provide a remedy for violations of rights.[34] Courts traditionally have fashioned remedies in the absence of legislative action, including the exclusionary rule for Fourth and Fifth Amendment violations and damage remedies under federal statutes. Moreover, as Justice Harlan argued, rights under federal law and the Constitution should not depend on the vagaries of state law but must be safeguarded and enforced by federal courts. Damage remedies are essential, both to compensate those whose rights have been violated and to provide a deterrent against future violations.

But over the past thirty-five years, the Supreme Court has consistently limited plaintiffs' ability to file *Bivens* suits. The dissenters in *Bivens* have triumphed. In *Correctional Services Corporation v. Malesko* (2001),[35] both Chief Justice Rehnquist's majority opinion and Justice Scalia's concurring opinion noted and praised this trend. The issue in *Malesko* was whether a privately operated prison could be sued in a *Bivens* action. In holding that such suits are not permitted, Rehnquist noted that "since *Carlson* [*v. Green* in 1980], we have consistently refused to extend *Bivens* liability to any new context or new category of defendants.[36] . . . In 30 years of *Bivens* jurisprudence we have extended its holding only twice, to provide an otherwise nonexistent cause of action against *individual officers* alleged to have acted unconstitutionally, or to provide a cause of action for a plaintiff who lacked *any alternative remedy* for harms caused by an individual officer's unconstitutional conduct. Where such circumstances are not present, we have consistently rejected invitations to extend *Bivens,* often for reasons that foreclose its extension here."[37]

Justice Scalia, in an opinion joined by Justice Thomas, went even further: he strongly suggested that he would overrule *Bivens.*[38] The four dissenting justices lamented that "the driving force behind the Court's decision is a disagreement with the holding of *Bivens* itself."[39]

A STATUTE, ANY STATUTE, MEANS THAT THERE IS NO CONSTITUTIONAL CLAIM

In *Bivens,* and again in the 1980 case *Carlson v. Green,* the Supreme Court identified two situations in which damage suits against federal officers will not be permitted. They are not available "when defendants show that Congress has provided an alternative remedy which it explicitly declared to be a *substitute* for recovery directly under the Constitution and viewed as equally effective";[40] and they are not allowed where there are "special factors counselling hesitation in the absence of affirmative action by Congress."[41]

These two circumstances, initially articulated as two distinct exceptions, have been combined over the past thirty-five years as the Court has found that congressionally created remedies *are* the special factors preventing the availability of *Bivens* suits. In fact, the Court has completely ignored the first exception, alternative remedies, and has focused entirely on the presence of special factors, even when it is considering whether the existence of a federal statute precludes a *Bivens* case. Thus, for clarity, analysis can be divided into two questions: When is the existence of a congressionally created remedy sufficient to prevent a *Bivens* suit? And what other special factors counsel hesitation and preclude *Bivens* remedies?

There have been five major Supreme Court decisions regarding the kind of congressional action that can foreclose a *Bivens* suit: *Davis v. Passman* (1979), *Carlson v. Green* (1980), *Bush v. Lucas* (1983), *Schweiker v. Chilicky* (1988), and *Hui v. Castaneda* (2010). In the first two cases, the Court found that the existence of a federal statute does not bar *Bivens* suits; in the last three, it decided the opposite. It now seems that the existence of any federal law, even when it provides no remedy, is enough to bar a *Bivens* suit.

The error in this is plain: a statute should not be able to preclude a constitutional remedy. The Constitution is the supreme law of the land, and as *Marbury v. Madison* told us long ago, the courts exist to provide a remedy when rights have been violated. In situations where, as Justice Harlan put it, the remedy is damages or nothing, precluding a *Bivens* suit is tantamount to foreclosing any remedy at all. *Bivens* thus should be interpreted to allow suits against federal officers who violate the Constitution, whether or not a statute exists. But the Supreme Court has taken exactly the opposite approach, greatly compromising the federal courts' ability to enforce the Constitution.

In *Davis v. Passman,* the Court considered whether a female aide could sue a congressman for gender discrimination based on a cause of action inferred directly from the Fifth Amendment's guarantee of equal protection.[42] Congressman Otto Passman had fired his administrative assistant, Shirley Davis, in 1974 because he wanted the position filled by a man. The Court held that, generally, federal officers could be sued for money damages for violations of the Fifth Amendment.

A crucial issue was that when Congress amended Title VII of the Civil Rights Act of 1964 to protect federal workers from employment discrimination, it specifically exempted employees of Congress.[43] The defendant alleged that this meant Congress had intended that its members not be subject to such suits.

The Court, however, rejected this argument, concluding that when it excluded its own members from Title VII, Congress did not mean to foreclose all other remedies.[44] Thus Davis could sue the now-former congressman for gender discrimination in violation of the Fifth Amendment even though a statutory provision indicated that members of Congress should not be liable for employment discrimination. In allowing the suit, the Court emphasized the judiciary's role in ensuring effective protection of constitutional rights. "We presume," the Court stated, "that justiciable constitutional rights are to be enforced through the courts. And, unless such rights are to become merely precatory, the class of those litigants who allege that their own constitutional rights have been violated, and who at the same time have no effective means other than the judiciary to enforce these rights, must be able to invoke the existing jurisdiction of the courts for the protection of their justiciable constitutional rights."[45]

In *Carlson v. Green,* the Supreme Court considered *Bivens* relief in an instance where an alternative federal law remedy existed.[46] Marie Green, whose son had died while serving a sentence in the Federal Corrections Center in Terre Haute, Indiana, sued prison officials on her son's behalf, claiming that his death was caused by gross inadequacies of medical facilities and staff and that this constituted cruel and unusual punishment. A remedy was available under the Federal Tort Claims Act, which allows suits against the United States for money damages for the negligent actions of federal officials. The issue before the Supreme Court was whether a *Bivens* suit should be allowed in light of this alternative.[47]

The Court ruled that *Bivens* suits were a "counterpart" to the Federal Tort Claims Act. The Act creates liability for the federal government, and *Bivens* permits recovery from the officers. It found no indication that Congress intended the Act to preempt *Bivens* suits.[48]

The Court also concluded that the remedies available under the Federal Tort Claims Act were not as effective as a *Bivens* suit. For instance, punitive damages and jury trials are available in *Bivens* litigation, but not under the Federal Tort Claims Act.[49] The Court emphasized that damages against individual officers were a more effective deterrent to constitutional violations.[50] And it noted that under the Federal Tort Claims Act, a cause of action exists only if liability arises under the laws of the state where the wrong occurred. The Court felt that the protection of federal rights should not depend on state law.

Almost certainly, neither *Davis* nor (especially) *Carlson* would be decided the same way today. In subsequent cases, the Court has insisted that the existence of a federal law, even if it provides no remedy, bars people who have suffered an injury at the hands of federal officers from filing a *Bivens* suit.

The first time the Court found that the existence of an alternative remedy foreclosed a *Bivens* suit was in a case in 1983, *Bush v. Lucas*.[51] William C. Bush, an aerospace engineer employed by the National Aeronautics and Space Administration, claimed that he had been demoted because he had made public statements that were highly critical of NASA. In 1975, he appealed his demotion to the Federal Employee Appeals Authority, which ruled against him, holding that his public statements were misleading and therefore fell outside the protections of the First Amendment. Two years later, Bush asked the Civil Service Commission Appeals Review Board to reopen the case. It did so, found in his favor on First Amendment grounds, and recommended reinstatement with back pay. The recommendation was accepted.

During the administrative appeals process, Bush filed suit in Alabama state court against his superiors, seeking damages for defamation and for violation of his First Amendment rights. The defendants removed the case to federal court. The district court found that there were no grounds for a *Bivens* suit because alternative remedies existed under the Civil Service Commission regulations, and the Supreme Court agreed. The Court stated at the outset that it assumed that Bush's First Amendment rights had been violated, that the civil service remedies were not as effective as a damages remedy, and that Congress had not explicitly precluded a *Bivens* suit. Nonetheless, it ruled that the existence of comprehensive civil service remedies prevented Bush from bringing a case directly under the First Amendment.

Before this decision, the Court had said that to preclude *Bivens* suits, Congress must have expressly declared that it had provided an alternative remedy that it deemed to be an equally effective substitute. In *Bush*, however, the Court said that Congress could "indicate its intent [to prevent judicial remedies] by statutory language, by clear legislative history, or perhaps even by the statutory remedy itself."[52] The question of whether a *Bivens* suit should be allowed "cannot be answered simply by noting that existing remedies do not provide complete relief for the plaintiff."[53] Rather, said the Court, Congress was in the best position to make policy judgments about what remedies should be available to federal employees. The Court found that these policy considerations were "special factors counselling hesitation" and refused to allow a *Bivens* suit.

Although the Supreme Court did not hold that all *Bivens* suits are precluded by the Civil Service Reform Act, lower courts have consistently applied *Bush* to bar *Bivens* suits by federal employees for matters covered by civil service act remedies.[54] One court concluded that "in the field of federal employment, even if no remedy at all has been provided by the Civil Service Reform Act, courts will not create a *Bivens* remedy."[55] In other words, even when the First Amendment rights of a federal government employee are violated, federal courts can provide no remedy whatsoever.

In *Schweiker v. Chilicky,* the Supreme Court again found that congressionally created remedies preclude a *Bivens* suit.[56] *Chilicky* arose from the Reagan Administration's illegal policy of disqualifying large numbers of Social Security disability recipients. Under a congressionally created program called Continuing Disability Review, the Social Security Administration wrongfully stopped disability payments to almost 200,000 individuals.[57] Congress then concluded that the Social Security Administration was abusing the review process and passed emergency legislation to stop the disqualifications. But many people went through months of financial hardship and the loss of medical benefits before the benefits were restored.

One of those people was James Chilicky, who was in the hospital recovering from open-heart surgery when he was informed that his heart condition was no longer disabling and that his disability benefits were discontinued. He sued one state and two federal officers in federal court in Arizona, claiming they had denied his benefits, causing him great suffering, without due process of law. The issue before the Supreme Court was whether the denial of a citizen's due process rights creates a cause of action for money damages against government officers.

The Court concluded that the existence of a congressionally created remedial scheme was a special factor counseling hesitation, and that it precluded a *Bivens* suit. "When the design of a government program," Justice O'Connor wrote for the majority, "suggests that Congress has provided what it considers adequate remedial mechanisms for constitutional violations that may occur in the course of administration, we have not created additional *Bivens* remedies."[58] After reviewing the administrative and judicial procedures that exist to correct wrongful denials of Social Security disability benefits, the Court declared that "the case before us cannot reasonably be distinguished from *Bush v. Lucas*."[59]

In a sharp dissent, Justices Brennan, Marshall, and Blackmun argued that "it is inconceivable that Congress meant by such mere silence to bar all redress for such injuries."[60] Noting how inadequate the existing procedures were to remedy the injuries Chilicky had suffered, they emphasized that there was no indication that Congress meant to deny recovery for constitutional violations. Once more, even with egregious constitutional violations that inflicted great injury, federal courts could provide no remedy.

The most recent decision precluding a *Bivens* suit because of a federal statute, *Hui v. Castaneda*, has deeply disturbing facts.[61] Francisco Castaneda was detained by the United States Immigration and Customs Enforcement authorities. He repeatedly sought treatment for a lesion on his penis that was growing, frequently bleeding, and emitting a discharge. It became very painful and a lump developed in his groin. A Public Health Service physician assistant and three outside specialists said that he needed to have a biopsy to see whether he had cancer. But because a Public Health Service physician and a Public Health Service officer considered this an "elective" procedure, he was denied the biopsy and was instead treated with ibuprofen and given an additional ration of boxer shorts.[62]

Almost a year after Castaneda complained of the lesion, a biopsy was performed. It disclosed he had penile cancer. His penis was amputated and he was treated with chemotherapy, but he died a year later. Before he died, he brought a *Bivens* suit against the Public Health Service officials who denied him a biopsy and medical treatment.

The Supreme Court unanimously ruled that a *Bivens* suit was not available because a federal statute gave Public Health Service officers immunity from liability. Justice Sotomayor, writing for the Court, stated: "Our inquiry in this case begins and ends with the text of §233(a)," a law that provides immunity for Public Health Service officers. Since this

statute creates absolute immunity for Public Health Service officers, Sotomayor wrote, there could be no *Bivens* claims against them. She concluded by declaring that the suit had to be dismissed because "§233(a)
plainly precludes a *Bivens* action against petitioners for the harms alleged in this case."[63] What distinguished this case from *Carlson v. Green*,
which also involved a claim against prison officials, was that *Carlson* did
not involve a statute creating immunity.

    Hui v. Castaneda goes further than any prior decision in allow-
ing Congress to preclude *Bivens* suits. In the earlier cases, the Court
demanded that alternative remedies, even if inadequate, had to be available. But *Hui v. Castaneda* does away with this requirement. Congress
can foreclose *Bivens* claims simply by declaring that federal officers are
immune to liability. But Congress, by statute, should not be able to preclude the federal courts from enforcing the United States Constitution
and from providing a remedy for constitutional violations. In *Bivens*,
the Court said that Congress could cut off *Bivens* suits by providing an
alternative remedy that it deemed to be an effective substitute for suits
against individual officers; but *Hui v. Castaneda* holds that Congress can
preclude *Bivens* suits without providing any remedy.

    There is a striking contrast between *Davis* and *Carlson*, on one
side, and *Bush, Chilicky*, and *Hui*, on the other. In *Davis* and *Carlson*,
the Court permitted *Bivens* suits because Congress had not explicitly
precluded relief. In *Bush, Chilicky*, and *Hui*, the Court denied *Bivens*
suits despite the inadequacy of other remedies, and in the absence of an
express declaration from Congress. In *Carlson*, the unavailability of punitive damages or a jury trial under the Federal Tort Claims Act was part
of the reason the Court permitted a *Bivens* suit. But in *Bush* the absence
of punitive damages and a jury trial under the Civil Service procedures
did not justify a *Bivens* suit.[64]

NO *BIVENS* SUITS FOR CLAIMS ARISING
FROM MILITARY SERVICE

The Supreme Court has applied the exception for "special factors counselling hesitation" to prevent suits arising from military service. In
Chappell v. Wallace, the Court addressed an allegation of discriminatory

practices by superior officers directed at minority enlisted personnel of the United States Navy.[65] Five African American enlisted men who served in the United States Navy on board a combat naval vessel sued the commanding officer of the vessel. The plaintiffs claimed that because of their race they were not assigned to desirable duties and they were threatened, given low performance evaluations, and given penalties of unusual severity.

The Supreme Court, in an opinion by Chief Justice Burger, concluded that the special nature of the military was a factor counseling hesitation. Burger wrote:

> Centuries of experience have developed a hierarchical structure of discipline and obedience to command, unique in its application to the military establishment and wholly different from civilian patterns. Civilian courts must, at the very least, hesitate long before entertaining a suit which asks the court to tamper with the established relationship between enlisted military personnel and their superior officers; that relationship is at the heart of the necessarily unique structure of the Military Establishment.[66]

This decision left the lower courts unsure whether the Court had barred all or only some *Bivens* suits arising out of military service.[67] The Court resolved this uncertainty in 1987 in *United States v. Stanley* where it made clear that all such suits are barred.[68]

James Stanley, as described in Chapter 1, was a former serviceman who sought damages because he had been given LSD, without his knowledge or consent, in an army experiment in 1958, causing lifelong psychological injury. The Supreme Court held that the United States government was immune from suit under the Federal Tort Claims Act because of the *Feres* doctrine, which prohibits suits against the federal government arising from military service. Moreover, the government officers who subjected Stanley to medical experimentation without his permission also could not be subject to a *Bivens* suit. In an opinion by Justice Scalia, the Court flatly declared "that no *Bivens* remedy is available for injuries that 'arise out of or are in the course of activity incident to service.'"[69] The Court concluded that under *Chappell v. Wallace,* all *Bivens* suits arising from military service were precluded by the need to preserve the military hierarchy.

Several justices wrote scathing dissents to this part of the opinion. Justice O'Connor said that while she agreed with *Chappell,* "conduct of the type alleged in this case is so far beyond the bounds of human decency that as a matter of law it simply cannot be considered a part of the military mission."[70] She contended that the defendants did not need insulation from liability resulting from the deliberate exposure of healthy individuals to medical tests without their consent. Justice Brennan drew parallels to Nazi medical experiments and argued that victims like Stanley must have a remedy for violations of their constitutional rights.[71]

There is no question that Stanley's constitutional rights were violated and that he suffered great harm as a result. But he could not sue the United States because of its sovereign immunity, and he could not sue the people who injured him. The law is now settled that *Bivens* suits are never permitted for constitutional violations arising from military service, no matter how severe the injury or how egregious the rights infringement. This is why Ariana Klay and Janet Galla and other women who were raped and sexually harassed while in military service were left with no remedy.

A total bar on suits is not necessary in order to protect military discipline and hierarchical authority.[72] Although the military presents a unique context, suits should be available at least in instances of deliberate and willful violations of constitutional rights. There is no evidence that liability for blatant, intentional constitutional violations would disrupt the military, or that immunity should exist for such grossly abusive behavior helps maintain military discipline.

STILL MORE LIMITS ON *BIVENS* SUITS

Yet the Supreme Court has gone further in precluding *Bivens* suits. It has said that even if the plaintiff can get past the obstacles described above, *Bivens* claims are not allowed if, on balance, it is not desirable to permit them. The 2007 case *Wilkie v. Robbins* articulated this new, very significant limit.[73]

Harvey Robbins was a Wyoming landowner who claimed that Charles Wilkie and other employees of the Federal Bureau of Land Management had unconstitutionally harassed and persecuted him for refusing to give the government an easement on his land. As Justice Ginsburg wrote in her dissent, when Robbins refused to grant the requested easement, "the BLM officials mounted a seven-year campaign of relentless harassment and intimidation to force Robbins to give in. They refused to maintain the road providing access to the ranch, trespassed on Robbins' property, brought unfounded criminal charges against him, canceled his special recreational use permit and grazing privileges, interfered with his business operations, and invaded the privacy of his ranch guests on cattle drives."[74]

The Court, however, said that a *Bivens* suit was not available *even if there were no alternative remedies* because, on balance, it was not desirable to allow such a claim. Justice Souter, writing for the Court, explained: "The decision whether to recognize a *Bivens* remedy may require two steps. In the first place, there is the question whether any alternative, existing process for protecting the interest amounts to a convincing reason for the Judicial Branch to refrain from providing a new and freestanding remedy in damages. But even in the absence of an alternative, a *Bivens* remedy is a subject of judgment: 'the federal courts must make the kind of remedial determination that is appropriate for a common-law tribunal, paying particular heed, however, to any special factors counselling hesitation before authorizing a new kind of federal litigation.'"[75]

Given that it was uncertain whether Robbins had an alternative remedy, the Court said, "this, then, is a case for Bivens step two, for weighing reasons for and against the creation of a new cause of action, the way common law judges have always done."[76] The Court concluded that allowing a *Bivens* suit was undesirable because it might lead to a flood of other litigation and because of the difficulty of proving whether government officers were acting out of a retaliatory motive. "The point here is not to deny that Government employees sometimes overreach, for of course they do, and they may have done so here if all the allegations are true. The point is the reasonable fear that a general *Bivens* cure would be worse than the disease."[77]

The Court acknowledged that there is little left of *Bivens:* "in most instances we have found a *Bivens* remedy unjustified." Indeed, if the concern over a "flood of litigation" is enough to preclude a *Bivens* suit, it is easy to imagine using this as a basis for denying almost any suit against federal officers who violate the Constitution. After all, it seems that there would be many fewer suits against officials of the Bureau of Land Management as compared to allowing *Bivens* suits against federal government law enforcement personnel, which is what *Bivens* itself involved. More important, the Court has made a value judgment: the efficiency gained by preventing suits is more important than keeping the federal courts available to remedy constitutional violations.

PRIVATE PRISONS AND THEIR GUARDS
CANNOT BE SUED AT ALL

Governments at all levels, including the federal government, increasingly make contracts with private companies to run prisons.[78] Astoundingly, the Supreme Court has held that neither private prisons nor private prison guards can be sued for constitutional violations when they are operating under contracts with the federal government.

In *Correctional Services Corp. v. Malesko,*[79] the Court held that a private entity that operates a prison cannot be sued in a *Bivens* action. The issue was whether a *Bivens* suit could be brought against a private company operating a halfway house under a contract with the Federal Bureau of Prisons. John Malesko, an inmate in the halfway house, had a serious heart condition but was not allowed to use the facility's elevator despite being housed on the fifth floor of the facility. In 1994, after he suffered a heart attack brought on by climbing the stairs, he brought a *Bivens* claim against the halfway house.

The Supreme Court, in a five-to-four decision, held that private entities may not be sued under *Bivens.* Chief Justice Rehnquist's majority opinion stressed that *Bivens* suits are available against individual federal officers, not against government or private entities. "Respondent . . . seeks a marked extension of *Bivens,*" Rehnquist wrote, "to contexts that would not advance *Bivens*' core purpose of deterring individual officers from engaging in constitutional wrongdoing. The caution toward extending *Bivens* remedies into any new context, a caution consistently and repeatedly recognized for three decades, forecloses such an extension here."[80]

Rehnquist noted that Malesko could have sought damages under the tort law in his state, but that was true in *Bivens* as well. The whole point of *Bivens* was that people who suffer from constitutional violations should not have to depend on state court remedies, which may or may not be available, and that federal courts must be able to address violations of the United States Constitution.

In *Minneci v. Pollard,* the Court restricted *Bivens* suits even further. It held that prison guards at a private prison operating under a contract with the federal government could not be sued in a *Bivens* action.[81] Richard Lee Pollard was an inmate at a private prison operating under a contract with the federal government. He suffered a broken arm for which he received inadequate treatment, causing him great pain and suffering. The law is clear that deliberate indifference to a prisoner's medical needs constitutes cruel and unusual punishment under the Eighth Amendment.[82] Pollard could not sue the private prison because of the Supreme Court's decision in *Correctional Services Corp. v. Malesko,* so he sued the prison guards instead.

But the Court said that no *Bivens* claim could be brought by a prisoner who suffered physical injuries and claimed an Eighth Amendment violation because state tort law provided some remedy, even though those remedies would not be the same as those available from a *Bivens* action. Justice Breyer, writing for the Court, stated: "Where, as here, a federal prisoner seeks damages from privately employed personnel working at a privately operated federal prison, where the conduct allegedly amounts to a violation of the Eighth Amendment, and where that conduct is of a kind that typically falls within the scope of traditional state tort law (such as the conduct involving improper medical care at issue here), the prisoner must seek a remedy under state tort law. We cannot imply a *Bivens* remedy in such a case."[83] Only Justice Ginsburg dissented.

This decision and *Correctional Services Corp. v. Malesko,* when taken together, mean that inmates whose constitutional rights are violated in private prisons, even when they suffer horribly as a result, cannot sue in federal court. Worse, these decisions create a significant new limitation: for the first time, the Court has said that the existence of *state* remedies can preclude a *Bivens* cause of action. In earlier cases, the Court said that the existence of a federal statutory remedy could preclude a *Bivens* action. In *Bivens* itself, the Court explicitly rejected the argument that a state tort remedy could be a reason to deny a federal lawsuit for a constitutional violation. State tort remedies usually exist, at least in theory. But the original *Bivens* decision was based on the premise that, for violations of the federal Constitution, federal courts must be able to provide a federal remedy. This has now been completely erased.

For thirty-five years, in decision after decision, the Supreme Court has made *Bivens* suits less and less available. People who are injured by federal officials are often left with no remedy, and federal courts are left unable to enforce the Constitution. The Court has not completely overruled *Bivens,* but it has dramatically restricted the ability to sue federal officers with those injured often left with no remedy.

The Immunity Defense

Although no statute authorizes suits against federal officers for money damages or for injunctive relief, there is a federal law that creates a cause of action against state and local officers who violate the Constitution: Section 1983 of the Civil Rights Act of 1871. The reason for this law can be inferred from the date. Following the Civil War and the adoption of the Thirteenth, Fourteenth, and Fifteenth Amendments, violence against the newly freed slaves was endemic throughout the South. The U.S. Senate conducted extensive investigations, especially focusing on the role of a then-new organization, the Ku Klux Klan. A six-hundred-page Senate report detailed the Southern states' unwillingness or inability to bring the Klan under control.[84] Congress adopted the Civil Rights Act of 1871, formally titled "An Act to Enforce the Provisions of the Fourteenth Amendment to the Constitution, and for other Purposes," in response to the report. As the Supreme Court described it almost a century later, the law was directed against "the campaign of violence and deception in the South, fomented by the Ku Klux Klan, which was denying decent citizens their civil and political rights."[85]

While the bill was under consideration, both houses of Congress engaged in lengthy discussions about the failure of state police and state courts to control the Klan. Section 1983 was meant to substantially alter the relationship between the federal government and the states. It empowered the federal government, and especially the federal courts, with the authority to prevent and redress violations of federal rights. As the Supreme Court declared: "the very purpose of §1983 was to interpose the federal courts between the States and the people, as guardians of the people's federal rights—to protect the people from unconstitutional action under color of state law, whether that action be executive, legislative, or judicial."[86]

Section 1983 is written in absolute language. It says, "*Every* person who, under color of any statute, ordinance, regulation, custom, or usage of any State or Territory or the District of Columbia, subjects, or causes to be subjected, *any citizen of the United States or other person* within the jurisdiction thereof to the deprivation of any rights, privileges, or immunities secured by the Constitution and laws, shall be liable to the party injured in an action at law, suit in equity, or other proper proceeding for redress." There are no exceptions.

But the Supreme Court disagrees. The Court has ruled over many decades that *all* government officials who are sued for money damages are immune from liability. Some have absolute immunity, meaning that they cannot be held liable at all, no matter how egregious their conduct or how horrible the injury they inflict. All other government officials are said to have "qualified immunity," meaning they be held liable only if they violate clearly established law that every reasonable officer should know.

Immunity doctrines are extremely important. The availability of relief against individual officers is often crucial because, as explained in Chapter 2, the government itself is often completely protected from liability. If injured individuals are to receive compensation, and if illegal government conduct is to be deterred, they must be able to sue individual officers.

It is widely believed that some immunity for individual officers is necessary. At minimum, it seems unfair to hold an officer personally liable if he or she had no reason to know that the actions taken were illegal. As the Supreme Court remarked, official immunity reflects "the injustice, particularly in the absence of bad faith, of subjecting to liability an officer who is required by the legal obligations of his position, to exercise discretion."[87] There is also concern that the absence of immunity might make it difficult to attract people into government service, or would chill the exercise of discretion. I am thus not arguing against all immunity for government officers. My objection is to the scope it has been given by the Supreme Court, and the extent to which it precludes enforcement of the Constitution.

ABSOLUTE IMMUNITY

The Supreme Court has said that some official tasks are protected by absolute immunity and thus cannot be the basis of any lawsuit for monetary relief. Judges performing judicial tasks, prosecutors performing prosecutorial tasks, legislators performing legislative tasks, law enforcement personnel testifying as witnesses, and the President performing presidential tasks can never be held liable for money damages, no matter how awful or clearly wrong their conduct or how horrific the resulting injury.

Absolute immunity is a creation of the Supreme Court. Its purpose is to protect the exercise of discretion by government officials. But *absolute* immunity is not necessary to achieve these goals. The choice is not limited to absolute immunity or no immunity. For example, certain functions could be protected by according immunity except for malicious acts or for intentional violations of rights. Such a standard would open the door to litigation, but other procedural devices are available to protect officials from meritless suits.

The impact of absolute immunity in keeping federal courts from enforcing the Constitution is evident in every area where the Supreme Court has created it.

Absolute judicial immunity. This chapter began with the story of *Stump v. Sparkman,* where the Court held that Linda Sparkman could not sue the judge who ordered her surgical sterilization, even though he unquestionably violated her constitutional rights and permanently took away her ability to have children. A similar case is *Mireles v. Waco.*[88]

Judge Raymond Mireles, upset that a lawyer did not show up in court despite a subpoena, told the bailiff to find the lawyer and forcibly bring him to court. He instructed the bailiff to rough up the lawyer to teach him a lesson. The lawyer, Howard Waco, filed a complaint against the judge alleging that the officers "by means of unreasonable force and violence seize[d] plaintiff and remove[d] him backwards" from another courtroom where he was waiting to appear, cursed him, and called him "vulgar and offensive names," then "without necessity slammed" him through the doors and swinging gates into Judge Mireles' courtroom.

The Supreme Court said that Waco's suit had to be dismissed because the judge possessed absolute immunity. The Court accepted Waco's allegations as true but said this did not matter: "judicial immunity is not overcome by allegations of bad faith or malice."[89]

Judges need some protection from being sued, but not for conduct like this or for ordering a girl's sterilization without legal authority. A judge who acts maliciously or without authority should be held liable. Those injured by the wrongdoing deserve compensation, and judges should be deterred from engaging in such behavior.

A very disturbing trend in the lower federal courts is extending absolute judicial immunity to administrative officials who never would be considered judges. For example, a federal court of appeals found that members of a county board that reviewed property tax assessments were entitled to absolute immunity when it was alleged that their decisions were politically biased.[90] The court reasoned that since these were "adjudicatory" decisions, the government officials—who were in no way judges—were protected by absolute judicial immunity.[91] Another federal court of appeals found that current and former Pennsylvania Gaming Control Board officials could not be sued for allegedly violating the Constitution in denying an application for a slot machine license.[92] The court explained that the board members were making individualized determinations and thus should be accorded absolute immunity. Courts have found that members of occupational licensing boards who allegedly have unconstitutionally denied professional licenses are also protected by absolute judicial immunity.[93]

These executive decision-makers are not by any definition judges. They have the capacity to violate the Constitution and inflict great injuries. Because it is so difficult to sue government entities, the victims usually have no other remedy. Yet the trend in the lower courts is to broadly accord absolute judicial immunity and preclude any litigation.

Absolute prosecutorial immunity. Prosecutors, too, have absolute immunity to suits for damages for prosecutorial misconduct. In *Imbler v. Pachtman,* the Supreme Court accorded absolute immunity to a prosecutor who knowingly used perjured testimony that caused an innocent person to be convicted and imprisoned for nine years.[94] The Court concluded that anything less than absolute immunity risked "harassment by unfounded litigation [that] would cause a deflection of the prosecutor's energies from his public duties, and the possibility that he would shade his decisions instead of exercising the independence of judgment required by his public trust."[95]

But something less than absolute immunity can achieve this goal without completely undermining enforcement of the Constitution. Prosecutors should not have absolute immunity when they knowingly use perjured testimony or otherwise intentionally violate people's constitutional rights.

Van de Kamp v. Goldstein is another illustration of the damage absolute prosecutorial immunity can inflict.[96] Thomas Lee Goldstein spent twenty-four years in prison for a murder that he did not commit. No eyewitnesses testified against him at his trial. There was no physical evidence linking him to the murder site. The primary evidence against Goldstein was the false testimony of a long-time jailhouse informant, Edward Floyd Fink. As the federal court of appeals explained: "Thomas Goldstein spent 24 years in prison after being convicted for murder based largely upon the perjured testimony of an unreliable jailhouse informant."[97]

At the time of his arrest, in 1979, Goldstein was an engineering student and a Marine Corps veteran with no criminal history. Once arrested on this basis, Goldstein awaited trial in the city jail in Long Beach, California, where he had the misfortune of being placed in a cell with Edward Fink. A heroin addict with a long criminal record, Fink had a long history of getting deals from prosecutors, such as reduced sentences, in exchange for testimony against his fellow inmates. He testified at Goldstein's trial that Goldstein admitted to the murder while they were together in the jail cell. On the basis of this testimony, Goldstein spent twenty-four years in prison.

In 1963, in *Brady v. Maryland*, the Supreme Court held that prosecutors have the constitutional duty to turn over to criminal defendants any evidence that might help show the defendant's innocence or impeach key prosecution witnesses.[98] Police and prosecutors often uncover exculpatory information when investigating crimes, and they should not be able to hide this evidence. The Supreme Court held and often reaffirmed that it violates due process of law if a prosecutor fails to disclose evidence that could materially assist the defendant at trial or at sentencing. Additionally, every state's code of professional responsibility, which regulates lawyer behavior, requires that prosecutors turn over to the defense any potentially exculpatory information, including any that might help reduce the defendant's sentence.

There is no dispute that the prosecutors in Goldstein's case had the constitutional duty to inform his defense counsel of Fink's history of making deals in exchange for reduced charges and sentences. This would have provided a crucial basis for impeaching the key witness against Goldstein. Obviously, there were lawyers in the Los Angeles District Attorney's office who knew of these deals, because they had negotiated them, and who could have informed Goldstein's attorneys. But they never did.

After he had spent over two decades in prison, a federal district court granted Goldstein's habeas corpus petition. The court concluded that there was no reliable evidence linking him to the murders and that Fink's testimony was so lacking in credibility that it could not be the basis for a conviction. The federal court of appeals agreed, and, finally, Tommy Lee Goldstein was a free man.

Goldstein then sued the District Attorney of Los Angeles County, John Van de Kamp, and other top officials, claiming they had violated his constitutional rights "by purposefully or with deliberate indifference" failing to create a system that would ensure that key evidence would be turned over to defendants. Goldstein also argued that the District Attorney violated Goldstein's constitutional rights by failing to adequately train and supervise deputy district attorneys to ensure that they shared information regarding jailhouse informants with their colleagues.

The federal court of appeals ruled that Goldstein's suit could go forward against Van De Kamp and others in his office. But the Supreme Court unanimously reversed this decision and ordered Goldstein's case dismissed. Justice Breyer wrote the opinion for the Court and said that prosecutors have absolute immunity to suits for money damages—they cannot be sued at all—and this extends even to the administrative practices that led to Goldstein's wrongful conviction. Tommy Lee Goldstein spent twenty-four years in prison for a murder he did not commit, but the Supreme Court said that the prosecutors were protected by absolute immunity. Such a clear injustice shows how absolute immunity keeps the federal courts from enforcing the Constitution.

Absolute legislative immunity. The Court has not only given legislators absolute immunity for their legislative tasks, but also has broadly construed who is protected by this. In *Bogan v. Scott-Harris,* an individual who worked as a police psychologist had his job eliminated by the mayor and city council as part of the city's budget process.[99] He sued, alleging that his firing was racially motivated and was in retaliation for speech activities.

The Supreme Court dismissed the suit against both the mayor and the members of the city council on the basis of absolute legislative immunity. It unanimously concluded that the process of proposing, voting for, and signing a budget are "integral steps in the legislative process" and thus safeguarded by absolute immunity. The psychologist's firing may or may not have been racially motivated; we will likely never find out. Even if it was blatantly unconstitutional, there was no remedy available.

Even if absolute immunity for legislators is justified—and I question whether *absolute* immunity is ever justified—there is no reason it should protect the mayor, an executive official. Presidents, governors, mayors all participate in the budgetary process, but as part of their executive duties. They are not legislators and should not have legislative immunity.

Law enforcement personnel testifying as witnesses. The Supreme Court has held that police officers and other law enforcement personnel have absolute immunity for the testimony they give as witnesses, even if they commit perjury. In general, police officers have only qualified, good faith immunity to suits under Section 1983 or in a *Bivens* action. But in *Briscoe v. LaHue,* the Court ruled that police officers who commit perjury have absolute immunity in suits against them for money damages.[100] Officers must be able to testify as witnesses without worrying about civil litigation, the Court reasoned; if absolute immunity did not exist, they would be sued frequently. Allowing such suits "might undermine not only their contribution to the judicial process but also the effective performance of their other public duties."[101] The Court emphasized that like all other witnesses, police officers can be criminally prosecuted for perjury (something that rarely occurs), and it argued that this provides an adequate deterrent to perjury. In other words, a police officer can lie under oath, cause an innocent person to be convicted and imprisoned, and then be totally immune to any civil liability.

The Supreme Court has extended this immunity to other witnesses for law enforcement, and beyond trials to other stages of criminal proceedings.[102] In 2004, Charles Rehberg, a certified public accountant in Albany, Georgia, sent anonymous faxes criticizing the management of a local hospital to several recipients. In response, apparently as a favor to the hospital's leadership, the local district attorney's office began a criminal investigation of Rehberg. The investigation was solely in retaliation for Rehberg's speaking out about the hospital's management; there was no indication that Rehberg had committed any crime.

James Paulk, the chief investigator in the district attorney's office, then went before a grand jury and lied about Rehberg. He testified that Rehberg had assaulted a hospital physician, Dr. James Hotz, after unlawfully entering the doctor's home. Rehberg was indicted for aggravated assault, burglary, and six counts of making harassing telephone calls. He challenged the indictment and a judge dismissed it for lack of any evidence to support it.

A few months later, Paulk returned to the grand jury, and Rehberg was indicted again for assaulting Dr. Hotz and for making harassing phone calls. Rehberg challenged the sufficiency of this second indictment, claiming that he was "nowhere near Dr. Hotz" on the date in question and that "there was no evidence whatsoever that [he] committed an assault on anybody." The indictment was dismissed again.

Undaunted, Paulk went before a grand jury a third time, and yet another indictment was returned. Rehberg was again charged with assault and making harassing phone calls. This indictment was dismissed as well.

Rehberg then sued Paulk for malicious prosecution in violation of the Fourth Amendment. This should have been an easy case. Paulk abused his power by three times lying before a grand jury to get a person indicted. Rehberg had financial costs for the lawyer he had to retain and for the emotional costs of being thrice falsely indicted. But when the case came before it in 2012, the Supreme Court unanimously ruled that Paulk was protected by absolute immunity.

In an opinion by Justice Alito, the Court held that it did not matter that the testimony was before a grand jury rather than at trial or by an investigator rather than a police officer: *Briscoe v. LaHue* stil applied. "We conclude that grand jury witnesses should enjoy the same immunity as witnesses at trial," Alito wrote. "This means that a grand jury witness has absolute immunity from any §1983 claim based on the witness' testimony."[103] Rehberg could not claim that Paulk had conspired to present false testimony or advance any other claim based on Paulk's testimony. "In the vast majority of cases involving a claim against a grand jury witness, the witness and the prosecutor conducting the investigation engage in preparatory activity, such as a preliminary discussion in which the witness relates the substance of his intended testimony. We decline to endorse a rule of absolute immunity that is so easily frustrated."[104]

Police and prosecutor's investigators cannot be sued for money damages, the Court ruled, even if they knowingly and intentionally lie under oath. They can be criminally prosecuted or administratively disciplined, of course, but the victims of their wrongdoing, who may have been egregiously injured and even falsely imprisoned for years, are left without any remedy. Once more the federal courts are left powerless to enforce the Constitution and provide redress.

Absolute presidential immunity. The final area where the Supreme Court has found absolute immunity is suits against the President for money damages for acts done while in office. In 1968, A. Ernest Fitzgerald was an analyst in the Defense Department who testified before Congress about cost overruns in building a transport plane. President Nixon was furious at him for embarrassing the Defense Department and ordered that Fitzgerald be fired. Fitzgerald sued Nixon for violating Fitzgerald's First Amendment rights to freedom of speech and to petition Congress for a redress of grievances.

The Supreme Court ruled in *Nixon v. Fitzgerald* that the President has absolute immunity and cannot be sued for money damages for actions committed in his official capacity.[105] In a 5–4 decision, the Court held that the President's "unique status under the Constitution" and the "singular importance" of his duties justified absolute immunity. As in other cases according absolute immunity, the Court emphasized the likelihood of frequent suits as a justification. The result, once more, is that even if the President blatantly violates the Constitution and imposes great harm, federal courts are powerless to provide a remedy.

Judges, prosecutors, legislators, police officers, and the President have enormous power. Although there is the need to protect them from frivolous suits, this protection does not require a complete bar on litigation. If these officers act maliciously, then like the rest of us, they should be held liable so as to compensate victims and deter wrongdoing. Otherwise, what is left of the assurance in *Marbury v. Madison* that no one is above the law and that "the government of the United States has been emphatically termed a government of laws, and not of men"?[106] Absolute immunity, by its very definition, puts some people above the law.

Qualified Immunity

The Supreme Court clearly believes that without the protection of absolute immunity, it would be far too easy to hold government officials liable for actions taken in good faith. The reality is just the opposite. *All* government officials—local, state, and federal—who are sued for money damages for constitutional violations are protected by qualified immunity if they are not accorded absolute immunity. The Court has recently redefined this standard to make it very difficult for plaintiffs to recover damages.

The Court first tried to define qualified immunity in *Scheuer v. Rhodes*.[107] On May 4, 1970, the Ohio National Guard killed four students participating in an antiwar demonstration at Kent State University. Litigation was commenced, on behalf of three of the students, against the governor of Ohio and several state officials, alleging that the defendants "intentionally, recklessly, willfully and wantonly" deployed the National Guard and instructed them to act illegally.

The Supreme Court ruled that the governor lacked absolute immunity and could claim only qualified immunity. In determining whether an act is in good faith, the Court wrote, "it is the existence of reasonable grounds for the belief formed at the time and in light of all the circumstances, coupled with good faith belief, that affords a basis for qualified immunity of executive officers."[108] This became known as the *Scheuer* test; it contained both an objective component (was the act reasonable?) and a subjective one (did this officer believe it was reasonable?). A plaintiff could refute the existence of good faith *either* by demonstrating that a reasonable officer would find the action impermissible or by showing that this particular officer knew his or her action was unreasonable. The Court apparently rejected a purely subjective standard, equating bad faith solely with malice or intent, because it might encourage perjury and would not set a high enough standard for official conduct. On the other hand, a purely objective standard, excluding liability based on the officer's actual state of mind, apparently was rejected because the purpose was to deter and punish those who knowingly act wrongfully.

The second major case developing the definition of good faith immunity was *Wood v. Strickland*.[109] Three students who had been expelled from the public high school in Mena, Arkansas, for the possession of alcohol claimed that they were denied procedural due process and sued school officials. The Supreme Court, in concluding that the officials were entitled to qualified immunity, clarified the test for determining whether an action was in good faith. An official is not immune if "he knew or reasonably should have known that the action" would violate constitutional rights, "or if he took the action with the malicious intention to cause a deprivation of constitutional rights or other injury."[110] Under this standard, an individual officer is liable if a plaintiff demonstrates that the officer acted either unreasonably or with impermissible intent. Interestingly, in light of subsequent developments, Justice Powell wrote a vehement dissent criticizing the *objective* component of the legal test because it was difficult to specify what law an officer should be expected to know.[111]

In 1982, in *Harlow v. Fitzgerald*, the Court revised the test for determining whether the officer acted in good faith.[112] Like *Nixon v. Fitzgerald*, this case concerned a lawsuit by A. Ernest Fitzgerald, who claimed that his job had been eliminated in retaliation for his exposing cost overruns in the Defense Department. Although in the companion case the Supreme Court found the President to possess absolute immunity, here it accorded other executive officials only good faith immunity.[113] The Court expressly discarded the subjective component of the *Scheuer* and *Wood* cases and left just one test of liability: "government officials performing discretionary functions generally are shielded from liability for civil damages insofar as their conduct does not violate clearly established statutory or constitutional rights of which a reasonable person would have known."[114]

The Court reasoned that the subjective element—allowing recovery upon proof of malice—would disrupt government operations. It was too easy for plaintiffs to allege malice in the hope of finding evidence during discovery. Discovery was time-consuming for the officer, and it would be difficult for trial courts to decide the case without a trial on the malice question because subjective intent is a factual matter for the jury to decide.[115] The Court felt that the benefits of the subjective component of the *Wood* test were outweighed by the burdens it would impose.

Still, Justice Powell's majority opinion allowed that the effect of this decision "may be to allow an unscrupulous official to engage in malicious misuse of public authority whenever the relevant legal standards are objectively unclear."[116] But the Court was more concerned with protecting officers from the costs of defending meritless suits than with ensuring that injured individuals receive compensation for wrongs they have suffered—or with enforcing the Constitution.

In a 2011 case, *Ashcroft v. Al-Kidd*, the Court again made it harder to hold government officers accountable.[117] Abdullah al-Kidd, a United States citizen and a married man with two children, was arrested at a Dulles International Airport ticket counter. Over the next sixteen days, he was confined in high-security cells in Virginia, Oklahoma, and then

Idaho, as well as strip-searched several times. Each time he was transferred to a different facility, al-Kidd was handcuffed and shackled about his wrists, legs, and waist. He was then released on "house arrest" and subjected to numerous restrictions on his freedom. By the time his confinement and supervision ended, fifteen months later, he had been fired from his job with a government contractor and had separated from his wife.

Al-Kidd was not arrested based on probable cause that he had committed a crime. Rather, he was held under the federal material witness statute, which allows the government to hold a person who has essential testimony and who otherwise is likely to be unavailable to testify. But the government was not holding Al-Kidd because it wanted to secure his testimony, as that statute requires. His detention had absolutely nothing to do with obtaining testimony. He was detained because federal officials wanted to investigate him, and the Justice Department used the material witness statute because it did not have enough evidence to arrest him on suspicion of any crime.

Al-Kidd was never charged, nor ever used as a material witness. He sued Attorney General John Ashcroft, who had authorized the detention. Ashcroft claimed that he was protected by qualified immunity and moved to dismiss the lawsuit. The federal court of appeals rejected this, saying that any government official, and especially the Attorney General of the United States, should know that arresting and detaining a person as a material witness, if there is no desire to use the person as a witness and no probable cause that the person has committed any crime, is a violation of the Fourth Amendment.[118]

The Supreme Court reversed this decision and held that Al-Kidd had no claim upon which he could recover damages. Justice Scalia, writing for the Court, said that former Attorney General Ashcroft was protected by qualified immunity because it was not clearly established law that his conduct was unconstitutional. Surely it does not take a case on point for the Attorney General of the United States to know that it is unconstitutional to detain someone as a material witness on false pretenses. It is clearly established law that it violates the Fourth Amendment to detain a person without probable cause, and this is exactly what the Justice Department did to Al-Kidd.

But the Court went even further. Justice Scalia, writing for the Court, declared: "A Government official's conduct violates clearly established law when, at the time of the challenged conduct, '[t]he contours of [a] right [are] sufficiently clear' that *every 'reasonable official* would have understood that what he is doing violates that right.' We do not require a case directly on point, but existing precedent *must have placed the statutory or constitutional question beyond debate.*"[119] Never before had the Supreme Court said that "every reasonable official" would have to have known that the conduct was impermissible. Never before had it said that a plaintiff could recover for a constitutional violation only if existing law placed the question "beyond debate." Scalia concluded his opinion with a very broad account of what is protected by qualified immunity. He wrote: "Qualified immunity gives government officials breathing room to make reasonable but mistaken judgments about open legal questions. When properly applied, it protects all but the plainly incompetent or those who knowingly violate the law."[120]

In case after case, the Court has found qualified immunity based on the absence of a case on point. Savannah Redding, a seventh grader at a public school in Safford, Arizona,[121] was suspected by a teacher of having given prescription-strength ibuprofen to another student. Two female school officials took Savannah into another room and strip-searched her. She was required to remove all of her outer clothes and to pull out her bra and underpants so that school officials could look inside. Nothing was found.

Savannah and her parents sued the school officials who subjected her to this degrading and humiliating search, contending that it violated the Fourth Amendment of the Constitution. It wasn't a close question: subjecting a seventh-grade girl to a strip search to look for ibuprofen, with no court order and no probable cause, is an obvious violation. In an 8–1 decision, the Court said that intrusiveness of the search violated the Fourth Amendment, especially given the minor nature of the suspected offense and the lack of any reason to believe that the girl had hidden drugs in her underwear.

But the Court then ruled, 7–2, that the school officials could not be held liable because they had qualified immunity. The law concerning strip searches, the Court said, was not clearly established at the time of the search because there were conflicting lower court cases about when strip searches in schools are permissible. But shouldn't any reasonable teacher or school official have "fair notice" that it is wrong to strip-search a seventh-grade girl, including looking in her underwear and at her breasts and genitals for ibuprofen, especially with no reason to believe she was hiding it there?

Three cases decided by the Supreme Court in 2014 exemplify the breadth of qualified immunity and the often insurmountable obstacle it presents to enforcing the Constitution. In *Lane v. Franks,* the Court unanimously held that a government employee's First Amendment rights were violated when he was fired for truthful testimony he gave in court pursuant to a subpoena.[122] Edward Lane, an official in the community college system in Alabama, discovered that there was a woman on his payroll who was doing no work. She was prosecuted in federal court and Lane testified as a witness. After he testified truthfully, he was fired by his supervisor. This seems so obvious a constitutional violation: of course, it is wrong to fire a person for testifying honestly in a criminal trial, especially when he was compelled to appear by a subpoena.

The Court found that the firing violated Lane's First Amendment rights, but it concluded that the defendant responsible for the firing was protected by qualified immunity. Justice Sotomayor, writing for the Court, said that "the relevant question for qualified immunity purposes is this: Could Franks [the supervisor] reasonably have believed, at the time he fired Lane, that a government employer could fire an employee on account of testimony the employee gave, under oath and outside the scope of his ordinary job responsibilities?" Reviewing the precedents, especially from the Eleventh Circuit, the Court found that none had clearly held that this particular action violated the First Amendment. Yet in an earlier case, *Hope v. Pelzer,* the Court had held that a case on point is not necessary.[123] Shouldn't every government officer know that it is wrong to fire a person for truthfully testifying in court? Why should there have to be a case holding such an obvious proposition in order for there to be liability?

In *Plumhoff v. Rickard,* the Court again found that government officials were protected by qualified immunity.[124] Police officers in West Memphis, Arkansas, pulled over Dennis Rickard because his car had only one operating headlight. Kelly Allen was in the passenger seat. When the officer asked if he had been drinking, Rickard replied that he had not. But because he failed to produce his driver's license upon request and appeared nervous, the officer asked Rickard to step out of the car. Rather than comply with the request, Rickard sped away.

A high-speed chase then occurred that lasted five minutes and reached speeds over 100 miles per hour. At one point, the officers appeared to have Rickard's car pinned. But when the car pulled away, officers shot at it, firing on the car a total of fifteen times. Both the driver and passenger were killed. The United States Court of Appeals for the Sixth Circuit concluded that the police had used excessive force and violated the Fourth Amendment.

The United States Supreme Court unanimously reversed this ruling, holding that there was no violation of the Fourth Amendment. Justice Alito wrote for the Court that the driver's conduct posed a "grave public safety risk" and that the police were justified in shooting at the car to stop it. "It stands to reason that, if police officers are justified in firing at a suspect in order to end a severe threat to public safety, the officers need not stop shooting until the threat has ended." Moreover, the Court said, even if there were a Fourth Amendment violation, the officers were protected by qualified immunity in that the law was not clearly established that their conduct violated the Fourth Amendment.

This is a disturbing holding. The Supreme Court has now said that whenever there is a high-speed chase that the officers believe could injure others—which would seem to be true of virtually all high-speed chases—the police can shoot at the vehicle and keep shooting until it stops. The car was pulled over for having only one working headlight. Why not just let it go and track the driver down later? Why should Dennis Rickard be punished with death for making the foolish choice to flee? Why should Kelly Allen be killed for having the bad luck to be his passenger?

Finally, in *Wood v. Moss,* the Court found that Secret Service agents were protected by qualified immunity when they gave supporters of the President better treatment than detractors at a public speaking event.[125] When President George W. Bush gave a speech in Oregon, the agents allowed his supporters to be closer and pushed the opponents further away. The law is clear that the government cannot discriminate among speakers based on their views unless strict scrutiny is met.

Nonetheless, the Court, with the majority opinion written by Justice Ginsburg, unanimously found that the Secret Service agents were protected by qualified immunity, because there were no cases on point concerning when Secret Service agents violate the First Amendment. But why do there need to be specific cases, since it is clearly established that viewpoint discrimination by government officials violates the First Amendment?

All of these cases were unanimous. All found qualified immunity because of the absence of a case on point. Together they show a Court that is very protective of government officials who are sued, and that has made it very difficult for victims of constitutional violations to recover damages. Not only could the government officers not be sued; in every case it was unlikely that the government entity could be sued either. The federal courts were left unable to enforce the Constitution.

Holding Government Officers Accountable

What needs to be done? First, the law should allow federal officers to be sued for money damages or injunctive relief whenever they are alleged to violate the Constitution. The existence of a federal statute should not preclude such suits, though it can provide a supplemental remedy. Citizens should be able to bring suits against *all* federal government officials who violate the Constitution. There never should be a complete preclusion of suits. Private entities and their employees who contract with the federal government should be liable as well.

Second, absolute immunity should be eliminated as a defense. No government official should be above the law. For some tasks, there should be liability only for intentional or reckless violations of constitutional rights or acts in clear absence of authority. This would protect the exercise of discretion while still allowing liability for egregious violations.

Third, for government officers protected by qualified immunity, there should be liability if either the officer violates clearly established law that a reasonable officer should know, or if it is demonstrated that the officer acted in subjective bad faith. No longer should plaintiffs have to prove that the rights that were violated were ones that "every reasonable officer" would know, or that are established "beyond dispute." The law should return to the standard the Supreme Court established in *Hope v. Pelzer:* there does not have to be a case on point; an officer is liable so long as he or she has "fair warning" that the conduct violates the Constitution.

How can this be achieved? Certainly, the Supreme Court could do it by reformulating the law. Most of what's needed would require nothing more than a return to earlier holdings.

Or the reforms can be accomplished by Congress. Congress can enact a statute, like Section 1983 of the Civil Rights Act of 1871, that allows citizens to sue federal officers who violate the Constitution. Absolute and qualified immunity are entirely a result of the Supreme Court's interpretation of Section 1983; they are not constitutional doctrines. Congress can thus change the law of absolute and qualified immunity at any time.

Federal courts cannot enforce the Constitution if no one can be sued for violating it. The prior chapter described the barriers to suing government entities, and this chapter described the obstacles to suing government officers. Together, these doctrines often mean that no one can be sued. Linda Sparkman was forever denied her constitutional right to have a child and there was nothing she could do.

An Alleged Constitutional Violation Always Should Be Adjudicated

Around 2:00 A.M. on October 6, 1976, Los Angeles police officers stopped an African-American male motorist, twenty-four-year-old Adolpho Lyons, who was driving with a taillight out.[1] Four officers, with guns drawn, ordered him out of his car and told him to face the car, spread his legs, and clasp his hands over his head. Lyons followed these instructions and an officer conducted a pat-down search. When the search was over, he began to drop his hands but was quickly ordered to place them back above his head.

An officer then grabbed Lyons's hands and slammed them, along with the keys Lyons was holding, onto his head. When Lyons complained of the pain from his keys, the officer applied his forearm to Lyons's throat and proceeded to choke him. Even after Lyons was handcuffed, the officer continued to choke him until he passed out. When he regained consciousness, Lyons was lying face down on the ground, choking, and spitting up blood; he had urinated and defecated. The LAPD officers gave him a citation for his broken taillight and released him. Lyons suffered a larynx injury and subsequently realized that he had nearly died from a routine traffic stop.[2]

On February 7, 1978, Lyons filed a complaint in the United States District Court for the Central District of California that alleged seven counts of police misconduct and constitutional violations related to the stranglehold used by the police.[3] The LAPD had authorized a procedure called a "carotid hold,"[4] in which an officer wraps an arm around a person's neck and holds the wrist of that arm with his or her other hand. Pressure is then applied to both sides of the neck,[5] compressing the carotid artery and diminishing blood flow to the brain.[6] By this means, a victim can be rendered unconscious, or even killed, within eight to fourteen seconds.[7] Between 1975 and 1983, when the Supreme Court rendered its decision in *City of Los Angeles v. Lyons*, at least sixteen people were killed by LAPD officers using this stranglehold.[8] Even more disturbing, black men accounted for twelve of these deaths, or 75 percent, in a city where black men constituted just 9 percent of the population.[9]

Lyons maintained that the stranglehold employed by the LAPD violated the First, Fourth, Eighth, and Fourteenth Amendments.[10] His complaint included witness and expert testimony in support of three conclusions. First, use of the stranglehold is very dangerous to the person who is choked.[11] Experts stated that in addition to the high risk of death by asphyxiation, victims also could go into cardiac arrest as the inability to breathe induces a rush of adrenaline as they struggle to get free.[12] Although the LAPD contended its officers used the hold to subdue subjects, it actually has the opposite effect on the body. A stranglehold causes the victim to violently writhe for air, a reaction that officers sensitively nicknamed "doing the chicken."[13]

Second, the LAPD neither properly trained its officers on what circumstances called for such a dangerous submission tactic nor prohibited its use when inappropriate.[14] One witness testified that strangleholds could be used whenever an officer "felt" he might come under bodily attack.[15]

Finally, the complaint presented evidence that safer alternatives existed, especially in situations where there was no imminent threat of deadly force.[16] Notably, by the time the case reached the Supreme Court, the LAPD had stopped using the stranglehold.[17]

The Supreme Court, in a 5–4 decision, held that Lyons lacked standing to seek an injunction that would stop the LAPD from employing the stranglehold in nonthreatening situations. Lyons lacked standing, the Court said, because he could not demonstrate that he personally was likely to be choked again in the future. Justice Byron White, writing for the Court, explained: "Lyons' standing to seek the injunction requested depended on whether he was likely to suffer future injury from the use of the chokeholds by police officers."[18] The Court continued, "Absent a sufficient likelihood that he will again be wronged in a similar way, Lyons is no more entitled to an injunction than any other citizen of Los Angeles; and a federal court may not entertain a claim by any or all citizens who no more than assert that certain practices of law enforcement officers are unconstitutional."[19] *City of Los Angeles v. Lyons* thus establishes that in order to have standing to seek an injunction, the individual must demonstrate a substantial likelihood that he or she personally will be subjected to the allegedly illegal policy in the future.

This decision is wrong on many levels. First, the Court incorrectly assumed that Lyons would suffer an injury in the future only if he would be choked again. But he surely would continue to suffer psychological injury—fear of being subjected to a similar chokehold—so long as he lived in Los Angeles and the LAPD policy remained unchanged.[20]

Second, *Lyons* is a substantial departure from prior practice. Never before had the Supreme Court determined standing on the basis of the remedy sought. In fact, under the Federal Rules of Civil Procedure, a plaintiff is not even required to request injunctive relief in a complaint in order to receive it as a remedy.[21]

Third, and most important, the Court's decision meant that no one could sue the LAPD and the City of Los Angeles to stop this practice. No person would ever be able to demonstrate a sufficient future likelihood of being choked. More generally, in situations where there is a policy that will inevitably injure someone, but there is no way to know who specifically will be harmed, the decision leaves the federal courts unable to enforce the Constitution. Justice Marshall criticized this paradox in his dissent and concluded that the *Lyons* decision "removes an entire class of constitutional violations from the equitable powers of a federal court" and "immunizes . . . any policy that authorizes persistent deprivations of constitutional rights."[22]

Under the *Lyons* holding, plaintiffs have standing to seek injunctions only against ongoing practices that are likely to directly harm them. For example, a student would have standing to challenge an on-going public school practice of holding prayer sessions every morning. But in many instances, plaintiffs seek injunctions—as Adolpho Lyons did—against policies that are sure to affect someone, but where a particular victim cannot be identified in advance.

I believe a federal court must always be available to decide whether the Constitution has been violated and if so, to provide a remedy. *Lyons* is representative of many Supreme Court cases that restrict federal jurisdiction and prevent federal courts from adjudicating constitutional issues and providing relief. In this chapter, I focus on two such doctrines—standing and the political question doctrine—that often are referred to as "justiciability" requirements. One reason the Supreme Court created these requirements is because it interprets Article III of the Constitution as limiting federal courts to deciding "cases" and "controversies." They are also based on what the Court calls "prudential" considerations—what it believes is required for prudent judicial administration.

Standing is the determination of whether a specific person is the proper party to bring a matter to the court for adjudication. As the Supreme Court defines it, "in essence the question of standing is whether the litigant is entitled to have the court decide the merits of the dispute or of particular issues."[23] In other words, does the litigant have a sufficient interest in the outcome to have a reason to bring the suit? The "political question doctrine" concerns whether a matter is properly decided by the courts or better left to the elected branches of government. Neither of these doctrines is mentioned in Article III of the Constitution. They are entirely created by the Supreme Court. That, of course, does not make them illegitimate, but it does mean they need to be justified.

The Court often has said that the standing doctrine promotes separation of powers by restricting the availability of judicial review.[24] It noted in *Warth v. Seldin,* for instance, that standing "is founded in concern about the proper—and properly limited role—of the courts in a democratic society."[25] More recently, the Court explained in *Clapper v. Amnesty International:* "The law of Article III standing . . . serves to prevent the judicial process from being used to usurp the powers of the political branches."[26] By restricting who may sue in federal court, the reasoning goes, standing limits what matters the courts may address and minimizes judicial review of the other branches of government. The Supreme Court has said that the "standing inquiry is especially rigorous" when judges are asked "to decide whether an action taken by one of the other two branches of the federal government was unconstitutional."[27]

The problem with this argument is that it depicts separation of powers as being advanced only by restricting the availability of federal judicial review. That begs the question of the appropriate role of the federal courts in the constitutional system. As I argued in Chapter 1, a proper concept of separation of powers must also include preserving the federal judiciary's role in enforcing the Constitution.[28] Separation of powers can be undermined by overexpansion of the federal courts' role, but also by undue restriction. My thesis is that the central role of the federal courts is to enforce the Constitution. Justiciability doctrines are wrong where they prevent the courts from fulfilling this function.

The Court has also said that it is not troubled by situations where no one can seek judicial review because that means the matter is left to the political process. As the Supreme Court declared in *Schlesinger v. Reservists Committee to Stop the War* in 1974: "Our system of government leaves many crucial decisions to the political processes. The assumption that if respondents have no standing to sue no one would have standing, is not a reason to find standing."[29] But enforcement of the Constitution should never be left to the political process. The Constitution exists to limit the government, those limits have meaning only if they are enforceable, and to think that the political process will address such issues is usually to indulge a fiction. The kinds of complaints that get dismissed for lack of standing rarely draw the level of public attention needed to make them political issues.

Standing

The word *standing* is not mentioned in the Constitution. It is entirely a judicially created doctrine. The Supreme Court has announced several requirements for standing, all of which must be met in order for a federal court to adjudicate a case. Three of these requirements are constitutional—meaning that they are derived from the Court's interpretation of Article III—and as constitutional restrictions they cannot be overridden by statute.[30] The plaintiff must allege (1) that he or she has suffered or imminently will suffer an injury; (2) that the injury is fairly traceable to the defendant's conduct; and (3) that a favorable federal court decision is likely to redress the injury.

In addition, the Court has identified other "prudential standing principles," which are based not on the Constitution but on prudent judicial administration. Unlike constitutional barriers, these may be overridden by statute. First, a party may assert only his or her own rights and cannot raise the claims of third parties that are not before the court. Second, a plaintiff may not sue as a taxpayer or as a citizen who shares a grievance in common with all other taxpayers or citizens.

The result of these restrictions is that governments may commit constitutional violations that no person has standing to challenge in court, in which case the Constitution goes unenforced. This should be impermissible: it is what the "checks and balances" provided by separation of powers are designed to prevent. Yet the Supreme Court has interpreted standing in such a way that this is exactly what occurs.

The requirement that a plaintiff seeking injunctive relief show that he or she will personally be harmed again in the future, as applied in *City of Los Angeles v. Lyons,* is an especially egregious example. It puts a nearly impossible burden of proof upon plaintiffs. I have sat in countless discussions with civil rights lawyers in which we concluded that no one could sue to stop an unconstitutional government practice because no one could show that he or she personally would be injured in the future. Judges have thrown literally hundreds of cases out of court because of the *Lyons* decision. Lower federal courts have dismissed, for lack of standing, requests for injunctions to regulate the use of the chemical mace by police, challenges to a state practice of paying police officers a bonus if their arrest led to a conviction, and attempts to halt strip searches conducted at county jails of women arrested for minor crimes.[31]

In addition, the courts have imposed three other standing doctrines that effectively bar anyone from challenging an unconstitutional government action: narrowly defining what constitutes a sufficient injury for purposes of standing; imposing a restrictive requirement for showing causation; and denying standing for injuries suffered as a taxpayer or a citizen.

WHAT CONSTITUTES "INJURY"?

As mentioned above, in order to have standing, the plaintiff must show that he or she has been or imminently will be injured. But sometimes the Court has defined "injury" so narrowly that people who clearly have suffered harms were deemed to lack standing. *Clapper v. Amnesty International* is one such case.[32]

The Foreign Intelligence Surveillance Act of 1978 (FISA), as amended in 2008, permits the Attorney General and the Director of National Intelligence to intercept communications between people in the United States and those in foreign countries.[33] The government may listen to their conversations and read their emails. Attorneys, journalists, and business people in the United States brought a lawsuit alleging that their communications with individuals in foreign countries were chilled by the possibility that the government might intercept them. The plaintiffs said that they regularly needed to communicate with individuals in foreign countries but were inhibited from doing so because they could no longer ensure that their communications remained confidential.

In a 5–4 decision, the Supreme Court ordered that the case be dismissed for lack of standing. The Court, in an opinion by Justice Alito, stressed that none of the plaintiffs could show that their own communications had been or were likely to be intercepted. That, of course, is because the NSA keeps this information secret. The Court explained:

> First, it is speculative whether the Government will imminently target communications to which respondents are parties. . . . Second, even if respondents could demonstrate that the targeting of their foreign contacts is imminent, respondents can only speculate as to whether the Government will seek to use §1881a-authorized [i.e., FISA-authorized] surveillance (rather than other methods) to do so. . . . Third, even if respondents could show that the Government will seek the

Foreign Intelligence Surveillance Court's authorization to acquire the communications of respondents' foreign contacts under §1881a, respondents can only speculate as to whether that court will authorize such surveillance. . . . Fourth, even if the Government were to obtain the Foreign Intelligence Surveillance Court's approval to target respondents' foreign contacts under §1881a, it is unclear whether the Government would succeed in acquiring the communications of respondents' foreign contacts. And fifth, even if the Government were to conduct surveillance of respondents' foreign contacts, respondents can only speculate as to whether *their own communications* with their foreign contacts would be incidentally acquired.[34]

Justice Breyer, writing for the four dissenters, sharply disagreed, saying that the chance that the plaintiffs' communications would be intercepted was high enough to meet the requirement for standing. He wrote that there was "a very strong likelihood that the Government will intercept at least some of the plaintiffs' communications. Consequently, we need only assume that the Government is doing its job (to find out about, and combat, terrorism) in order to conclude that there is a high probability that the Government will intercept at least some electronic communication to which at least some of the plaintiffs are parties. The majority is wrong when it describes the harm threatened plaintiffs as 'speculative.'"[35]

Many things are troubling about the Court's ruling. First, the majority opinion says that for standing to exist, the injury has to be "certainly impending."[36] This raises the bar: as Justice Breyer says, past cases required a "reasonable probability" or "high probability."[37] There is no reason to demand more. Requiring that the harm be "certainly impending" will often mean that no one has standing to challenge an unconstitutional government practice.

Second, the plaintiffs met the Court's requirement. They claimed their speech was being chilled by the very existence of the authority and program developed to intercept communications between those in the United States and foreign countries. The harm they suffered was not speculative or probable but certain. For example, some of the plaintiffs were lawyers who said that in order to protect attorney-client confidentiality, they had to refrain from electronic communications with their clients. They could communicate only by traveling to foreign countries to meet their clients in person. Other plaintiffs were business people and journalists who said their communications with people in foreign countries were chilled. The law effectively prevented them from using the phone or Internet, which is a harm by itself.

Finally and most important, the Court's decision makes it very unlikely that anyone can challenge the constitutionality of the FISA law. No one ever will be able to show that the NSA has intercepted his or her personal communications or is likely to do so. If the government chooses to use evidence gained from such surveillance against a criminal defendant, he or she could object to its introduction. But in any other circumstance, no one will likely be able to show that the NSA intercepted his or her communications. This means that even if the Foreign Intelligence Surveillance Act violates the Constitution, the federal courts will never be able to adjudicate it.

RESTRICTING CAUSATION

In *Allen v. Wright*,[38] parents of black public school children brought a class action suit against the Internal Revenue Service because they said it failed to carry out its statutory obligation to deny tax-exempt status to racially discriminatory private schools. Federal law is clear—racially discriminatory schools cannot get tax breaks—but the IRS chose not to enforce it.

The plaintiffs claimed two injuries. One was that they and their children were stigmatized by government financial aid given to schools that racially discriminate. The plaintiffs also claimed that their children's chances of receiving a racially integrated education were diminished by the tax breaks given to discriminatory schools. If the IRS enforced the law, the parents argued, the schools would either stop discriminating or would have to charge higher tuition because of the lost tax breaks. Either way, more white students likely would attend the public schools.

These are serious allegations: the federal government was fostering segregation by giving illegal tax breaks to racially discriminatory private schools. But the Supreme Court ordered the case dismissed for lack of standing.

On the first claim, the Court said the plaintiffs' assertion that they were stigmatized by the government's policy did not constitute an injury for standing purposes. The Court explained that stigmatic injury "accords a basis for standing only to those persons who are personally denied equal treatment. . . . If the abstract stigmatic injury were cognizable, standing would extend nationwide to all members of the particular racial groups against which the Government was alleged to be discriminating by its grant of a tax exemption to a racially discriminatory school."[39]

Here the Court assumes its conclusion. It is undesirable, the Court asserts, to define standing in a way that permits such a large group to challenge an illegal or unconstitutional government action. I would argue just the opposite: where the government is violating the Constitution or federal laws, it is important to ensure that *someone* has standing. In its concern about allowing too many people to sue, the Court has defined standing in such a way that no one can sue.

As for the second claim, that the IRS was increasing segregation in the public schools, the Supreme Court acknowledged that this claim stated a serious, concrete injury. But it nonetheless denied standing, because "the injury alleged is not fairly traceable to the Government conduct respondents challenge as unlawful. . . . From the perspective of the IRS, the injury to respondents is highly indirect and results from the independent action of some third party not before the court."[40] In a footnote, the Court stated that even though a change in IRS policy might redress the injury, this possibility is still insufficient for standing because the IRS did not cause the segregation.[41]

Simple supply-and-demand economics refutes this conclusion. The plaintiffs alleged that without the tax breaks, racially discriminatory schools would have to charge more and this would cause fewer students to attend. Perhaps with a service as crucial as education and a factor as emotionally laden as racial integration, the higher tuitions might not have reduced attendance as expected. But the plaintiffs should at least have had the chance to introduce evidence and try to prove their claim. Because the case was dismissed, they never had that chance.

The Court's decision in *Allen v. Wright* meant that no one would have standing to challenge an IRS policy that violated federal law and likely increased the racial imbalance of public schools. The Court invoked separation of powers to justify limiting standing, but its decision actually weakened the separation of powers. It prevented the judiciary from acting as a check on the unconstitutional and illegal action of the executive branch.

DENYING STANDING WHEN THE PLAINTIFF
IS A CITIZEN OR A TAXPAYER

The Supreme Court has created a "prudential principle" that denies standing "when the asserted harm is a generalized grievance shared in a substantially equal measure by all or a large class of citizens."[42] This principle stops individuals from suing if their only injury is as a citizen or as a taxpayer concerned with having the government follow the law.

The term "generalized grievance" is confusing because it implies that no one would have standing to challenge a blatantly unconstitutional law that applied to everyone in the country. For example, would it be a generalized grievance if Congress passed a law prohibiting all religious worship? In that case, the Court tells us, standing would exist even though this injury would be shared by a large class of citizens. "Nor . . . could the fact that many persons shared the same injury," the Court declared in 1973, "be sufficient reason to disqualify from seeking review . . . any person who had in fact suffered injury. . . . To deny standing to persons who are in fact injured simply because many others are also injured, would mean that the most injurious and widespread Government actions could be questioned by nobody."[43] A later Court explained that "where a harm is concrete, though widely shared, the Court has found injury in fact."[44]

The number of people affected by a government action, then, does not determine whether a grievance is generalized. Rather, a generalized grievance exists when plaintiffs sue solely as citizens concerned with having the government follow the law, or as taxpayers interested in restraining allegedly illegal government expenditures.

This doctrine means that there will be constitutional claims that no individual may litigate. The Supreme Court first articulated the barrier to taxpayer and citizen standing during the 1920s and 1930s. In *Frothingham v. Mellon,* a Massachusetts resident named Frothingham, suing as a taxpayer, sought to restrain expenditures under the Federal Maternity Act of 1921, which provided financial grants to the states in order to reduce maternal and infant mortality.[45] Ms. Frothingham asserted that the expenditures violated the Tenth Amendment's reservation of powers to the state governments. The Supreme Court ruled that she lacked standing because her "interest in the moneys of the treasury ... is comparatively minute and indeterminable."[46] The Court held that federal court review must be based on a plaintiff's allegation of a direct injury and "not merely that he suffers in some indefinite way in common with people generally."[47] Ms. Frothingham's claim—challenging a program to reduce maternal and infant mortality—admittedly does not arouse our sympathies (at least not mine). But a federal court should have heard it.

A few years later, in *Ex parte Levitt,* the Supreme Court ruled that a person could not gain standing as a citizen claiming a right to have the government follow the law.[48] Albert Levitt sued to have Hugo Black's appointment to the United States Supreme Court declared unconstitutional, contending that Black could not be appointed to the Court because, as a senator, he had voted to increase Supreme Court justices' retirement benefits. This, Levitt alleged, violated Article I, Section 6 of the Constitution, which states that "No Senator shall during the time for which he was elected, be appointed to any civil office the emoluments whereof shall have increased during such time." The Court held that the plaintiff lacked standing because "it is not sufficient [for standing] that he has merely a general interest common to all members of the public."[49]

Frothingham and *Levitt* establish the bar to taxpayer and citizen standing. The effect of these decisions is that no one in the country may sue the government on this basis, even to press a claim that the Constitution has been violated.

The primary case deviating from this rule was the Warren Court's decision in *Flast v. Cohen*.[50] In *Flast*, the Court upheld the right of a taxpayer, Florence Flast, to challenge federal subsidies to parochial schools as violating the First Amendment's prohibition against government establishment of religion. Under the Elementary and Secondary Education Act of 1965, the federal government gave funds to parochial schools to support instruction in secular subjects. Based on *Frothingham*, the lower court dismissed Flast's challenge, concluding that her only claim was as a taxpayer and that such standing was not permitted.

The Supreme Court reversed this ruling. Both the majority and the dissent agreed that the rule preventing plaintiffs from asserting generalized grievances was prudential rather than constitutional.[51] Chief Justice Warren wrote for the Court that Flast's ability to sue as a taxpayer depends on "whether there is a logical nexus between the status asserted and the claim sought to be adjudicated."[52]

To demonstrate that "logical nexus," Warren wrote, Flast needed to establish two factors. First, "the taxpayer must establish a logical link between that status and the type of legislative enactment attacked."[53] A taxpayer could challenge only the expenditure of funds under the Taxing and Spending Clause of the Constitution, not "an incidental expenditure of tax funds in the administration of an essentially regulatory statute."[54] Second, the "taxpayer must establish a nexus between that status and the precise nature of the constitutional infringement alleged."[55] In other words, the taxpayer must argue that the expenditure violates a particular constitutional provision, not just that Congress has exceeded the scope of its constitutional powers.

Flast was different from *Frothingham*, Warren argued, because although both cases involved challenges to government spending programs, the First Amendment is a limit on Congress's taxing and spending authority, whereas the Tenth Amendment, at issue in *Frothingham*, is not.[56] The ruling raised speculation that the Court had substantially expanded the availability of taxpayer standing.[57]

Since then, however, the Court has without exception rejected taxpayer standing. *Flast v. Cohen* has not been overruled—though Justices Scalia and Thomas have urged this—but its holding is limited to its facts. The bottom line is that taxpayer standing is allowed only if a person is challenging a government expenditure because it violates the Establishment Clause of the First Amendment.

In *United States v. Richardson*, the plaintiff, an insurance adjuster, William B. Richardson, claimed that the statutes keeping the Central Intelligence Agency budget classified violated the Constitution's requirement for a regular statement and accounting of all expenditures.[58] The Court ruled that he lacked standing because he did not allege a violation of a personal constitutional right but instead claimed injury only as a citizen and taxpayer. Richardson, the Court held, was "seeking to employ a federal court as a forum in which to air his generalized grievances about the conduct of government."[59]

Richardson's claim that if he could not sue, no one could, was ruled irrelevant. Chief Justice Burger wrote: "It can be argued that if respondent is not permitted to litigate this issue, no one can do so. In a very real sense, the absence of any particular individual or class to litigate these claims gives support to the argument that the subject matter is committed to the surveillance of Congress, and ultimately to the political process."[60]

In a decision handed down the same day, the Court denied citizen and taxpayer standing in *Schlesinger v. Reservists Committee to Stop the War*.[61] The plaintiffs had sued to enjoin members of Congress from serving in the military reserves. Article 1, Section 6 of the Constitution prevents a senator or representative from holding civil office. This case arose in the context of the Vietnam War when some members of Congress also were in the armed forces reserves. Again, the Court refused to rule on the claim of unconstitutionality, holding that the matter posed a generalized grievance. The plaintiffs had not alleged any specific violation of their constitutional rights, only an interest, as citizens or taxpayers, in having the government follow the law. The Court stated: "Respondents seek to have the Judicial Branch compel the Executive Branch to act in conformity with the Incompatibility Clause, an interest shared by all citizens. . . . Our system of government leaves many crucial decisions to the political processes. The assumption that if respondents have no standing to sue no one would have standing, is not a reason to find standing."[62]

These decisions mean that no one has standing to challenge a government practice that violates the Constitution. Contrary to what the Court says, the fact that no one would have standing is exactly the reason for finding standing. Otherwise, the federal courts cannot enforce the Constitution.

After *Richardson* and *Schlesinger,* taxpayer standing was restricted to the one area where it had been approved in *Flast:* alleged violations of the Establishment Clause of the First Amendment. Even this exception has not held up; the Supreme Court has continually narrowed it.

In *Valley Forge Christian College v. Americans United for Separation of Church and State,* the Court denied taxpayer standing to challenge a federal government grant of surplus property as violating the Establishment Clause of the First Amendment.[63] The United States Department of Health, Education, and Welfare gave a seventy-seven-acre tract of land, worth over $500 million, to Valley Forge Christian College. Americans United for Separation of Church and State sued to enjoin the transfer of the property on the ground that it was government aid to religion in violation of the Establishment Clause. The Supreme Court held that the plaintiffs lacked standing because they sued solely as taxpayers interested in having the government follow the law.[64]

The result under *Flast v. Cohen* should have been clear: taxpayers have standing to challenge federal actions that they believe violate the Establishment Clause of the First Amendment. But the Court distinguished *Flast* from *Valley Forge* on two grounds, both spurious. First, the plaintiffs in *Valley Forge* were challenging a property transfer by the Department of Health, Education, and Welfare, not a congressional statute.[65] This distinction should not matter. Both Congress and the executive branch are bound to obey the First Amendment. In fact, in *Flast* the named defendant was Wilbur Cohen, then the Secretary of Health, Education, and Welfare.

Second, the Court said that, unlike Florence Flast, the *Valley Forge* plaintiffs were objecting to a government action pursuant to Congress's power over government property, Article IV, Section 3 of the Constitution, not to a spending program under Article I, Section 8.[66] Again, this distinction should make no difference. All congressional actions, whatever part of the Constitution empowers them, must comply with the First Amendment and the entire Bill of Rights. If *Flast* establishes that taxpayers have standing to halt violations of the Establishment Clause, it is hard to see why it matters whether the objectionable action was authorized by Article I or Article IV.[67]

The Court further restricted taxpayer standing in *Hein v. Freedom from Religion Foundation.*[68] Upon taking office, President George W. Bush created a White House Office of Faith-Based and Community Initiatives to provide government funds to "faith-based institutions." The intent was to give money directly to churches, synagogues, and mosques to provide social services. Taxpayers brought a suit challenging this as violating the Establishment Clause.

The Court ruled, without a majority opinion, that the taxpayers lacked standing. Justice Alito announced the judgment for the Court and distinguished *Flast v. Cohen* as involving expenditures under a specific federal statute, whereas the money for the White House Office of Faith-Based and Community Initiatives came from general executive revenue. Alito's opinion, joined by Chief Justice Roberts and Justice Kennedy, explained: "The link between congressional action and constitutional violation that supported taxpayer standing in *Flast* is missing here. Respondents do not challenge any specific congressional action or appropriation; nor do they ask the Court to invalidate any congressional enactment or legislatively created program as unconstitutional. That is because the expenditures at issue here were not made pursuant to any Act of Congress. . . . Those expenditures resulted from executive discretion, not congressional action."[69]

In other words, the plurality opinion in *Hein v. Freedom from Religion Foundation* concluded that taxpayers lack standing to challenge expenditures of funds from general executive revenue. But the distinction between spending from general revenue and spending under a specific federal statute makes no sense. The President, just like Congress, must comply with the First Amendment. Moreover, this distinction is doubly nonsensical because *all* spending by the federal government must be authorized by a federal statute.

The other six Justices sharply criticized the plurality's reasoning. Justices Scalia and Thomas concurred in the judgment but called for

Flast v. Cohen to be overruled. Scalia lamented the "meaningless distinctions" and wrote: "If this Court is to decide cases by rule of law rather than show of hands, we must surrender to logic and choose sides: Either *Flast v. Cohen* should be applied to (at a minimum) *all* challenges to the governmental expenditure of general tax revenues . . . , or [it] should be repudiated. For me, the choice is easy. *Flast* is wholly irreconcilable with the Article III restrictions on federal-court jurisdiction that this Court has repeatedly confirmed are embodied in the doctrine of standing."[70] Justice Souter, in a dissent joined by Justices Stevens, Ginsburg, and Breyer, agreed that there was no meaningful distinction between money from general executive revenue and spending under a specific federal statute, but these justices would have followed *Flast* and allowed taxpayer standing.[71]

Most recently, in *Arizona School Tuition Organization v. Winn,* the Court again rejected a claim of taxpayer standing to challenge an alleged Establishment Clause violation.[72] Arizona law allowed taxpayers who voluntarily contributed money to a "student tuition organization" (STO) to receive a dollar-for-dollar tax credit up to $500 a year. The challengers argued that this program provides $50 million a year for private, almost entirely religious schools.

The Court, in a 5–4 decision, ordered the suit dismissed for lack of standing. Once again, it found a few millimeters of difference between this case and *Flast* and that was enough to deny standing. Justice Kennedy, writing for the majority, distinguished government expenditures from tax credits: "The distinction between governmental expenditures and tax credits refutes respondents' assertion of standing. When Arizona taxpayers choose to contribute to STOs, they spend their own money, not money the State has collected from respondents or from other taxpayers."[73] Justice Scalia, joined by Justice Thomas, concurred and again urged that *Flast v. Cohen* be overturned: "*Flast* is an anomaly in our jurisprudence, irreconcilable with the Article III restrictions on federal judicial power that our opinions have established. I would repudiate that misguided decision and enforce the Constitution."[74]

Justice Kagan wrote a vigorous dissent, joined by Justices Ginsburg, Breyer, and Sotomayor. She stated:

This novel distinction in standing law between appropriations and tax expenditures has as little basis in principle as it
has in our precedent. Cash grants and targeted tax breaks are
means of accomplishing the same government objective—
to provide financial support to select individuals or orga-
nizations. Taxpayers who oppose state aid of religion have
equal reason to protest whether that aid flows from the one
form of subsidy or the other. Either way, the government has
financed the religious activity. And so either way, taxpayers should be able to challenge the subsidy. Still worse, the
Court's arbitrary distinction threatens to eliminate *all* occasions for a taxpayer to contest the government's monetary
support of religion. Precisely because appropriations and tax
breaks can achieve identical objectives, the government can
easily substitute one for the other.[75]

There is no basis for distinguishing government subsidies from
government tax credits as they relate to the Establishment Clause. In
both instances, the government uses its resources in a manner that violates the Constitution. Yet the effect of the *Arizona School Tuition Organization* decision is that so long as the government structures its aid to
religious institutions as a tax credit rather than a direct subsidy, no one
has standing to challenge it.

CAN THE RESTRICTIONS ON STANDING BE JUSTIFIED?

For the federal courts to enforce the Constitution, there must always
be someone with standing to challenge a constitutional violation. This
sounds basic, but it would be a significant change in the law. Are there
any reasons not to do so? Several traditional defenses for the standing
doctrine might be invoked against my proposal.

First, it can be argued that Article III commands that federal courts
not hear such cases. But Article III does not mention standing, let alone
the specific rules such as injury, causation, redressability, and the bar
against hearing generalized grievances. The only constitutional basis for

the standing doctrine is the language in Article III, Section 2, which says that the federal courts may hear nine categories of "cases" and "controversies." This is the language that the Supreme Court has interpreted as giving rise to the standing doctrine, even though nothing in the history of Article III suggests such a limit.

Indeed, in every example I have described in this chapter, there unquestionably was a "case" or "controversy." Adolpho Lyons had been nearly killed by an LAPD officer's use of the chokehold, and he had a case against the City of Los Angeles to stop its use, except when necessary to protect the officer's safety. Attorneys, business people, and journalists contended that the warrantless electronic eavesdropping authorized by the Foreign Intelligence Surveillance Act violated their First Amendment and Fourth Amendment rights. The plaintiffs in *Allen v. Wright* claimed that the federal government's policy of providing tax credits to racially discriminatory private schools directly harmed their children. Each of the generalized grievance cases involved a plaintiff who alleged that the government was acting unconstitutionally. By any commonsense understanding of the words "cases" and "controversies" all of these cases met this Article III requirement.

A second argument is that standing serves judicial efficiency by preventing a flood of lawsuits by those who have only an ideological stake in the outcome.[76] But in light of the high costs of litigation, I question how large the burden really would be. The risk is that there might be a large number of suits challenging the same government practice. But there are procedural devices, such as consolidation, that can be used to deal with this. More important, this argument erroneously places a higher value on efficiency than on enabling the federal courts to enforce the Constitution.

Standing is also justified in terms of conserving the Court's political capital. The Court once stated: "Should the courts seek to expand their power so as to bring under their jurisdiction ill-defined controversies over constitutional issues, they would become the organs of political theories. Such abuse of judicial power would properly meet rebuke and restriction from other branches."[77] But this wrongly assumes that hearing a case constitutes judicial abuse. I contend that when there is a claim that the Constitution has been violated, someone must have standing to challenge it in federal court. Claims that the government has violated a specific constitutional provision are not "ill-defined controversies."

Third, standing is said to improve judicial decision-making by ensuring that there is a specific controversy before the court, and an advocate with sufficient personal concern to effectively litigate the matter. The Supreme Court has often quoted its words from *Baker v. Carr,* that standing requires a plaintiff to allege "such a personal stake in the outcome of the controversy as to assure that concrete adverseness which sharpens the presentation of issues upon which the court so largely depends for illumination of difficult constitutional questions."[78]

But courts need varying degrees of fact to decide different cases; some cases present pure questions of law, in which the factual context is largely irrelevant. If tomorrow, for example, a city government banned all abortions within its borders, the facts in the legal challenge would be immaterial. Also, a plaintiff's personal stake in the outcome of litigation is no guarantee of high-quality advocacy. The best litigator in the country, who cared deeply about an issue, could not raise it without a plaintiff who had personally suffered an injury; but a pro se litigant with no legal training could pursue the matter on his or her own behalf. Nothing in my argument would prevent courts from using standing doctrines to say that there is a better plaintiff available. But it makes no sense to have a situation where no one can sue because of a hypothetical concern over wanting to make sure that there is the best plaintiff. I am especially concerned with situations where the Court defines standing so restrictively as to prevent there being any plaintiff at all.

Fourth, standing requirements are said to promote fairness by ensuring that people will raise only their own rights and concerns and not meddle with the rights of others who do not want the protection offered. The Court explained, "the courts should not adjudicate such rights unnecessarily, and it may be that in fact the holders of those rights either do not wish to assert them, or will be able to enjoy them regardless of whether the in-court litigant is successful or not."[79] This is a legitimate concern, but again, it is not a reason to define standing in a way that prevents anyone from being able to sue. In all of the examples that

I have described, people were asserting their own rights to sue but were denied that ability for lack of standing.

Finally, and most significantly, my position might be opposed on separation-of-powers grounds. Some might disagree with my premise that federal courts must always be able to adjudicate constitutional issues; they may view the judicial role as solely to prevent and remedy specific injuries suffered by individuals. Under this view, the federal courts have no authority to halt government violations of the Constitution unless there is a plaintiff whose personal rights have been infringed. In *Richardson, Schlesinger, Valley Forge, Lujan,* and *Freedom from Religion Foundation,* the Court expressly noted that the "generalized grievance" barrier reserves certain matters for the political branches of government, thereby promoting the separation of powers. Moreover, this barrier excludes plaintiffs who sue entirely out of ideological interests and not on the basis of specific, concrete injuries.[80]

But I have a very different vision of the federal courts' role. I see its primary purpose in the constitutional system as upholding the Constitution. I believe the Supreme Court has inappropriately deemed some parts of the Constitution to be enforceable only through the political process. No one can have standing to challenge the practices objected to in *Richardson, Schlesinger, Valley Forge,* and *Freedom from Religion Foundation.* The constitutional provisions involved there—the Statements and Accounts Clause, the Incompatibility Clause, and the Establishment Clause—could be blatantly disregarded by Congress and the President, and the courts would be powerless to halt the violations. This is deeply troubling because the purpose of judicial review is to safeguard constitutional matters from majority rule—a function that is lost when key provisions are taken out of the courts' hands and reserved for the political process. The generalized grievance doctrine effectively reads these clauses out of the Constitution, except to the extent that political branches choose to voluntarily comply with them.

Furthermore, the Court's distinction between parts of the Constitution is unjustified. The Court draws a distinction between constitutional provisions that protect individual rights—such as the Equal Protection Clause, the violation of which creates standing—and provisions pertaining to the structure of government, such as the Statements and Accounts Clause, the violation of which is considered a general-ized grievance. The desirability of this distinction is highly questionable. Structural parts of the Constitution are integral to individual rights. For example, if Congress were to adopt a law designating the current presi-dent as President-for-Life, in violation of Article II, would anyone have standing to sue? Perhaps this could be challenged as infringing the right to vote. But under a strict reading of the generalized grievance cases, no citizen or group of citizens could challenge such a law, because any plaintiff would be presenting a claim common to all.

Ultimately, two competing visions of the federal judiciary are at stake. There is no more fundamental disagreement over the role of the federal courts than this. Under one view, the federal courts are limited to remedying specific injuries suffered by particular individuals. The logic of this position leads to great deference to the political branches of government and fear of the federal courts as an antimajoritarian in-stitution. The majority opinions in *Richardson, Schlesinger,* and *Valley Forge,* and the plurality opinion in *Freedom from Religion Foundation* endorsed this view. The dissents, however, embraced the other position: that the federal judiciary exists to ensure government compliance with the Constitution. In this view, judicial deference does not include toler-ating constitutional violations. When governments violate the Consti-tution, there must always be someone with standing to challenge them in federal court.

The Political Question Doctrine

Certain allegations of unconstitutional government conduct, according to the Supreme Court, are "political questions" that should not be ruled on by the federal courts, even when all of the jurisdictional and other jus-ticiability requirements are met. The Court has said that constitutional interpretation in these areas should be left to the politically accountable branches of government, the President and Congress. In other words, the "political question doctrine" refers to matters that the Court deems inappropriate for judicial review. Despite an allegation that the Consti-tution has been violated, the federal courts refuse to rule and instead dismiss the case. In essence, the political question doctrine says that the federal judiciary cannot enforce some parts of the Constitution.

I believe that this doctrine is inconsistent with the federal courts' primary mission of enforcing the Constitution. There should be no allegations of constitutional violations that federal courts cannot adjudicate. Professor Martin Redish contends that "the political question doctrine should play no role whatsoever in the exercise of the judicial review power."[81] I agree.[82] As I explained in Chapter 1, matters are placed in a Constitution to insulate them from majoritarian control, and therefore it is inappropriate to entrust constitutional issues to the majoritarian branches of government. Politically accountable bodies cannot be relied on to enforce a document that is meant to restrain them. The federal courts certainly can and should give deference to the choices of the other branches of government, but they should do so in rulings on the merits of individual cases, not through dismissals on justiciability grounds.

To develop this argument, I begin by briefly reviewing the areas where the Court has found cases to be nonjusticiable political questions. Then I explain why the political question doctrine should be eliminated to ensure judicial enforcement of the Constitution.

WHAT CASES ARE DISMISSED AS POLITICAL QUESTIONS?

The Court has used the political question doctrine to dismiss cases involving such matters as challenges to partisan gerrymandering, objections to presidential actions in foreign policy, and claims that Congress was violating the Constitution in its procedures for impeachments. The unifying thread among these and similar cases—what makes them "political questions"—is somewhat answered by the classic formulation provided in *Baker v. Carr*.[83] Virtually every case considering the political question doctrine quotes this language:

> Prominent on the surface of any case held to involve a political question is found a textually demonstrable commitment of the issue to a coordinate political department; or a lack of

judicially discoverable and manageable standards for resolving it; or the impossibility of deciding without an initial policy determination of a kind clearly for nonjudicial discretion;
or the impossibility of a court's undertaking independent
resolution without expressing lack of the respect due coor-
dinate branches of government; or an unusual need for un-
questioning adherence to a political decision already made;
or the potentiality of embarrassment from multifarious pro-
nouncements by various departments on one question.[84]

Many of these criteria are unclear. Moreover, these criteria are
useless in identifying what constitutes a political question. For example,
nowhere does the Constitution state that the legislature or executive
should decide whether a particular action constitutes a constitutional
violation. The Constitution does not mention judicial review, much less
limit it by creating "textually demonstrable commitments" (a phrase
never defined by the Court) to other branches of government. Nothing
in the Constitution restricts enforcement of any provision to the political branches of government.

The most important constitutional provisions are written in broad
language and do not include what the Court has termed (but never defined) "judicially discoverable and manageable standards." The Court
is constantly creating standards for areas that are inherently vague. It
has to decide, for instance, what is "cruel and unusual punishment" or
"due process" or an "establishment of religion." It is hard, if not impossible, to identify an area where the courts could not create judicial
standards.

The Court also speaks of questions that depend on "initial policy determination[s] of a kind clearly for nonjudicial discretion," but
that is hardly a criterion that can be used to separate political questions
from justiciable cases. My position is that if there is an allegation of
a constitutional violation then it is an appropriate area for a judicial
determination.

Another famous articulation of the political question doctrine
came from Professor Alexander Bickel over a half century ago:

Such is the foundation, in both intellect and instinct, of the political question doctrine: the Court's sense of lack of capacity, compounded in unequal part of

(a) the strangeness of the issue and its intractability to principled resolution;

(b) the sheer momentousness of it, which tends to unbalance judicial judgment;

(c) the anxiety, not so much that the judicial judgment will be ignored, as that perhaps it should but will not be;

(d) finally ("in a mature democracy"), the inner vulnerability, the self-doubt of an institution which is electorally irresponsible and has no earth to draw strength from.[85]

But Bickel's criteria are no more useful than those from *Baker v. Carr* in deciding what is a political question. Some of them are just wrong. Why should the "strangeness of the issue" cause the Court not to enforce the Constitution, and what makes an issue sufficiently strange for the courts to be unable to decide it? "Sheer momentousness" should not be a reason for the courts to avoid a question; quite the contrary. The notion that judicial decisions could or should be "ignored" is inconsistent with the very idea of having federal courts. In *United States v. Nixon,* the Court rightly found justiciable a request by the Watergate Special Prosecutor for tapes of White House conversations, even though it was truly momentous and there was a risk that President Nixon would ignore the court's order.[86]

POLITICAL QUESTIONS AND THE ELECTORAL PROCESS

There are several major areas where the Supreme Court has applied the political question doctrine to rule that constitutional claims cannot be adjudicated. One of the most notable examples is cases brought under Article IV, Section 4 of the Constitution, which states, "The United States shall guarantee to every State in this Union a Republican form of government." The Court has consistently held that cases alleging a violation of this clause—also known as the Guarantee Clause—present nonjusticiable political questions. Several scholars have urged the Court to reconsider this rule.[87] It has not yet done so, but Justice O'Connor once remarked, "the Court has suggested that perhaps not all claims under the Guarantee Clause present nonjusticiable political questions" and that "contemporary commentators have . . . suggested that courts should address the merits of such claims, at least in some circumstances."[88]

In fact, this clause was involved in the first Supreme Court case to proclaim that a matter was a political question. In *Luther v. Borden,* in 1849, the Court held that a challenge to the validity of the Rhode Island state government—which had no state constitution and still operated under a 1663 charter from King Charles II—was a political question.[89] A dispute arose when the existing government refused to allow a new government, under a state constitution approved by the voters, to take office. The Supreme Court held that the case could not be decided by a federal court. "Under this article of the constitution," the Court wrote, "it rests with Congress to decide what government is the established one in a State. For as the United States guarantee to each state a republican government, Congress must necessarily decide what government is established in the State before it can determine whether it is republican or not."[90] In the Court's view, the case posed a political question because if the state's government was declared unconstitutional, then all of its actions would be invalidated, creating chaos in Rhode Island.[91] Additionally, the Court, in siding with the existing Rhode Island government, spoke of a lack of criteria for deciding what constitutes republican government.

Since *Luther v. Borden,* the Supreme Court has never deemed a state government or state action to violate the Republican Form of Government Clause.[92] In *Taylor & Marshall v. Beckham,* the Court refused to decide whether a state's resolution of a disputed gubernatorial race violated this clause.[93] In *Pacific States Telephone & Telegraph Co. v. Oregon,* it again held that cases under this clause are not justiciable.[94] *Pacific States* involved a challenge to a state law, passed through a voter initiative, that taxed certain corporations. The defendant, a corporation sued by the state of Oregon for failure to pay taxes due under this law, argued that the statute was unconstitutional because the initiative process, as a form of direct democracy, violated the Republican Form of

Government Clause. The Supreme Court held that the matter was not justiciable, calling the issue "political and governmental, and embraced within the scope of powers conferred upon Congress, and not therefore within the reach of judicial power."[95]

These precedents led the Court to dismiss as nonjusticiable the first challenges to the drawing of state legislative districts. By the middle of the twentieth century, many state legislatures were badly malapportioned. Legislative districts had not been reapportioned to reflect the growth of urban areas, leaving rural residents overrepresented and urban dwellers substantially underrepresented in state legislatures. Legislators who benefited from this system were not about to redraw districts to eliminate their own seats, and the rurally dominated state legislatures drew district lines for their states' congressional representatives that also favored their areas.

In *Colegrove v. Green*, in 1946, the Supreme Court declared nonjusticiable a challenge to the congressional districting in Illinois.[96] Justice Frankfurter wrote for the majority: "The appellants ask of this Court what is beyond its competence to grant. Effective working of our government revealed this issue to be of a peculiarly political nature and therefore not fit for judicial determination. Authority for dealing with such problems resides elsewhere."[97] Justice Frankfurter famously declared, "Courts ought not to enter this political thicket."[98] Four years later, in *South v. Peters*, the Court held that "federal courts consistently refuse to exercise their equity powers in cases posing political issues arising from a state's geographical distribution of electoral strength among its political subdivisions."[99] Only cases alleging racial discrimination in the drawing of election districts or in holding elections merited federal court involvement.[100]

But in 1962, in the landmark decision of *Baker v. Carr*, the Supreme Court reversed itself. Claims that malapportionment violates the Equal Protection Clause became justiciable.[101] Interestingly, the Court did not overrule *Luther v. Borden*, but instead distinguished cases brought under the Equal Protection Clause from those brought under the Republican Form of Government Clause. Justice Brennan explained that whereas "the Guaranty Clause is not a repository of judicially manageable standards . . . judicial standards under the Equal Protection

Clause are well-developed and familiar."[102] This is a fatuous distinction. The two clauses are equally vague, and the principle of one-person one-vote could have been articulated and enforced under either provision.[103] Nonetheless, the Court's holding that challenges to malapportionment are justiciable was one of the most important rulings in American history.[104] The political process was unlikely ever to correct the constitutional violation, and judicial review restored an important democratic principle.[105]

The effect of the Supreme Court's decisions since *Luther v. Borden* is that the Republican Form of Government Clause is essentially read out of the Constitution. The Court has never enforced this provision.

Challenges to partisan gerrymandering are another type of claim that the Court has ruled nonjusticiable. Gerrymandering occurs when the political party that controls the legislature draws election districts to maximize its own safe seats. In *Vieth v. Jubelirer* in 2004,[106] in dismissing an equal protection challenge to partisan gerrymandering, a plurality of justices said that such suits are inherently nonjusticiable political questions. Republicans controlled the Pennsylvania legislature and drew election districts to maximize Republican seats. This, of course, is unique neither to Republicans nor to Pennsylvania. Except in places with independent district commissions, election districts for all levels of government are drawn to maximize seats for the party drawing the districts.

In a 1986 case, *Davis v. Bandemer,* the Court had held that challenges to gerrymandering are justiciable.[107] But in *Vieth,* the plurality concluded that *Davis* had proved impossible to implement. The plurality opinion, written by Justice Scalia and joined by Chief Justice Rehnquist and Justices O'Connor and Thomas, argued that challenges to partisan gerrymandering are political questions with no judicially discoverable or manageable standards. There is, Scalia wrote, no basis for courts to decide when partisan gerrymandering offends the Constitution.

Justice Kennedy provided the fifth vote for the majority. He agreed to dismiss the case because of the lack of judicially discoverable or manageable standards, but he said he did not believe such standards could not be developed in the future. Thus, he disagreed with the plurality opinion that challenges to partisan gerrymandering are always political questions: such cases can be heard when standards are developed. Justices Stevens, Souter, and Breyer each wrote dissenting opinions, which Justice Ginsburg joined, arguing that the standards already exist.

Two years later, in *League of United Latin American Citizens v. Perry*,[108] the Court did not offer any more clarity. It again dismissed a challenge to partisan gerrymandering. After Republicans gained control of the Texas legislature in 2002, they replaced a congressional district map drawn up by a federal district court in 2001 with one designed to maximize Republican seats. The new map was very successful. The Texas congressional delegation went from seventeen Democrats and fifteen Republicans in the 2002 election to eleven Democrats and twenty-one Republicans in 2004.

Many lawsuits challenged the Texas gerrymandering, and once more, the Court did not hand down a majority opinion. Justice Kennedy wrote for the plurality: "We do not revisit the justiciability holding but do proceed to examine whether appellants' claims offer the Court a manageable, reliable measure of fairness for determining whether a partisan gerrymander violates the Constitution."[109] The challengers had claimed that mid-decade redistricting for openly partisan reasons provided a "reliable standard" by which the Court could invalidate the Texas plan, but Kennedy rejected this argument.

Justices Scalia and Thomas reiterated their view, expressed in *Vieth*, that challenges to partisan gerrymandering are always nonjusticiable political questions. Chief Justice Roberts and Justice Alito agreed with the dismissal of the suit but did not specify whether they found the issue nonjusticiable or whether they thought partisan gerrymandering did not violate equal protection. Roberts wrote:

> I agree with the determination that appellants have not provided "a reliable standard for identifying unconstitutional political gerrymanders." The question whether any such standard exists—that is, whether a challenge to a political gerrymander presents a justiciable case or controversy—has not been argued in these cases. I therefore take no position on that question, which has divided the Court, and I join the Court's disposition in Part II without specifying whether

appellants have failed to state a claim on which relief can be granted, or have failed to present a justiciable controversy.[110]

Justices Stevens, Souter, Ginsburg, and Breyer again dissented from the finding that partisan gerrymandering was nonjusticiable. They would have ruled on the merits of the equal protection claim.

Although there still has not been a majority opinion holding that challenges to partisan gerrymandering are always political questions, after *Vieth* and *Perry* it was hard to imagine such a case succeeding. The result was that there is an allegation of a politically very significant constitutional violation, but no court can rule on its constitutionality. But now, with Justice Scalia's death and a new Justice joining the Court, that could change.

The Court should have reaffirmed its holding in *Davis v. Bandemer* that partisan gerrymandering is unconstitutional. States should be required to draw their election districts on the basis of population or geography or community of interests, not to maximize the political control over those in power in the legislature. We all were taught that voters should choose their elected officials; partisan gerrymandering means that elected officials get to choose their voters.

THE POLITICAL QUESTION DOCTRINE AND FOREIGN POLICY

Challenges to the President's conduct of foreign policy are a second major area where the Supreme Court has used the political question doctrine.[111] In *Oetjen v. Central Leather Co.,* in 1918, the Court declared: "The conduct of the foreign relations of our Government is committed by the Constitution to the Executive and Legislature 'the political' Departments of the Government, and the propriety of what may be done in the exercise of this political power is not subject to judicial inquiry or decision."[112]

Yet the Court has also emphasized that "it is error to suppose that every case or controversy which touches foreign relations lies beyond judicial cognizance."[113] For example, it has upheld, on the merits, the President's use of executive agreements instead of treaties to implement major foreign policy agreements.[114] It has also upheld the constitutionality of the President's use of the treaty power for specific purposes.[115]

Most recently, in *Zivotofsky v. Clinton,* the Court ruled that the constitutionality of a federal law allowing American parents with a child born in Jerusalem to have the passport indicate Israel as the country of birth is not a political question.[116] The Court explained: "Resolution of Zivotofsky's claim demands careful examination of the textual, structural, and historical evidence put forward by the parties. . . . This is what courts do. The political question doctrine poses no bar to judicial review of this case."[117] Later, by a 5–4 margin, the Court declared the federal law unconstitutional as infringing on the President's power to decide whether to recognize foreign governments.[118]

It is difficult to find any principle in the Court's rulings that defines which foreign policy issues are justiciable and which present political questions. Sometimes it has said that foreign policy disputes cannot be adjudicated, but at other times they can be. The best that can be done is to describe the areas where the political question doctrine has been applied in the realm of foreign affairs. There are four such areas.

First, the Supreme Court has held that the determination of when a war begins or ends is left to the political branches of government. In *Commercial Trust Co. v. Miller,* the question was whether a congressional declaration that World War I had ended prevented application of the Trading with the Enemy Act, a federal statute that barred commerce with nations with whom the United States was at war.[119] In 1921, Congress, with the approval of the President, passed a joint resolution ending the war with Germany and proclaiming peace. The issue arose over whether this congressional proclamation was enough to suspend the Act. The Court stated that the power to decide when a war ends is vested exclusively in Congress.[120] In other cases, it has held that the political branches decide when hostilities begin, and hence when it is appropriate to call up the militia.[121]

Second, the Court has held that recognition of foreign governments is a political question,[122] as is the diplomatic status of individuals claiming immunity.[123] In other words, issues concerning who represents a foreign state, and in what capacity, are not justiciable.

Third, the Court has held that many issues surrounding the ratification and interpretation of treaties are political questions. In the 1902 case of *Terlinden v. Ames,* for example, the Court held that it is a political question whether a treaty survives when one country is annexed by another.[124] Many decades later, in *Goldwater v. Carter,* a plurality of the Court held that a challenge to President Carter's rescission of the United States' treaty with Taiwan posed a nonjusticiable political question. Senator Barry Goldwater had argued that[125] just as the President cannot unilaterally repeal a law, neither can he rescind a treaty without the Senate's consent. Justice Rehnquist, writing for a plurality of four Justices, ruled this a political question, saying that there were no standards in the Constitution governing rescission of treaties and that the matter was a "dispute between coequal branches of our Government, each of which has resources available to protect and assert its interests."[126]

Fourth, challenges to the President's use of the war powers have often been found to be political questions. During the Vietnam War, several dozen cases were filed in the federal courts arguing that the war was unconstitutional because there was no congressional declaration of war. The Supreme Court did not take up any of these cases, but almost all of the lower courts ruled that these challenges were political questions.[127] In the 1980s, the lower courts dismissed challenges to the constitutionality of President Reagan's military activities in El Salvador on the same grounds.[128] Lower courts later dismissed challenges to the war in Iraq as nonjusticiable as well.[129]

OVERSIGHT OF OTHER BRANCHES OF GOVERNMENT

A third area where the Court has invoked the political question doctrine is the courts' oversight and control of the other branches of the federal government. In *Gilligan v. Morgan,* the Court dismissed a lawsuit claiming that the government was negligent in failing to adequately train the Ohio National Guard.[130] Students at Kent State University initiated the suit after the shooting of four students during an anti–Vietnam War protest on May 4, 1970, contending that grossly inadequate training of the Guard had caused the unjustified use of lethal force.

The Supreme Court, in an opinion by Chief Justice Burger, dismissed the case as posing a political question. Allowing review, Burger wrote, "would plainly and explicitly require a judicial evaluation of a wide range of possibly dissimilar procedures and policies approved by different law enforcement agencies or other authorities. It would be inappropriate for a district judge to undertake this responsibility, in the unlikely event that he possessed the requisite technical competence to do so."[131] The Court emphasized that relief would require ongoing supervision and control of Ohio National Guard activities.

A case from 1892, *Field v. Clark,* involved the claim that a section of a bill passed by Congress was omitted from the final version of the law authenticated by the Speaker of the House and the Vice President, and signed by the President.[132] The Court ruled that judicial review was unnecessary because Congress could protect its own interests by adopting additional legislation.

But a key case rejecting the application of the political question doctrine to internal congressional decisions is *Powell v. McCormack*.[133] In 1967, the House of Representatives refused to seat Representative Adam Clayton Powell even though his constituents had elected him. A House subcommittee found that Powell had deceived Congress by presenting false travel vouchers for reimbursements and had used government funds to make illegal payments to his wife. Powell and thirteen of his constituents sued, arguing that the refusal to seat him was unconstitutional because he was properly elected and met all of the constitutional requirements for service as a representative.

The Constitution specifically provides, in Article I, Section 5, that each house of Congress may, by a two-thirds vote, expel a member. But the Court noted that the issue in *Powell v. McCormack* was not expulsion but exclusion.[134] The defendants argued that the case posed a political question because Article I, Section 5 states that each house of Congress shall "be the Judge of the Qualifications of its Members." But the Court held that the House of Representatives had discretion only to determine if a member met the qualifications stated in Article I, Section 2—requirements of age, citizenship, and residence.[135] In declaring that the case was justiciable and did not pose a political question, the

Court stressed the importance of allowing people to select their legislators. It "concluded that Art. I. §5, is at most a 'textually demonstrable commitment' to Congress to judge only the qualifications expressly set forth in the Constitution."[136]

The defendants urged the Court to dismiss the case rather than risk conflict with another branch of government. Rejecting the notion that such considerations should influence its ruling, the Court did not apply the political question doctrine and instead stated, "Our system of government requires that federal courts on occasion interpret the Constitution in a manner at variance with the construction given the document by another branch. The alleged conflict that such an adjudication may cause cannot justify the courts' avoiding their constitutional responsibility."[137] Here as in the area of foreign policy, however, the Court has been inconsistent as to when cases should be dismissed as political questions.

CHALLENGES TO IMPEACHMENT

The final area where the Court has dismissed cases as nonjusticiable political questions is challenges to the impeachment process. *Nixon v. United States* involved federal district court judge Walter Nixon, who had been convicted of making false statements to a grand jury.[138] He refused to resign from the bench and continued to collect his judicial salary while in prison. The House of Representatives adopted articles of impeachment, and the Senate created a committee to hold a hearing and make a recommendation to the full Senate. The committee recommended removal from office, and the entire Senate voted accordingly.

Nixon argued, however, that the Senate's procedure violated Article I, Section 3 of the Constitution, which provides that the "Senate shall have the sole Power to try all Impeachments." He maintained that this meant that the entire Senate had to sit and hear the evidence, and that the use of a committee to hear testimony and make a recommendation was unconstitutional.

Chief Justice Rehnquist, writing for the Court, held that the language and structure of Article I explicitly entrust impeachment to the Senate rather than the courts. The framers, he wrote, "deliberately separated the two forums to avoid raising the specter of bias and to ensure independent judgments. . . . Certainly, judicial review of the Senate's trial would introduce the same risk of bias as would participation in the trial itself."[139] Judicial review would be inconsistent with the framers' views of impeachment as the only legislative check on the judiciary; the courts' involvement would undercut this independent check on judges.[140] As with all areas where the Supreme Court has deemed a matter to be a political question, this means that even blatantly unconstitutional actions would go unreviewed.

THE POLITICAL QUESTION DOCTRINE
SHOULD BE ELIMINATED

My central thesis by now should be familiar: the Constitution exists to restrict what the government may do. As *Marbury v. Madison* recognized long ago, these restrictions have little meaning if they cannot be enforced.[141] In all of the areas I have described, the application of the political question doctrine prevents judicial enforcement of key constitutional provisions. This is inconsistent with the Constitution's very purpose and with the role of the judiciary in our constitutional system.[142]

To develop the meaning of the Constitution in an orderly, coherent manner and ensure that its mandates are observed, society needs an authoritative interpreter of the document's provisions. In Chapter 1, I described why the Supreme Court and the federal judiciary are best suited to fulfill this role. This means that the Court must be the authoritative interpreter of *all* constitutional provisions.

In part, this is because the other branches are unlikely to do the job. History shows that Congress is generally unwilling to restrain the President. Professor Arthur S. Miller, in a 1973 study of the separation of powers, wrote that "congressional review of executive policy-making is sporadic, and the executive frequently makes policy without Congress either taking responsibility for it or repudiating it. The result is a system sharply skewed towards executive policymaking."[143] Paul Gewirtz offers many reasons why Congress may not contravene the President even though a majority of its members may disagree with him: "when . . . faced with an executive policy that is in place and functioning, Congress often acquiesces in the executive's action for reasons which have nothing to do with the majority's preferences on the policy issues involved. . . . In such a situation, Congress may not want to be viewed as disruptive; or Congresspersons may not want to embarrass the President; or Congress may want to score political points by attacking the executive's action rather than accepting political responsibility for some action itself; or Congresspersons may be busy running for reelection or tending to constituents' individual problems; or Congress may be lazy and prefer another recess."[144]

The framers' intention of preventing the accumulation of power in one branch of government is thwarted when matters are deemed to be political questions. I believe that when there are claims that the President is acting in excess of the Constitution's grant of power and unconstitutionally usurping legislative power, these matters should be resolved by the judiciary. This calls for abandoning the justiciability doctrines that reserve interpretation of parts of the Constitution to the political branches. Judicial review exists to protect the Constitution from majority rule, and this includes the parts of the Constitution that define the structure of government. Given that these provisions often directly affect the distribution of governmental power, they are the parts we should be most reluctant to entrust to the majoritarian branches. To ensure that the Constitution is protected from majoritarian pressures, the judiciary should be empowered to interpret all of its provisions.

I can envision several objections to this conclusion. First, it might be argued that my approach is inconsistent with a two-hundred-year tradition of judicial declarations that certain subjects pose a political question. Initially it should be noted that this tradition is inconsistent with how the Court initially defined political questions. The political question doctrine, as set forth in *Marbury v. Madison,* provides that the courts should not review an official's performance of duties in which he or she has discretion. Only the exercise of lawful discretion should be unreviewable—not because of the political question doctrine, but because such challenges fail on the merits. Claims that an official is acting without constitutional authority or is violating a constitutional provision are not political questions.

Phrased differently, in every case involving a separation of powers issue, the question is whether the official has the power to act, and if so, whether the act is discretionary or mandated by some external authority and whether the action interferes or usurps the powers of another branch of government. Whether an official has the authority to act, and whether he or she is obligated to act in a particular manner, are not political questions. Only if the act is discretionary—meaning it is within the official's permissible authority—is the conduct unreviewable. As the Court declared in *Baker v. Carr*: "Deciding whether a matter has in any measure been committed by the Constitution to another branch of government, . . . whether the action of that branch exceeds whatever authority has been committed, is itself a delicate exercise in constitutional interpretation, and is a responsibility of this Court as ultimate interpreter of the Constitution."[145]

The political question doctrine should not prevent a court from determining whether the executive's conduct is an unconstitutional usurpation of judicial or legislative power. Justice William Brennan explained that the political question "doctrine does not pertain when a court is faced with the antecedent question whether a political branch has been constitutionally delegated as the repository of political decision-making power. The issue of decision-making authority must be resolved as a matter of constitutional law, not political discretion; accordingly it falls within the competence of the courts."[146]

Second, it can be argued that the allocation of constitutional decision-making to the legislature or executive is desirable because these branches have special expertise for some subjects. For example, it is often said that the President has special expertise in foreign policy. The Supreme Court once stated: "the very nature of executive decisions as to foreign policy is political, not judicial. Such decisions . . . are delicate, complex, and involve large elements of prophecy. . . . They are decisions of a kind for which the Judiciary has neither aptitude, facilities nor responsibility."[147]

This, however, only justifies deference to the executive's foreign policy choices. There is no reason why presidential expertise requires complete abdication and total deference, which is what the political question doctrine entails, when there are allegations of unconstitutional actions. Deference to expertise is appropriate when the question is whether an action was wise or is likely to succeed; but foreign-policy expertise cannot determine whether an action is constitutionally permitted.

In any case, the political question doctrine is most often invoked in situations where expertise is irrelevant. The question of whether the Vietnam War was unconstitutional because the President was waging war without a congressional declaration does not turn on foreign policy expertise. It poses a standard constitutional question concerning the meaning of two abstract provisions: the President's power as commander-in-chief of the armed forces and the congressional power to declare war. Similarly, expertise does not justify judicial abdication in generalized grievance cases. The question of whether it is unconstitutional for members of Congress to serve in the army reserves, the issue in the *Schlesinger* case, turns on the interpretation of a constitutional provision, not factual information possessed by an expert.

Also and quite important, the constitutional provisions governing foreign policy are largely meaningless without judicial enforcement. Although in some instances the other branches of government might try to uphold the Constitution even in the absence of judicial review, this is often impossible. In *Goldwater v. Carter,* Senator Goldwater contended that rescission of a treaty required approval of two-thirds of the Senate; that is, one-third of the senators should be able to block rescission.[148] Yet there is no way that one-third of the senators can enforce their position—even if it is impeccably correct constitutional law—without judicial review.

A third objection is that in some instances, the stakes are too high and the basis for judicial decisions too unclear to permit court involvement. An example of this is impeachment. If a President were impeached, could the Court review the case to determine if there was a "high crime or misdemeanor" or whether the procedures specified in Article I were followed? The argument is that the Court would exacerbate a constitutional crisis if it declared a presidential impeachment unconstitutional. It is a nightmare to imagine a situation where the House impeached a President and the Senate voted to convict, but the Court ruled that the President should remain in office. To avoid this possibility, it could be argued that the judiciary should deem itself to lack authority to review all impeachment cases.

I would argue that this situation would require great caution and judicial deference, but not total noninvolvement. What if a President were impeached for an act that was completely lawful and within his constitutional powers? Although this is unlikely, it is equally unlikely that the Court would declare an impeachment unconstitutional in the absence of compelling circumstances. Moreover, it must not be forgotten that Andrew Johnson was impeached and almost removed from office for exercising the chief executive's prerogative to remove cabinet officers. He was impeached for violating a statute—the Tenure in Office Act, which prohibited presidential firing of cabinet members—that was almost certainly unconstitutional. Or what if the Senate declared a President to be convicted by less than a two-thirds vote, perhaps entirely on the basis of a committee's determination?

The significance of such an event is hardly an argument for judicial abdication. In such circumstances, judicial review is essential to uphold the Constitution. The constitutional provisions dealing with impeachment become meaningless if the legislature can impeach by whatever procedures or standards it desires. Judicial involvement is also necessary to uphold the separation of powers. If the legislature could disregard the Constitution and impeach whenever it chose, there is a danger of a great shift in power toward the legislature and a threat to the structure of government.

Again, to say that there is a judicial role does not speak to the substantive standards of review that the Court should use. Especially in situations like impeachment, judicial deference to Congress on the merits is appropriate. But there is an enormous difference between hearing the case with a strong presumption in favor of the legislature's action and automatically denying review.

Finally, it might be argued that judicial restraint, as urged by people like Felix Frankfurter, Alexander Bickel, and Jesse Choper, is needed to protect the Court's legitimacy and credibility. They contend that the courts must preserve their institutional credibility by avoiding decisions that will draw the other branches' ire. The judiciary's limited power to enforce its decisions, they argue, means that the courts must depend on voluntary compliance by the legislature and the executive. They urge judicial restraint so as to preserve the Court's legitimacy and not risk defiance of its decisions.

I have several problems with this argument. First, I see little evidence that the Supreme Court's legitimacy or credibility is fragile. Further, I see no evidence that the areas where the Court dismisses cases because of the political question doctrine make any real difference in its overall credibility. If deciding cases in these areas would have an effect, there is no way to know whether it would be positive, and enhance the Court's overall credibility, or negative and diminish it. The unstated assumption is that doing less is best for the Court's credibility. There is no basis for that premise. Some very controversial rulings, like *Brown v. Board of Education* and *United States v. Nixon,* enhanced the Court's institutional credibility over the long term.

Even the most disputed decisions have done little damage to the Court's credibility. Many predicted that the decision in *Bush v. Gore*[149] would harm the Court's credibility. Justice Stevens wrote in his dissent that the decision "can only lend credence to the most cynical appraisal of the work of judges throughout the land. . . . Although we may never know with complete certainty the identity of the winner of this year's Presidential election, the identity of the loser is perfectly clear. It is the Nation's confidence in the judge as an impartial guardian of the rule of law."[150]

But the nation did not lose confidence in the Court. According to Gallup polls, 65 percent of Americans expressed confidence in the Court as an institution in September 2000, three months before the decision, and 62 percent expressed confidence in June 2001, six months after the ruling.[151] Why was there not the loss of legitimacy that so many predicted?

One explanation is that *Bush v. Gore* enhanced the Republicans' view of the Court and lessened that of Democrats, so it evened out. Again, the Gallup polls provide some support for this. Approval of the Court among Republicans went from 60 percent in August 2000 to 70 percent after the decision in December, while approval among Democrats shrank from 70 percent in August to 42 percent in December.

Any harm to the Court's credibility was likely short-lived. The country quickly accepted that George W. Bush was President, no matter how he got there, and moved on. In such a close election, most people were willing to accept the result. The margin of statistical error was larger than the number of votes that decided the election. Most people understood that our system of voting and counting votes is not precise enough to definitively resolve such a close election. More generally, most people accept that the Court is deciding hard cases where there is no clear right answer, and that the justices are applying their political and legal philosophies in good faith.

Bush v. Gore shows that the Supreme Court's legitimacy is robust, not fragile, and no single decision or group of rulings is likely to make much difference in the public's appraisal of the Court. The Court's credibility has been built up over two hundred years of American history; it is the result of confidence in the Court's methods and overall decisions. It reflects popular understanding of the desirability of resolving disputed questions in the courts and under the Constitution, even though everyone knows that, at times, they will be on the losing side.

For the Constitution to serve as a restraint on political majorities, we need the Court to enforce its strictures. That is why the political question doctrine should be eliminated.

The Way Forward

The Supreme Court has caused the problems I have identified, and it can rectify them. The Court can and should hold that someone must always have standing to raise a constitutional issue, and the standing question becomes who is the best plaintiff. The Court can eliminate the generalized grievance doctrine and the political question doctrine on the ground that both doctrines effectively prevent judicial enforcement of the Constitution and instead leave it to the political branches, where it does not belong.

I, of course, recognize that the Supreme Court is not likely to follow this recommendation. That raises the question: to what extent could Congress accomplish this reform? For areas where the Court has deemed the standing requirements to be constitutional, Congress cannot act. It could not, for example, pass a law to change how the Court has defined the requirements for injury, causation, and redressability—reflected in cases such as *Lyons v. Los Angeles* and *Allen v. Wright*—because these are based on the Court's interpretation of Article III of the Constitution.

It is less clear whether Congress can eliminate the generalized grievance or the political question doctrines. The Court has never specified whether these are constitutional or prudential requirements. In *Warth v. Seldin,* the Supreme Court declared that the generalized grievance doctrine's bar on citizen and taxpayer suits was "prudential," not constitutional.[152] It apparently reasoned that while citizens and taxpayers are hurt when the government violates the law, it was prudent for the federal courts not to hear such cases.

But in *Lujan v. Defenders of Wildlife,* the Court treated the bar on citizen standing as constitutional.[153] The Endangered Species Act provided that "any person may commence a civil suit on his own behalf (A) to enjoin any person, including the United States and any other governmental instrumentality or agency . . . who is alleged to be in violation of any provision of this chapter."[154] The plaintiffs invoked this authority to challenge a federal regulation providing that the United States would not comply with the Act outside the country except on the high seas. The Court, in an opinion by Justice Scalia, held that the plaintiffs were asserting a generalized grievance and that Congress has no power to authorize standing in such an instance. The Court characterized the prohibition against citizen-standing as derived from Article III and not susceptible to a statutory override. *Lujan* has dramatic implications for the many federal statutes that authorize citizen suits as an enforcement mechanism.[155] Such provisions are especially common in environmental statutes: they are included in the Clean Water Act,[156] the Surface Mining Control and Reclamation Act of 1977,[157] the Safe Drinking Water Act of 1974,[158] the Comprehensive Environmental Response, Compensation, and Liability Act,[159] the Clean Air Act,[160] the Noise Control Act,[161] and the Energy Conservation Act.[162] *Lujan* appears to strike down all of these provisions except where the plaintiff can otherwise demonstrate an injury sufficient for standing.

In a later case addressing the generalized grievance doctrine, however, the Court reaffirmed that plaintiffs have standing if they can show a personal, concrete injury. In *Federal Election Commission v. Akins,* the Court held that plaintiffs had standing to challenge a decision of the Federal Election Commission that the American Israel Political Affairs Committee is not a "political committee" subject to the regulation and reporting requirements under the Federal Election Campaign Act of 1971.[163] The federal statute permitted standing to any "aggrieved party." The dissent argued that the plaintiffs presented a generalized grievance in that their desire for enforcement of the law was the same as everyone else's in the world.[164]

Justice Breyer, writing for the majority, expressly rejected this argument and emphasized that the federal statute created a right to information. The denial of this right, he argued, was a concrete injury sufficient for standing. He explained that unlike *Richardson,* "there is a statute which . . . does seek to protect individuals such as respondents from the kind of harm that they say that they have suffered, i.e., failing to receive particular information about campaign-related activities."[165] *Federal Election Commission v. Akins* is an important post-*Lujan* clarification of the generalized grievance requirement because it clearly holds that Congress can create, by statute, rights that would not otherwise exist, and that an alleged violation of those rights is sufficient for standing, even under a broad citizen suit provision and even where the injury is widely shared in society.

Ultimately, then, on the question of whether the generalized grievance standing doctrine is constitutional or prudential, the Court has been inconsistent. Still, this is preferable to its silence on whether the political question doctrine is constitutional or prudential. Could Congress direct the federal courts to adjudicate a matter that the Supreme Court has deemed a political question? Unlike the other justiciability doctrines, the political question doctrine is not derived from Article III's limitation of judicial power to "cases" and "controversies." If this doctrine is determined to be based on separation of powers or textual commitments to other branches of government, it might be treated as constitutional. On the other hand, if it reflects the Court's concerns about preserving judicial credibility and limiting the judiciary's role in a democratic society, it is prudential.

The political question doctrine should be regarded as prudential, and Congress should eliminate it. Since it is not based on Article III of the Constitution, the only constitutional basis for its application would be separation of powers. But as I have argued throughout this book, the Court's role in relation to the other two branches is to enforce the Constitution. A doctrine that prevents it from fulfilling this role is a violation of separation of powers and thus has no place in American law.

The Great Writ

How Habeas Corpus Has Been Suspended

On November 4, 1995, Leandro Andrade, a nine-year Army veteran and father of three, was caught shoplifting five children's videotapes worth a total of $84.70 from a K-Mart in Ontario, California. The store's loss prevention officer observed his actions, stopped him, and confiscated the tapes. Andrade was arrested for shoplifting.

Two weeks later, on November 18, 1995, Andrade went to a different K-Mart, in Montclair, California, and was caught shoplifting four children's videotapes worth $68.84. Again, security observed Andrade on store video cameras, stopped him, confiscated the tapes, and arrested him for shoplifting.

Under California law, each crime by itself would be regarded as a petty theft,[1] a misdemeanor punishable by a fine, a jail sentence of six months or less, or both.[2] But California law also provides that petty theft with a prior conviction for a property offense is a felony.[3]

Andrade had been a drug addict while in the Army. After his discharge he committed a series of minor property crimes, including shoplifting. His most serious offenses were in 1983, twelve years before his K-Mart thefts, when he robbed three houses on the same day. He was unarmed, and in no instance was anyone home. He was caught, convicted of burglary, and sentenced to two and a half years in prison, which he served. Because of those convictions, Andrade's shoplifting was charged as the felony crime of petty theft with a prior.[4]

The way California's sentencing structure works, two counts of petty theft with a prior is punishable by a maximum of three years and eight months in prison.[5] That would have been a significant punishment for stealing $153 worth of children's videotapes.

But that is not what Andrade got as a punishment. In 1994, California adopted a law called "three strikes and you're out."[6] The three strikes law mandates a sentence of twenty-five years to life upon a defendant's third felony conviction.[7] It requires that the first two felonies be "serious" or "violent,"[8] but at the time of Andrade's trial, the third strike could be any crime, however minor.[9] Andrade, convicted of two counts of petty theft with a prior, was sentenced to two consecutive sentences of twenty-five years to life imprisonment.[10] His sentence, properly phrased, was an indeterminate life sentence with no possibility of parole for fifty years.[11] Thirty-seven years old when he was convicted in 1996, he would become eligible for parole in 2046, at the age of eighty-seven.[12]

Andrade's sentence was not unique. At the time of his appeal, 344 individuals were serving sentences of twenty-five to life or more for shoplifting—for petty theft with a prior—under California's three strikes law.[13] Hundreds more were serving life sentences for possessing small quantities of drugs.

The California Court of Appeal affirmed the judgment against Andrade, finding that the sentence did not violate the Eighth Amendment's prohibition of cruel and unusual punishment.[14] The California Supreme Court denied review.[15]

Andrade, on his own, then filed a timely habeas corpus petition in the United States District Court for the Central District of California.[16] The district court denied the petition,[17] and Andrade appealed.[18] I was appointed to represent him in the Ninth Circuit Court of Appeals and did so successfully; the Ninth Circuit held that Andrade's sentence was cruel and unusual punishment.[19] The Supreme Court has long held that "grossly disproportionate" sentences are cruel and unusual punishment in violation of the Eighth Amendment. The federal court of appeals concluded that fifty years to life for stealing $153 worth of videotapes was grossly disproportionate.

The State of California petitioned for Supreme Court review, which was granted.[20] In a 5–4 decision, the Court reversed the Ninth Circuit and ruled that Andrade was not entitled to a writ of habeas corpus.

Habeas corpus is a basic element of American law that allows a federal court to provide relief to a person who was convicted or sentenced in violation of the Constitution and laws of the United States. It derives from English law and is assured by Article I, Section 9 of the Constitution. In 1996, Congress amended the federal statutes concerning habeas corpus to greatly restrict its availability. One provision says that a federal court may grant habeas corpus only if a state court decision is "'contrary to' or an 'unreasonable application' of clearly established federal law."[21]

The Supreme Court held that Andrade was not entitled to habeas corpus relief under this provision because there was not clearly established federal law showing that his sentence was "grossly disproportionate." Yet there was a Supreme Court case directly on point: *Solem v. Helm* in 1983,[22] in which the Court held that it was grossly disproportionate to sentence a person to life imprisonment for passing a bad check for $100 because of six prior nonviolent offenses. Justice Powell, writing for the Court, observed that "the Court has continued to recognize that the Eighth Amendment prohibits grossly disproportionate punishments."[23] He announced a three-part test for determining whether a sentence is grossly disproportionate: "A court's proportionality analysis under the Eighth Amendment should be guided by objective criteria, including (i) the gravity of the offense and the harshness of the penalty; (ii) the sentences imposed on other criminals in the same jurisdiction; and (iii) the sentences imposed for commission of the same crime in other jurisdictions."[24]

In a subsequent case, *Harmelin v. Michigan* in 1991, seven of the justices reaffirmed the test from *Solem v. Helm* even while the Court upheld a life sentence for possession of more than 650 grams of cocaine.[25] Seven justices reaffirmed the principle that grossly disproportionate sentences are unconstitutional. Only Chief Justice Rehnquist joined Justice Scalia's opinion arguing otherwise.[26] Expressly disagreeing with their view, Justice Kennedy endorsed the Court's "adherence to the narrow proportionality principle that has existed in our Eighth Amendment jurisprudence for 80 years."[27] Justices O'Connor and Souter joined this opinion. Four dissenting justices, actually the plurality in the case, argued that "gross disproportionality" was too restrictive a constitutional standard and that courts should be more willing to find criminal sentences cruel and unusual punishment.[28] In other words, seven of the justices agreed that at the very least, grossly disproportionate sentences violate the Eighth Amendment.

In upholding Ronald Allen Harmelin's life sentence, Kennedy stressed the harms caused by the defendant's conduct: Harmelin had possessed enough cocaine for between 32,500 and 65,000 doses.[29] This, Kennedy wrote, distinguished his offense from the "relatively minor, nonviolent crime at issue in *Solem*." Harmelin's crime was "as serious and violent as the crime of felony murder without specific intent to kill."[30]

Under the three-part test from *Solem*, there should have been no doubt that Andrade's sentence was cruel and unusual punishment. The crime was minor and nonviolent, but the punishment was huge: life in prison with no possibility of parole for fifty years. In California, only murder and a few violent crimes could receive as large a punishment. Second-degree murder was punishable by fifteen years to life; voluntary manslaughter by up to eleven years; rape by up to eight years. As the Ninth Circuit pointed out: "Most violent crimes . . . are punished much less severely. . . . Andrade's sentence is grossly disproportionate when compared to . . . sentences for violent crimes."[31] Comparison with other jurisdictions made the gross disproportionality of Andrade's sentence even more apparent. Prior to California's three strikes law, no one in the United States ever had received a life sentence for shoplifting.

In light of all of this, it was disturbing that the Court found Andrade not entitled to habeas corpus. First, the Court's conclusion that there was no clearly established law is surprising given the existence of clearly established law: the three-part test from *Solem* and *Harmelin*, a test the Court has often cited with approval.[32] Moreover, as O'Connor's majority opinion in Andrade's case stated, under Eighth Amendment jurisprudence, a gross disproportionality principle "emerges as 'clearly established.'"[33] But she never explained why a life sentence for shoplifting is not grossly disproportionate.

Second, the Court ruled that the state court decision against Andrade was not "contrary to" or an "unreasonable application" of clearly established federal law. The Court has said that under Section 2254(d), a federal court also can grant habeas corpus if the state court "decides a case differently than we have done on a set of materially indistinguishable facts."[34] It is hard to see how the facts in Andrade's case and *Solem v. Helm* are distinguishable, and the Court's explanation strains credulity.

Both Andrade and Helm were in their mid-thirties when sentenced to life in prison. Both had received their first felony convictions approximately fifteen years earlier, each for residential burglary. Both had purely nonviolent prior records, principally financial and property crimes. Both received life sentences under state recidivist statutes for minor offenses: Jerry Helm for writing a bad check for approximately $100; Andrade for shoplifting $153 worth of videotapes.

Justice O'Connor said that the difference between Andrade and Helm is that Andrade was eligible for parole in fifty years, whereas Helm was sentenced to life in prison with no possibility of parole.[35] She thus concluded that Andrade's case was similar to *Rummel v. Estelle*,[36] where the defendant was sentenced to life in prison for misappropriating approximately $100 worth of property but was eligible for parole in twelve years. Realistically, a life sentence with no possibility of parole for fifty years is the same as a life sentence with no chance of parole. By the time Andrade would be eligible for parole—at the age of eighty-seven, in 2046 after 50 years in prison—the actuarial tables tell us he very likely would be dead. After Justice O'Connor's opinion, a state can immunize its sentences from Eighth Amendment analysis by setting parole in seventy-five or one hundred years.

In 2012, California voters passed an initiative to revise the three strikes law to require that the third strike be a serious or violent felony. This applied retroactively, and Andrade was released from custody. Without this initiative, he would have spent the rest of his life in prison.

Lockyer v. Andrade is just one of many Supreme Court cases restricting the availability of habeas corpus. Congress, through its 1996 statute,[37] and the Court through its restrictive interpretations of that law, have made habeas corpus relief extremely unlikely. A crucial vehicle for the federal courts to enforce the Constitution has thus been taken away. United States Court of Appeals Judge Stephen Reinhardt powerfully expressed this when he wrote: "The collapse of habeas corpus as a remedy for even the most glaring of constitutional violations ranks among the greater wrongs of our legal era. Once hailed as the Great Writ, and still feted with all the standard rhetorical flourishes, habeas corpus has been transformed over the past two decades from a vital guarantor of liberty into an instrument for ratifying the power of state courts to disregard the protections of the Constitution."[38]

Why Habeas Corpus Matters

Because it protects individuals against arbitrary and wrongful imprisonment, it is not surprising that habeas corpus long has been viewed as the "great writ of liberty."[39] It allows a person who alleges that he or she has been convicted in violation of the Constitution and laws of the United States to be heard and to receive a remedy.[40] Blackstone referred to habeas corpus as "the most celebrated writ in English law."[41] The framers of the Constitution, recognizing its importance, provided in Article I, Section 9 that "The Privilege of the Writ of Habeas Corpus shall not be suspended, unless when in Cases of Rebellion or Invasion the public Safety may require it."[42] The Judiciary Act of 1789 made habeas corpus available to prisoners who claim that they are held in custody by the federal government in violation of the Constitution, treaties, or laws of the United States.[43] After the Civil War, at a time of great distrust in the ability and willingness of state courts to protect federal rights, Congress provided habeas corpus relief to state prisoners if they were held "in custody in violation of the Constitution or laws or treaties of the United States."[44]

It is in the nature of any human system that mistakes will be made: constitutional violations will lead to convictions; innocent people will be convicted. Habeas corpus exists to let the federal courts provide a remedy. Judge Reinhardt expressed it well:

Although in most cases it serves our society honorably and admirably, the modern American criminal justice system all too often does not produce fair and just outcomes. In fact, recent studies as well as newly developed scientific techniques suggest that it fails to live up to our ideals more frequently than most of us would hope. Some of the major structural problems include insensitivity to the causes and effects of racial discrimination, inadequate public defender services, and a lack of adequate oversight and transparency in law enforcement. These problems manifest themselves in any number of ways, from racially disparate enforcement of the criminal law, to trials marked by fundamental constitutional errors, to the tragedy of wrongful convictions.[45]

This explains why it is so important that a person who believes he or she has been wrongly convicted should have access to habeas corpus. This is especially crucial for those who have been convicted in state court. There long has been a debate about whether state courts are as willing as federal courts to enforce the Constitution.[46] Those who believe they are not point to the two judicial systems' differing institutional characteristics.[47] For example, the federal judicial system has greater insulation from political pressure because federal judges have life tenure and their salaries cannot be decreased, whereas thirty-nine states have some form of judicial election. Many studies have shown that elected state court judges are much more likely to uphold death sentences than judges with lifetime appointments.[48] Some also believe that federal courts attract superior judges, provide more institutional support, and are more committed than state courts to protecting federal rights.[49] Others claim that state courts are equal to federal courts in their willingness and ability to enforce the Constitution.

I think this debate is unresolvable.[50] But as I have argued throughout this book, it is essential that the federal courts be available to enforce the Constitution. Habeas corpus is a crucial vehicle for this. For a person who has been convicted in state court, it is virtually the only way for the federal court to hear the matter and ensure that federal constitutional

rights are upheld.[51] The only other avenue for federal court review of a
state court criminal conviction is through direct Supreme Court review
of the state court decision. But the Court hears and decides fewer than
seventy-five cases a year; in its 2014–15 term, it decided sixty-six, and
in its 2015–16 term, it decided sixty-three cases after briefing and oral
argument. Realistically, for a person convicted in state court who wants
a federal court to decide whether his or her conviction violates the Constitution, it is habeas corpus or nothing. The rules created by Congress
and the Supreme Court almost always make it nothing.

Restricting the Availability of Habeas Corpus

The Supreme Court and Congress have created so many limits on the
federal courts' ability to hear constitutional claims via writs of habeas
corpus that I will just describe some of the most important restrictions. I begin with those created by the Court itself and then consider
those stemming from the Antiterrorism and Effective Death Penalty Act
(AEDPA) in 1996, which the Supreme Court has interpreted to greatly
restrict the availability of habeas corpus relief.

NO FOURTH AMENDMENT CLAIMS

Forty years ago, the Supreme Court said that federal courts could no
longer enforce the Fourth Amendment via writs of habeas corpus. In
Stone v. Powell, the Court concluded that Fourth Amendment claims
that had been raised and decided in state courts generally could not be
heard in federal habeas corpus review.[52] Claims that a state court improperly failed to exclude evidence as being the product of an illegal
search or seizure could not be relitigated, the Court ruled, if the state
court had provided an opportunity for a hearing: "where the State has
provided an opportunity for full and fair litigation of a Fourth Amendment claim, a state prisoner may not be granted federal habeas corpus
relief on the ground that the evidence obtained in an unconstitutional
search or seizure was introduced at his trial."[53]

     The Court emphasized that the exclusionary rule—the rule that
bars prosecutors from using improperly obtained evidence in a crimi-

nal trial—does not relate to the accuracy of the fact-finding process but instead exists to deter illegal police practices. The Court said that this deterrence would be increased marginally, if at all, by allowing exclusionary rule claims to be raised on habeas corpus.[54] The Court also stressed the exclusionary rule's costs in permitting guilty defendants to go free and in undermining respect for the criminal justice system.[55]

The Court also rejected the assertion that state judges would be less vigilant than federal court judges in upholding the Fourth Amendment. Earlier, in the 1953 case *Brown v. Allen,* the Court had held that constitutional claims could be relitigated on habeas corpus even if there had been a full and fair opportunity to be heard in state court.[56] In reaching this decision it explicitly noted that state courts often disregard the Constitution. But Justice Powell, writing for the majority in *Stone v. Powell,* said that the Court was "unwilling to assume that there now exists a general lack of appropriate sensitivity to constitutional rights in the trial and appellate courts of the several States."[57] Powell wrote that there is no "intrinsic reason" why the fact that someone is a federal judge rather than a state judge "should make him more competent or conscientious or learned" regarding Fourth Amendment claims.[58]

The holding that Fourth Amendment claims cannot be relitigated on habeas corpus is wrong for many reasons.[59] First, it violates the separation of powers: the Court exceeded its proper judicial role in deciding that certain constitutional claims could not be heard on habeas corpus review. Federal statutes make habeas corpus available for *any* denial of a constitutional right.[60] There is no indication that Congress intended Fourth Amendment claims to be treated differently from other constitutional issues. The Court should not have decided on its own that certain constitutional claims could not be raised on habeas corpus.[61]

Second, *Stone* wrongly assumes that federal and state courts are equal in the protection of constitutional rights. Taken to its logical conclusion, this raises the question of why federal courts need to exist at all, if state courts are their equal in every way. In fact they are not equal: federal courts are uniquely situated to decide constitutional claims, and this justifies relitigation of constitutional issues on habeas corpus.[62] Throughout this book, I have argued that the federal courts' role is to enforce the Constitution; *Stone v. Powell* means that they cannot enforce the Fourth Amendment.

Third, *Stone* mistakenly concluded that habeas corpus review of exclusionary rule claims would serve little purpose. The Supreme Court emphasized that the exclusionary rule does not bear on the reliability of the evidence or the defendant's actual guilt or innocence. But those who are convicted in violation of the Constitution should have a remedy whether or not they committed a crime. In another decision, a plurality of the Court stated that the "central reason for habeas corpus [is to afford] a means . . . of redressing an *unjust* incarceration."[63] But illegally obtained evidence does not have to be false for its admission to be unconstitutional. Although a central purpose of individual liberties is to prevent the conviction of innocent persons, the Fourth Amendment rights against unreasonable searches and seizures also exist to protect our privacy and dignity from government infringement. Justice Brennan stated this view forcefully in his dissent in *Stone:* "Procedural safeguards . . . are not admonitions to be tolerated only to the extent they serve functional purposes that ensure that the 'guilty' are punished and the 'innocent' freed."[64] In Brennan's view, habeas corpus exists to ensure that no person is jailed in violation of the Constitution.

PROCEDURAL DEFAULTS

When may a defendant raise a constitutional issue that was not presented in earlier proceedings? Imagine, for example, that a person was convicted in state court primarily on the basis of a confession. He did not challenge the confession during his trial or when he appealed his conviction to a higher state court. But now he wants to argue on habeas corpus that the confession was coerced and therefore that the conviction violates his Fifth Amendment privilege against self-incrimination. May the federal court hear that claim?

The law on this has changed dramatically over time. Under the Warren Court's decisions, a defendant was allowed to raise matters not argued in the state courts unless the government could show that the defendant deliberately chose to bypass the state court procedures. In other words, there was a strong presumption that procedural defaults—

the failure to comply with state procedural rules—would not bar federal habeas corpus review.

In sharp contrast, the Burger Court held—and it has been the law ever since—that a defendant may present matters on habeas corpus that were not raised at trial only if he or she can demonstrate either actual innocence or show good "cause" for the procedural default and also "prejudice" to the federal court's refusal to hear the matter. This approach creates the opposite presumption from that of the Warren Court: procedural defaults in state court now preclude habeas corpus litigation.

The Warren Court's major ruling on this issue came in the 1963 case of *Fay v. Noia.*[65] Three co-defendants had been convicted of felony murder in connection with a killing that occurred during an armed robbery. The only evidence against the defendants was a confession that each signed. Two of the defendants appealed to the New York State Court of Appeals and succeeded in getting their convictions overturned because of how their confessions were obtained. Noia, the third defendant, then tried to have his conviction overturned as well. But the New York courts denied his motion because of his failure to appeal along with his co-defendants; the court said that this constituted a procedural default precluding review.

The U.S. Supreme Court rejected the argument that failure to comply with state procedures bars federal court review on habeas corpus. The Court concluded that "a forfeiture of remedies does not legitimize the unconstitutional conduct by which . . . [a] conviction was procured."[66] In *Fay,* the Court saw the purpose of habeas corpus as preventing the detention of individuals whose conviction resulted from unconstitutional conduct. A state could prevent a habeas petitioner from raising an issue on the ground that it was not presented at trial only if he or she "deliberately bypassed the orderly procedure of the state courts."[67]

The Burger Court, however, adopted a dramatically different standard. In *Davis v. United States*[68] and *Francis v. Henderson,*[69] it refused to allow habeas petitions challenging the composition of grand juries when no challenge was made at the time of trial. The Court held in both cases that the defendants would be allowed to present the claims only if they could demonstrate "cause"—a persuasive reason for not having complied with the state procedural rule—and "prejudice"—a harm to not having the matter heard on habeas corpus.

A year after *Francis*, in the 1977 case of *Wainwright v. Sykes*, the Court made it clear that the "deliberate bypass" standard of *Fay* no longer applied; rather, defendants had to show cause and prejudice before presenting a matter on habeas corpus that was not raised at trial.[70] John Sykes was convicted of third-degree murder in Florida state court; he filed a habeas corpus petition in federal court challenging the constitutionality of the admission of his confession at trial. On appeal, the state court refused to rule on the question because Sykes had not raised it at trial, and under state law, a failure to make a contemporaneous objection to the admission of evidence is deemed a waiver.

The Supreme Court considered whether the procedural default prevented Sykes from challenging the admissibility of the confession in a federal court habeas proceeding. Under the *Fay v. Noia* standard, Sykes would have been barred from raising the issue on habeas corpus only if the state could demonstrate that he had deliberately bypassed state procedures. But the Court rejected this approach and instead adopted the "cause" and "prejudice" test.

Justice Rehnquist, writing for the majority, offered several reasons for preferring the cause and prejudice rule. He argued that the state's contemporaneous objection rule is very important to the orderly administration of the state's courts and that the *Fay* approach does not sufficiently encourage defendants to raise all of their objections at the time of the trial.[71] The *Fay* test, he contended, "may encourage 'sandbagging' on the part of defense lawyers, who may take their chances on a verdict of not guilty in a state court with the intent to raise their constitutional claims in a federal habeas court if their initial gamble does not pay off."[72] The deliberate bypass test encouraged both litigants and state court judges to view the state court proceedings as a "'tryout on the road' for what will later be the determinative federal habeas proceeding."[73] The "cause" and "prejudice" test, by contrast, would elevate the importance of the state court proceedings, prevent sandbagging, maximize efficiency, and serve the interests of justice.

Fay v. Noia and *Wainwright v. Sykes* thus articulated very different tests for when a matter can be raised on habeas corpus that was not litigated in state court. *Fay* puts a strong presumption in favor of allowing the constitutional claim to be heard on habeas corpus, whereas *Wainwright* puts a strong presumption against it. The basis of this difference is that the two decisions are premised on radically disparate assumptions. First, the *Fay* Court assumed that when matters are not raised in state courts, it is likely because of an inadvertent omission or error by the defense attorneys. Justice Brennan, the author of the majority opinion in *Fay* and a dissenter in *Wainwright,* explained that "any realistic system of federal habeas corpus jurisdiction must be premised on the reality that the ordinary procedural default is born of the inadvertence, negligence, inexperience, or incompetence of trial counsel."[74] But in *Wainwright,* the Court assumed that when there was an omission in state court, it was usually because of a strategic decision by a defense attorney attempting to sandbag claims until the later proceedings. This was a major concern for the *Wainwright* Court.

But it is difficult to see what an attorney might gain by sandbagging. If the objection is presented at trial, there is a chance that the court will rule in the defendant's favor and thus help acquit the defendant. If the court rules against the defendant, the objection is preserved and can be raised on appeal. But if the objection is sandbagged for a habeas petition, the defendant is giving up use of the objection at trial and on appeal for no apparent gain. Even under the *Fay v. Noia* standard, if it could be shown that the defendant deliberately bypassed review in state proceedings, he or she was barred from presenting the objection on habeas corpus. And given the low rate of success on habeas, it is hard to imagine attorneys strategically choosing to take a chance on a possible later reversal at that stage.[75]

I also question, as an empirical matter, the assumption that procedural defaults are more likely the result of deliberate sandbagging rather than attorney error. The reality of criminal representation, especially when it is done by overworked public defenders and by appointed counsel of often questionable competence, suggests the opposite conclusion.

Fay and *Wainwright* are also based on differing assumptions about the fairness of binding defendants to strategic choices made by their attorneys. The *Fay* approach says that a defendant should be deemed to have waived the right to present an issue only if he or she made a knowing and voluntary decision to forgo the state procedures. Justice Brennan explained that *Fay*'s "bypass test simply refuses to credit what is essentially a lawyer's mistake as a forfeiture of constitutional rights."[76] *Wainwright,* on the other hand, presumes that individuals are represented by competent, alert attorneys and that it is completely appropriate to bind clients to their counsel's choices.

Third, *Fay* and *Wainwright* differ on the importance of ensuring compliance with state procedures. The *Fay* Court recognized the desirability of ensuring that defendants raise all of their objections in state court, but considered it more important to ensure that no person is put in prison because of a constitutional violation. *Wainwright* stressed the crucial importance of enforcing contemporaneous objection rules and ensuring the use of state court procedures.

Although *Wainwright* implicitly overruled *Fay,* it was not until *Coleman v. Thompson,* in 1991, that *Fay* was explicitly overturned and the Court held that all procedural defaults must be evaluated under the cause and prejudice test.[77] Justice O'Connor, writing for the majority, declared:

> We now make it explicit: in all cases in which a state prisoner has defaulted his federal claims in state court pursuant to an independent and adequate state procedural rule, federal habeas review of the claim is barred unless the prisoner can demonstrate cause for the default and actual prejudice as a result of the alleged violation of federal law, or demonstrate that the failure to consider the claim will result in a fundamental miscarriage of justice.[78]

Roger Coleman was convicted of third-degree murder in a Virginia court; he filed a state habeas corpus petition that was denied by the state court of appeals because he had filed the notice three days late. The issue was whether this procedural error precluded federal habeas review. After explaining that *Wainwright v. Sykes* had overruled *Fay v. Noia,* the Court ruled that the petitioner's procedural default would preclude federal habeas review unless he could show cause and prejudice or a likelihood of actual innocence.

In May 1992, Coleman was executed in Virginia despite some evidence that he was actually innocent.[79] No federal court ever heard his claim.

Beginning with two decisions decided on the same day in 1986 —*Murray v. Carrier*[80] and *Smith v. Murray*[81]—the Supreme Court has held that as an alternative to demonstrating cause, a habeas petitioner may raise matters not argued in the state courts by demonstrating that he or she is probably innocent of the charges. But surprisingly the Court has suggested that a showing of likely innocence is not enough for a federal court to overturn a conviction on habeas corpus; it is only a basis for raising constitutional errors when there has been a procedural default. In 1993, in *Herrera v. Collins,* a majority of the Court joined Chief Justice Rehnquist's conclusion that "'actual innocence' is not itself a constitutional claim, but instead a gateway through which a habeas petitioner must pass to have his otherwise barred constitutional claim considered on the merits."[82]

Leonel Torres Herrera was convicted of murder. Ten years later, shortly before his scheduled execution, he brought a habeas petition claiming that newly discovered evidence showed that he was actually innocent of the murders and that his now-deceased brother was the actual perpetrator. A Texas rule, which required that newly discovered evidence be presented within thirty days of conviction, prevented the claim from being brought in state court.

Rehnquist's opinion stated that actual innocence is a basis for a federal court hearing on constitutional claims even when the cause and prejudice test is not met. Actual innocence, however, is not a basis for habeas corpus relief by itself. The "traditional remedy for claims of innocence based on new evidence, discovered too late in the day to file a new trial motion," Rehnquist wrote, "has been executive clemency."[83] In other words, a person can use a claim of actual innocence to raise some other claim, such as a confession being improperly obtained, but proof that a convicted person is truly innocent would not be a basis for habeas corpus relief.

This harsh result—that if executive clemency is denied, innocent people could be executed because state and federal courts refuse to hear newly discovered evidence—is called into question by Justices O'Connor and Kennedy. Although they concurred in Rehnquist's opinion, they declared that "the execution of a legally and factually innocent person would be a constitutionally intolerable event."[84] Indeed, they concluded their opinion by stating that they understood the majority opinion as assuming "that a truly persuasive demonstration of actual innocence would render any such execution unconstitutional and that federal habeas relief would be warranted if no state avenue were open to process the claim."[85] Reviewing the evidence against Herrera, O'Connor and Kennedy concluded that it was appropriate to deny his habeas petition because he "is not innocent, in any sense of the word."[86]

Justices Scalia and Thomas, meanwhile, argued that even if an individual presented compelling evidence of "actual innocence," that by itself would be insufficient for habeas relief.[87] Scalia wrote: "There is no basis in text, tradition, or even in contemporary practice (if that were enough), for finding in the Constitution a right to demand judicial consideration of newly discovered evidence of innocence brought forward after conviction."[88]

This is astounding and deeply disturbing: five justices joined an opinion stating that it does not violate the Constitution to imprison or even execute an innocent person. And this holding never has been overturned by the Court.

LIMITING THE FEDERAL COURTS' POWER ON HABEAS

Teague v. Lane, in 1989, is another Supreme Court decision that substantially limits the federal courts' ability to hear constitutional claims raised in habeas corpus petitions.[89] Simply put, *Teague* held that a petition must be based on existing constitutional rules and cannot raise "new rights" that have not yet been recognized by the Supreme Court. More specifically, the Court ruled that when a habeas petition asks a federal court to create a new rule recognizing a constitutional right, the court may not decide the matter unless the right would be applied retroactively. "Retroactivity," the Court declared, "is properly treated as a threshold question."[90]

The Supreme Court virtually never finds that a right applies retroactively. This means that a person can present in a habeas corpus request only the rights that existed at the time of the conviction. It also leads to harsh results based on accidents of timing: if the Supreme Court declares a police or prosecutorial action unconstitutional, those who were previously convicted because of these actions are out of luck.[91] For example, in *Ring v. Arizona,* the Court held that the Constitution requires a jury, not a judge, to decide whether a death sentence is appropriate in a criminal case.[92] But it held that this requirement does not apply retroactively, so that those who were sentenced to death before *Ring v. Arizona* could not bring a habeas corpus petition challenging their death sentences.[93]

Before *Teague,* the federal courts considered habeas corpus petitions alleging constitutional violations, even when they asked the Court to recognize a new constitutional right that would not be applied retroactively to other cases. When the Supreme Court articulated a new right it would benefit the habeas petitioner and future criminal defendants. The Court would subsequently decide, in another case, whether this new right was to be applied retroactively. But in *Teague,* the Supreme Court ruled that retroactivity must be determined first; federal courts may not hear habeas petitions asking the Court to recognize new rights unless such rights would be retroactively applied in all cases.

The Court in *Teague* broadly defined what counts as a "new" right, thus limiting the constitutional claims that can be presented to a federal court on habeas corpus. The Court said that a "case announces a new rule when it breaks new ground or imposes a new obligation on the States or Federal government. . . . A case announces a new rule if the result was not *dictated* by precedent existing at the time the defendant's conviction became final."[94]

Because very few criminal procedure rights have retroactive application, the effect has been to restrict habeas petitions from presenting claims except for rights that are already established.[95] The Court recognized only two situations in which rights have retroactive effect. One is where the new rule places "certain kinds of primary, private individual conduct beyond the power of the criminal law-making authority to proscribe."[96] The other is when a new rule adopts a procedure that is "implicit in the concept of ordered liberty,"[97] a designation that is "reserved for watershed rules of criminal procedure."[98]

In other words, *Teague* says that an individual cannot present a claim on habeas corpus review unless either it is an already established right or it is a right that passes the very high bar for retroactive application. Because the latter is rare and the Court broadly defined what is a "new right," *Teague* very substantially limits what can be raised on habeas corpus. Habeas corpus long has been a primary vehicle for federal courts, especially the Supreme Court, to identify and protect new constitutional rights.[99] After *Teague*, it no longer can serve this function.[100]

It would be hard to overstate *Teague*'s importance in limiting the federal courts' power to enforce the Constitution. Justice Brennan explained, in a strongly worded objection:

> This extension means that a person may be killed although he or she has a sound constitutional claim that would have barred his or her execution had this Court only announced the constitutional rule before his or her conviction and sentence became final. It is intolerable that the difference between life and death should turn on such a fortuity of timing and beyond my comprehension that a majority of this Court will so blithely allow a State to take a human life though the method by which the sentence was determined violates our Constitution.[101]

What Justice Brennan feared came to pass: *Teague* applies in death penalty cases. In *Saffle v. Parks*, the Court used *Teague* to preclude a defendant from challenging the constitutionality of the jury instructions in a capital case.[102] Robyn Leroy Parks, convicted and sentenced to death in 1983 for shooting and killing a gas station attendant in Oklahoma City, objected that the jury was instructed to "avoid any influence of sympathy." The defendant maintained that the Eighth Amendment requires that the jury, after hearing the mitigating evidence, be allowed to base its sentencing decision on sympathy for the defendant.

In an opinion by Justice Kennedy, the Court concluded that the defendant was seeking to create a new rule because precedent did not "dictate" that result. Moreover, the Court found that the case did not fit either of the situations where rules are retroactively applied. Parks could not challenge the jury instructions on habeas corpus. Parks was executed by lethal injection in Oklahoma on March 10, 1992.

In *Sawyer v. Smith,* the Supreme Court again applied *Teague* to preclude a habeas corpus challenge to a death sentence.[103] In 1985, in *Caldwell v. Mississippi,* the Supreme Court held that prosecutors, during the penalty phase of a capital case, cannot minimize the importance of the jury's responsibility by emphasizing the existence of judicial review of the jury's decision.[104] A year before *Caldwell,* Robert Sawyer was convicted of murder and at the penalty phase, the prosecutor told the jury that others would review their decision. Sawyer sought habeas corpus relief on the grounds that the prosecutor's statement violated *Caldwell* and violated the Eighth Amendment.

The Supreme Court said that this issue could not be raised on habeas corpus because Sawyer was asserting a right not yet in existence when he was convicted; it was recognized by the justices a year after he was convicted. Justice Kennedy wrote for the majority: "Examination of our Eighth Amendment authorities that preceded *Caldwell* shows that it was not dictated by prior precedent existing at the time the defendant's conviction became final."[105] Although *Caldwell* relied on many prior Eighth Amendment cases and many state constitutions had already recognized the *Caldwell* right, the Court concluded that the outcome in *Caldwell* was not "dictated" by precedent and that "no case prior to *Caldwell* invalidated a prosecutorial argument as impermissible under the Eighth Amendment."[106] In other words, the Court agreed that Sawyer's conviction violated the Constitution, but ruled that he could be executed because he was relying on a decision that came down after he was convicted. He was put to death because of an accident of timing.

It is clear that the Court generally defines "new rule" expansively and instances where rules have retroactive application narrowly. Thus *Teague* means that habeas corpus can virtually never be used—as it had been for decades—to recognize new constitutional rights. It also means that timing is everything when it comes to habeas corpus petitions. Individuals can raise only the rights that existed before their convictions became final; rights articulated even days later cannot provide the basis for habeas corpus relief. People may be executed because they were unlucky enough to face judicial proceedings before practices were challenged.

ONLY EVIDENCE PRESENTED IN STATE COURT

The restrictions I have described so far—the preclusion of Fourth Amendment claims being heard on habeas corpus, the strict rule with regard to procedural default, the bar on presenting claims of new rights on habeas corpus—were all imposed by the Burger and Rehnquist Courts in the 1970s and 1980s. But the Supreme Court's view of habeas corpus was not limited enough to satisfy Congress. In 1996, the Antiterrorism and Effective Death Penalty Act imposed many new restrictions on the ability of federal courts to hear habeas corpus petitions. This law was passed after the Oklahoma City bombing and was supported by President Bill Clinton at a time when his reelection was in doubt and appearing tough on crime was seen as helping his campaign.

A California jury convicted Scott Lynn Pinholster of two counts of first-degree murder for the stabbing deaths of Thomas Johnson and Robert Beckett.[107] Pinholster and two accomplices had broken into an acquaintance's house to steal drugs and money but were interrupted by Johnson and Beckett, who were housesitting. Pinholster was convicted of stabbing Johnson while one of his accomplices stabbed Beckett, taking money from both victims, and fleeing the scene. After Pinholster's conviction, the prosecutors asked for the penalty phase to be scheduled where the jury would consider whether to impose a death sentence. Pinholster's lawyers objected that they were never notified that the prosecution would present aggravating evidence during the penalty phase, and so they had not prepared mitigating evidence to defend Pinholster.[108] The trial court overruled the defense lawyers' objection but offered the attorneys a continuance to do further research and prepare for the penalty phase. The lawyers declined this offer and said they were ready to proceed with the penalty phase,[109] which was scheduled for six days later. The same jury then sentenced Pinholster to death on both counts of murder.[110]

Pinholster was not a sympathetic defendant. He bragged about having made a career of violent crime and about his white-power affiliations.[111] After his conviction, sentence, and appeal, he filed habeas corpus petitions in both federal and state court that quite compellingly alleged his attorneys, Harry W. Brainard and Wilbur G. Dettmar, had provided ineffective assistance at the penalty phase of his trial. Specifically, he presented substantial new evidence that his attorneys had failed to investigate and present mitigating evidence about his mental health.[112]

In his federal habeas petition, Pinholster's new lawyers presented testimony from an expert witness and psychologist, Dr. John M. Stahlberg, whom Pinholster's attorneys had consulted before the penalty phase of his trial. Stahlberg stated that he would have made further inquiry into Pinholster's mental health "before concluding that he had merely a personality disorder," had Pinholster's attorneys given him an accurate family history.[113] Pinholster's counsel only billed a total of 6.5 hours of preparation for the penalty phase of his trial, never contacted Dr. Stahlberg again or consulted any other mental health expert, never researched Pinholster's family history or medical and academic records, and called only one witness—Pinholster's mother—to testify on his behalf.[114]

Pinholster's habeas corpus petition came before the federal district court, where an evidentiary hearing was granted on the claim of ineffective assistance of counsel during the penalty phase of the trial.[115] Had Pinholster's counsel done any research into his mental health and family history, they would have discovered that his childhood was unstable and filled with drugs and violence. His biological father, grandmother, and stepfather beat him regularly during his childhood. His mother neglected him and his siblings, very often leaving them with little to eat. Pinholster's attorneys would also have discovered a long family history of mental illness, drug abuse, and suicide. His father was diagnosed as having paranoid and narcissistic personality disorder, while his siblings had psychiatric diagnoses ranging from bipolar disorder to schizophrenia.

Pinholster himself was diagnosed as having brain damage and epilepsy brought on by frontal lobe injuries sustained in two serious childhood car accidents. Pinholster's childhood history further showed that he had been placed in special education classes, was institutionalized at one point, and several times had been sent to homes for mentally disturbed children. He was eventually diagnosed with organic personality disorder. All of these were relevant mitigating circumstances for the jury to consider in deciding whether to impose a death sentence.

The district court granted Pinholster's petition for habeas corpus based on the "inadequacy of defense counsel in investigating and presenting mitigation evidence at the penalty phase" of his trial.[116] The U.S. Court of Appeals for the Ninth Circuit ultimately affirmed this decision.[117]

But the Supreme Court, in an opinion by Justice Thomas, reversed the Ninth Circuit's judgment and once more severely limited the federal courts' role in preventing injustice through the writ of habeas corpus.[118] The Court held that habeas corpus review by a federal court is "limited to the record that was before the state court that adjudicated the claim on the merits."[119] Therefore, all of the mitigating evidence about his family history and mental health diagnoses that Pinholster presented in his habeas petition was inadmissible for review in the federal district court. Pinholster's jury had been deprived of the opportunity to deliberate on all the facts of his case during the trial phase of his case, and Pinholster was now deprived of a just and thorough review of his case at the federal level. In fact, it was *because* the facts had not been given to the jury—precisely the injustice Pinholster was complaining of—that he was not allowed to present them to a federal court.

The federal court thus could not enforce the Sixth Amendment's assurance of adequate assistance of counsel. The result of this ruling is that someone like Pinholster, who can provide "substantial evidence of ineffective assistance of counsel, or of a prosecutor's failure to disclose exculpatory evidence, or even of actual innocence, will be unable to present this material on habeas corpus."[120] A person who has new evidence that he or she was wrongly convicted in state court cannot be heard in federal court. The evidence must be presented to the state court, assuming it even has a procedure to make this possible. As Judge Reinhardt declared: "This decision appears to be flatly wrong."[121] The statute does not justify the Court's restrictive interpretation. Reinhardt again: "The Court ignored § 2254(e)(2), the provision that limits the instances in which a federal court may hold an evidentiary hearing on a petitioner's claim. This provision would be unnecessary if Congress did not believe that federal habeas petitioners might rely on evidence not presented in state court, including in cases governed by AEDPA."[122]

Even more important, Judge Reinhardt explains, "*Pinholster* makes sense only if one accepts the Court's view that habeas corpus is primarily concerned with ensuring that state courts did not completely botch a criminal case. . . . This view—that habeas corpus is about the federal court interfering with the state system, and not about the federal court adjudicating the constitutional rights of the petitioner—reflects a profound misunderstanding of the proper function of the Great Writ. To explain why, I cannot improve on the words of Justice Brennan: 'Habeas lies to enforce the right of personal liberty; when that right is denied and a person confined, the federal court has the power to release him. Indeed it has no other power; it cannot revise the state court judgment; it can act only on the body of the petitioner.' Understood in this light, it is difficult to comprehend why the Court has become so preoccupied with asking whether there was an 'extreme malfunction' in state court. The proper question is, and always should have been, whether the detainee has a constitutional right to be free."[123]

THE BAR TO SUCCESSIVE PETITIONS

One of the most important changes in habeas corpus law in the last quarter century has been the imposition, by both the Supreme Court and Congress, of strict bans on successive petitions. As originally drafted, the habeas corpus statutes did not bar individuals from filing repeated petitions presenting the same claims. In the 1948 revisions of the habeas corpus laws, a provision was added excusing a federal court from ruling on a petition when the matter contained in it had already been presented and decided. Section 2244(a) provided that a judge need not entertain a petition for a writ of habeas corpus when the legality of the detention "has been determined by a judge or court of the United

States on a prior application for a writ of habeas corpus and the petition presents no new ground . . . , and the judge or court is satisfied that
the ends of justice will not be served by such inquiry." This, of course,
makes sense; once an issue has been decided on federal habeas review,
there is no need for the court to hear it again.

But in *McCleskey v. Zant* in 1990, the Supreme Court imposed a
new and much more troubling limit. It held that an individual who has
previously filed a habeas corpus petition challenging a conviction may
file a subsequent petition presenting a *new* issue only if he or she can
show good cause for filing a new petition and prejudice to not being allowed to file a successive petition.[124] Warren McCleskey, who had been
sentenced to death for killing a police officer while robbing a furniture
store, learned after filing his first habeas corpus petition that there had
been an informant in his cell. He then filed a second habeas corpus petition, arguing that the government's coaching and use of the informant
violated the Fifth Amendment under *Massiah v. United States*,[125] which
held that the government may not deliberately elicit statements from
a person under indictment who is represented by a lawyer, unless the
lawyer is present.

In *McCleskey v. Zant*, the Supreme Court held that the defendant
could not raise this issue in the second habeas petition.[126] Thus, the
Court concluded, "we have held that a procedural default will be excused
only upon a showing of cause and prejudice. . . . We now hold that the
same standard applies to determine if there has been an abuse of the writ
through inexcusable neglect."[127] In this case, the Court held, the petitioner knew enough even without the wrongly withheld information that
he should have pursued his *Massiah* claim in his earlier habeas petition.

Justice Marshall, joined by Justices Blackmun and Stevens, strongly
criticized the decision. Marshall wrote in dissent, "Today's decision de-
parts drastically from the norms that inform the proper judicial function. Without even the most casual admission that it is discarding long-
standing legal principles, the Court radically redefines the content of
the abuse of the writ doctrine."[128] He especially objected to precluding
a second habeas petition based on information the defendant did not
have available when he filed the first petition, precisely because the government wrongly withheld it.

The overwhelming majority of habeas petitions are filed by inmates without legal representation. There is generally no right to a lawyer on habeas corpus. Limiting inmates to one habeas petition unless there are extraordinary circumstances will mean that meritorious claims will go unheard because the inmate did not know the law when filing the first petition.

But Congress went even further in the Antiterrorism and Effective Death Penalty Act: it created an almost complete ban on successive habeas corpus petitions. An individual who has filed one habeas petition may not file another without first obtaining permission from the United States Court of Appeals. The Act states: "Before a second or successive application permitted by the section is filed in the district court, the applicant shall move in the appropriate court of appeals for an order authorizing the district court to consider the application."[129] Moreover, "the grant or denial of an authorization by a court of appeals to file a second or successive application shall not be appealable and shall not be the subject of a petition for rehearing."[130]

Under the Act, a court of appeals may allow a successive petition only in two circumstances. First, a successive petition may be allowed if "the applicant shows that the claim relies on a new rule of constitutional law, made retroactive to cases on collateral review by the Supreme Court that was previously unavailable."[131] In *Tyler v. Cain*, the Supreme Court ruled that only itself, and no lower court, can make a decision retroactive for purposes of allowing a successive habeas petition.[132] A criminal defendant challenged his conviction on the grounds of an impermissible jury instruction, which was clearly unconstitutional under the Supreme Court's decision in *Cage v. Louisiana*.[133] Nonetheless, the Supreme Court held that habeas relief could not be granted because it had never declared that *Cage* applies retroactively. Justice Thomas, writing for the Court in a 5–4 decision, focused on the literal language of the habeas statute, which allows a successive habeas petition based on rules "made retroactive to cases on collateral review by the Supreme Court."[134] The result, as the dissent lamented, is that people will be held in prison even though it is clear that their conviction was unconstitutional because the Supreme Court had not made the rule retroactive. This leaves the federal courts powerless to enforce the Constitution even when it is clear that people have been unconstitutionally convicted or sentenced.

The second ground for allowing successive habeas petitions is if "the factual predicate for the claim could not have been discovered previously through the exercise of due diligence and the facts underlying the claim, if proven and viewed in light of the evidence as a whole, would be sufficient to establish by clear and convincing evidence that, but for the constitutional error, no reasonable factfinder would have found the applicant guilty of the underlying offense."[135] In other words, new evidence clearly pointing to a convicted person's innocence can justify a claim, but only if it could not have been discovered earlier.

The law's very title, the Antiterrorism and Effective Death Penalty Act, shows that it was motivated by Congress's desire for finality. Multiple habeas corpus challenges to a conviction were seen as a source of significant costly delays, especially in capital cases. But the restrictions on successive petitions mean that some state prisoners will never get a meaningful hearing on their constitutional claims. Prisoners are not entitled to legal assistance in preparing habeas corpus claims; thus many file self-drafted petitions and omit important claims because they have little understanding of the law. They are then prevented from filing another petition with the help of counsel or other inmates. The restrictions on successive petitions provide efficiency and finality at the cost of justice.

A STATE COURT DECISION MUST BE "CONTRARY TO" OR AN "UNREASONABLE APPLICATION OF" CLEARLY ESTABLISHED FEDERAL LAW

I have recounted only some of the restrictions on habeas corpus. For example, I have not discussed the one-year statute of limitations the Antiterrorism and Effective Death Penalty Act placed on habeas petitions.[136] Nor have I discussed the rule that a habeas petition must be dismissed unless every claim within it has been presented first to the state court,[137] a requirement that causes most petitions to be dismissed.

But let's assume the habeas petitioner is one of the few who manages to overcome all of these obstacles: the habeas petition is not filed too late; it is the first habeas petition by this individual; all of its claims have been properly exhausted in state court; it seeks application of existing law and not the recognition of a new rule; and it does not seek a factual hearing. Even in this rare instance, there is no assurance that the petition will be granted. The Antiterrorism and Effective Death Penalty Act imposed a significant new restriction on the ability of a federal court to grant relief to state prisoners: habeas may be granted only if the state court "decision . . . was contrary to, or involved an unreasonable application of clearly established federal law, as determined by the Supreme Court." This is clearly meant to create much greater deference to state courts and to limit the instances in which federal court can grant habeas corpus review.

Can Congress intrude so deeply into the courts' prerogatives? The Supreme Court first addressed this question in *Williams v. Taylor*.[138] Terry Williams was convicted of murder in Virginia state court and sentenced to death. A state trial court, on a motion for postconviction relief, found that Williams had had ineffective assistance of counsel, but the Virginia Supreme Court disagreed, finding that there was not sufficient prejudice. The Fourth Circuit found that 42 United States Code Section 2254(d)(1) precluded habeas review unless the state court "decided the question by interpreting or applying the relevant precedent in a manner that reasonable jurists all would agree is unreasonable."

The Supreme Court reversed the Fourth Circuit and expressly rejected its conclusion that a state court judgment is unreasonable only if all reasonable jurists would agree that the state court was unreasonable. Justice O'Connor wrote for the majority:

> But the statute says nothing about "reasonable judges," presumably because all, or virtually all, such judges occasionally commit error; they make decisions that in retrospect may be characterized as "unreasonable." Indeed, it is most unlikely that Congress would impose such a requirement of unanimity on federal judges. As Congress is acutely aware, reasonable lawyers and lawgivers regularly disagree with one another. Congress surely did not intend that the views of one such judge who might think that relief is not warranted in a

particular case should always have greater weight than the contrary, considered judgment of several other judges.[139]

O'Connor emphasized that "contrary to" and "unreasonable application" are independent bases for habeas relief. For a state court's decision to be reviewable because it is "contrary to" clearly established federal law, the decision must be "substantially different" from the relevant Supreme Court precedent."[140] A state court decision is contrary to Supreme Court precedent if it contradicts that decision or reaches a different result on materially indistinguishable facts. As for the second phrase, in assessing whether a state court decision involves "an unreasonable application of . . . clearly established" federal law, the question is "whether the state court's application of federal law was objectively unreasonable."[141] O'Connor stressed that "the most important point is that an *unreasonable* application of federal law is different from an *incorrect* application."[142]

The Court applied this standard again in *Lockyer v. Andrade,* the case in which it upheld Leandro Andrade's two consecutive sentences of twenty-five years to life for stealing $153 worth of videotapes.[143] O'Connor, again writing for the Court, focused on the standard under Section 2254(d), saying that the only "clearly established" doctrine that applied to Andrade's case was a "gross disproportionality principle, the precise contours of which are unclear, applicable only in the 'exceedingly rare' and 'extreme case.'"[144] Thus there was not, in her view, clearly established law.

Nor was the Court amenable to Andrade's argument that the state court decision was "contrary to" a Supreme Court decision. Earlier, in *Solem v. Helm,* the Court had held that it was cruel and unusual punishment to sentence Jerry Helm to life in prison with no possibility of parole for passing a bad check worth $100.[145] But in *Lockyer v. Andrade,* the Court said that *Solem* was distinguishable because Helm had no possibility of parole, whereas Andrade was eligible for parole in 2046, when he would be eighty-seven years old.[146]

More recently, in *Harrington v. Richter,* the Supreme Court held that the deferential standard of Section 2254(d) applies even if the state court does not explain its decision.[147] The California Supreme Court denied a constitutional claim in a one-sentence summary order. The Court held that relief could be granted only if the requirements of Section 2254(d) were met. Justice Kennedy, writing for the Court, explained: "determining whether a state court's decision resulted from an unreasonable legal or factual conclusion does not require that there be an opinion from the state court explaining the state court's reasoning."[148] The Court then found that habeas corpus relief was unwarranted because the state court decision was not an unreasonable application of clearly established federal law. "As a condition for obtaining habeas corpus from a federal court, *a state prisoner must show that the state court's ruling on the claim being presented in federal court was so lacking in justification that there was an error well understood and comprehended in existing law beyond any possibility for fairminded disagreement.*"[149]

This seems identical to the standard the Court had earlier rejected in *Williams v. Taylor*. Under *Harrington v. Richter*, habeas relief can be granted only if there is an error that leaves no possibility for "fairminded disagreement." If reasonable judges could disagree, habeas corpus cannot be granted.

Judge Stephen Reinhardt explains why this standard is unduly restrictive: "Even putting the lack of precedent aside, it is apparent that if the 'fairminded jurist' rule were taken literally, it would mean that a federal court could *never* grant habeas relief. That is because, in order to grant habeas relief, we would need to find that each of the state court judges who denied the petitioner's claim was not fairminded. . . . In fact, under the Court's rationale, if only a single Supreme Court justice agreed with the state court, the rest of the Court would have to adopt the view that the dissenting Justice was not 'fairminded' in order to grant habeas relief."[150]

The Way Forward

Taken all together, these limitations make it almost impossible for a federal court to grant a petition for habeas corpus, even when there is clear evidence that the Constitution has been violated. Every one of the limitations I have described—and others that I did not—must be overcome in order for a federal court to hear and grant a habeas corpus petition.

Today, as a result, habeas corpus rarely functions as a vehicle for federal courts to enforce the Constitution. A 2007 study found that the federal district courts granted only 12.4 percent of habeas petitions for capital cases, and 0.29 percent—less than three-tenths of 1 percent—for non-capital cases.[151]

All of the restrictions I have described in this chapter should be overturned. The law of habeas corpus should be changed to allow those who claim that they are in custody in violation of the Constitution or laws of the United States to have their petitions heard and decided. Specifically:

- Federal courts should be able to hear on habeas corpus all claims of a constitutional violation, even those that have been previously litigated in state court. This was the law under the Supreme Court's 1953 decision in *Brown v. Allen* and it should be restored.[152] The courts should no longer be prevented from hearing claims of Fourth Amendment violations on habeas corpus.
- Individuals should be able to raise on habeas corpus matters not previously raised unless it is shown that there was a "deliberate bypass" of the earlier, available procedures. This was the law under *Fay v. Noia* and it should be restored.
- A federal court should be able to hear and give relief on habeas corpus to those showing a violation of the Constitution and laws of the United States without consideration of whether it is a new right or one that would apply retroactively. This was the law prior to *Teague v. Lane* in 1989 and it should be restored.
- Federal courts should be able to hold factual hearings to determine whether there has been a constitutional violation. This was the law prior to *Cullen v. Pinholster* and it should be restored.
- Prisoners should not be limited to one habeas petition, especially since they do not have a right to an attorney for habeas corpus. Successive petitions should be allowed unless there is proof of "abuse of the writ," which should be

defined to prevent only petitions that raise frivolous issues
or those that already have been litigated. This was the law
prior to *McCleskey v. Zant* in 1990 and AEDPA in 1996, and
it should be restored.

- A federal court should grant a habeas petition on a finding of a violation of the Constitution or laws of the United
  States. Period. The restrictive standard of AEDPA, that the
  state court decision must be "contrary to" or an "unreasonable application" of clearly established law as articulated by the Supreme Court, should be repealed. This was
  the law prior to 1996 and it should be restored.

- The rule of complete exhaustion for habeas corpus petitions should be eliminated. Under the 1982 decision in *Rose
  v. Lundy,* a habeas petition must be dismissed unless every
  claim within it has been presented to the state court. The
  law before that was that a federal court could hear and decide any specific claim that had been exhausted; it should
  be restored.

- The one-year statute of limitations created by AEDPA in
  1996 should be repealed.

All of these proposals would restore the law to what it was relatively recently.
None requires a novel or radical change. They would enable the federal
courts to use habeas corpus, as they once did, to enforce the Constitution.

How could this be accomplished? In my ideal, the Supreme Court
would conclude that the restrictions imposed by Congress (as interpreted by the judiciary) are an unconstitutional suspension of the writ
of habeas corpus. Article I, Section 9 of the Constitution prohibits Congress from suspending the writ of habeas corpus except when there is a
rebellion or invasion. The restrictions described in this chapter, taken
together, have effectively suspended the writ of habeas corpus. Some
federal judges have argued that AEDPA is an unconstitutional suspension of the writ of habeas corpus.[153] If it cannot bring itself to make
such a broad ruling, the Court should overturn its decisions restricting
habeas corpus in specific cases, such as *Stone v. Powell, Teague v. Lane,
Cullen v. Pinholster,* and *Harrington v. Richter.*

But even if that does not happen (and obviously it is highly un-likely from the current Court), Congress can cure the problem. The availability of habeas corpus is governed by federal statutes. Congress could repeal the restrictions contained in the Antiterrorism and Effec-tive Death Penalty Act and replace it with a law that contains all of the reforms I have described. Lest this seem radical, federal Court of Ap-peals Judge Alex Kozinski recently wrote: "AEDPA is a cruel, unjust and unnecessary law that effectively removes federal judges as safeguards against miscarriages of justice. It has resulted and continues to result in much human suffering. It should be repealed."[154]

Obviously, some will disagree. They might argue that habeas cor-pus should be available only for those who are actually innocent.[155] I disagree with this view. No one, innocent or guilty, should be incarcer-ated in violation of the Constitution. Never has the Supreme Court held that habeas corpus is reserved for those who can demonstrate factual innocence. Nor should it be restricted in this way. The protections of the Constitution serve many purposes in addition to protecting the in-nocent from wrongful conviction: they prevent abusive prosecutorial and police practices, uphold the dignity of individuals, and safeguard privacy. Besides, the restrictions I describe in this chapter also apply to the innocent.

Others will object to my proposal on federalism grounds: that it gives federal courts too much authority to review state court deci-sions.[156] Of course, any federal court habeas relief for state prisoners has a federal court overturning state court decisions. Ultimately we must decide which is more important, deference to the states or enforcing the rights of those who have been convicted in violation of the Constitution and laws of the United States. It really is that stark a choice. The restric-tions on habeas corpus that I describe in this chapter have meant that far fewer state court criminal convictions are overturned. The price is that habeas corpus relief is denied even when the Constitution has been violated. Federal courts have no vehicle other than habeas corpus to en-force the Constitution for those convicted in state court. Under present law, they don't even have that.

Opening the Federal
Courthouse Doors

I n November 2001, FBI and Immigration and Naturalization Service agents arrested Javad Iqbal on charges of conspiracy to defraud the United States in relation to identification documents. A Muslim citizen of Pakistan, Iqbal was working as a cable television installer in Hicksville, New York. While awaiting trial he was housed at the Metropolitan Detention Center (MDC) in Brooklyn, New York, where the FBI deemed him a person "of high interest" in its investigation of the September 11 terrorist attacks. Under this designation, Iqbal was transferred to a section of the MDC known as the Administrative Maximum Special Housing Unit (ADMAX SHU). Detainees in ADMAX SHU were kept in lockdown twenty-three hours a day. For the one hour per day they were allowed outside their cells, they were forced to remain in handcuffs and leg irons and were accompanied by four officers.

Iqbal claimed that while at ADMAX SHU, he was severely abused and mistreated by his jailors. According to Iqbal, the jailors "'kicked him in the stomach, punched him in the face, and dragged him across' his cell without justification."[1] On multiple occasions, he alleged, he was ordered to strip and subjected to body cavity searches, even though "he posed no safety risk to himself or others."[2] Iqbal further alleged that he and other Muslim detainees were not allowed to pray "because there would be 'No prayer for terrorists.'"[3]

Iqbal had not been convicted of any crime. The FBI and Department of Justice imprisoned him at the MDC and ADMAX SHU because he was designated a person "of high interest." He eventually pled guilty to using another man's Social Security card, served a term of imprisonment, and was removed to his native country.

Iqbal is not alone in describing such injuries. Many other detainees at the MDC have also alleged physical and verbal abuse at the hands of jailors. A study by the Justice Department's Office of the Inspector General found "a pattern of physical and verbal abuse against some September 11 detainees held at the MDC by some correctional officers, particularly during the first months after the terrorist attacks."[4] The Inspector General's inspection team interviewed nineteen detainees who were being held at the MDC and found that all nineteen detainees complained of some form of abuse, with twelve reporting physical abuse and ten reporting verbal abuse.[5] The latter included jailors using slurs like "Bin Laden Junior" to address detainees and threats such as "you're going to die here" and "you're never going to get out of here."

In October 2001, a newspaper article was published in which a September 11 detainee alleged severe physical abuse at the hands of his jailors. This prompted the Office of Inspector General to initiate another investigation of the MDC, the results of which are also detailed in the report. All four of the detainees who were interviewed complained of physical abuse such as officers slamming them into walls or being dragged by their handcuffs.[6] The OIG also interviewed eight officers, whom the detainees identified as their abusers. Nearly all of the officers denied "physically or verbally abusing any of the detainees or witnessing any other officer abuse the detainees." Only one of the officers who was interviewed told the OIG that he "witnessed officers 'slam' inmates against walls" and that this "was a common practice before the MDC began videotaping the detainees."[7] The officer informed the OIG that he believed these actions were unwarranted and that when he reported his concerns to his supervisor, the supervisor told him the behavior was "all part of being in jail and not to worry about it." The officer signed a sworn affidavit concerning everything he reported to the OIG about these abusive practices.

Four additional cases of alleged abuse were referred to the FBI for investigation. In all four instances, detainees claimed they were injured when guards slammed them against a wall or door. Two detainees "alleged that they were threatened by MDC correctional officers and incurred additional physical abuse, such as being kicked by officers or having the chain on their leg restraints stepped on by officers."[8] One detainee complained that he was also subjected to unnecessary strip searches and verbal abuse. In light of the numerous instances of abuse documented by the OIG's and FBI's investigations, Iqbal's claims are quite credible.

Moreover, the majority of the mistreated detainees at the MDC were Muslim men from the Middle East. Following September 11, the FBI and the DOJ commenced an extensive investigation to identify those who had aided the attacks. The FBI questioned more than 1,000 people with suspected links to the 9/11 attacks or to terrorism generally.[9] Of these, 762 were held on immigration charges, of whom 184 were deemed to be "of high interest."[10] The largest number of detainees—making up around one-third of the total—came from Pakistan. Other countries with high Muslim populations, including Egypt, Turkey, Jordan, and Yemen, were also well represented. About 64 percent of the detainees were arrested in New York.

Iqbal filed a complaint in federal district court alleging violation of his constitutional rights. He named as defendants Attorney General John Ashcroft, FBI Director Robert Mueller, and many other government officials who were responsible for his detention and treatment.

The Supreme Court, in a 5–4 decision, ordered that his complaint be dismissed for "failure to state a claim upon which relief can be granted."[11] In an opinion by Justice Kennedy, the Court held that Iqbal had not stated sufficient facts to make it "plausible" for a court to conclude that his constitutional rights had been violated.

It is hard to imagine what other facts Iqbal could have put in his complaint to make it more plausible. I have read the complaint many times. Iqbal describes in specific terms how he was improperly treated, why this violated the Constitution, and how the defendants were responsible. I have no idea what else the Court wanted the complaint to contain in order for the lawsuit to go forward. The dismissal means that Iqbal can never have his constitutional claims heard by any American court.

In this chapter, I want to consider three developments in procedure that, once again, limit the federal courts' ability to enforce the Constitution: the imposition of greater pleading requirements for suits in federal court, requirements that federal courts abstain even though all other jurisdictional requirements are met, and the restrictions on class action suits. These developments affect all litigation in federal courts, not just adjudication of constitutional claims. But the heightened pleading standard imposed in *Ashcroft v. Iqbal* has had its greatest effect in causing the dismissal of civil rights cases, including constitutional claims. The abstention doctrine also keeps federal courts from hearing constitutional claims, and the restrictions on class action suits often keep civil rights cases, where the damages to specific individuals are small, from going forward. When a large number of people each have a relatively small monetary claim, it usually is a class action suit or nothing because no one person has enough to gain to bring a lawsuit. Class actions are a crucial device for systematic reform. All of these procedural developments keep federal courts from being able to hear cases and provide relief.

Pleading Requirements

Over the past decade, the Supreme Court has made it much harder for injured individuals to get into federal court by significantly increasing the facts that the lawyer must know and allege in a complaint in order for a lawsuit to go forward in federal court. A seemingly technical decision about court procedures that received little public attention has had a profound effect on the ability of injured plaintiffs to sue and has systematically favored defendants, especially in civil rights cases.

For as long as courts and civil suits have existed, they have had to confront the issue of how much detail should be required in a complaint. If a great deal of detail is required, then many plaintiffs with meritorious claims will be out of luck because they do not have all of the facts. Often, key facts are in the control of the defendants, and would-be plaintiffs cannot get at them until there is a lawsuit and they have a chance to take depositions, ask interrogatories, and request documents—the process known as "discovery" in which both plaintiffs and defendants are permitted to gather facts from each other in order to assemble their respective cases. On the other hand, making it easier for plaintiffs to get into court means some defendants will have to deal with frivolous suits and the attendant costs.

American courts initially followed the English rules for complaints, which were quite strict in requiring detailed facts in order to get into court. In the mid-nineteenth century, American courts began to devise their own rules for pleadings, but these standards still required plaintiffs to provide very specific facts to support their claims. In the late 1930s, the Federal Rules of Civil Procedure ushered in a new system of procedures, which came to be called "notice pleading." This system strongly favored plaintiffs. All that was required to get into federal court was a short, plain statement of the facts, enough to inform the defendants and the court as to the nature of the claim, and enough to show that it was not impossible that the plaintiff could recover damages. In 1957, in *Conley v. Gibson*, the Supreme Court explained that under these rules, a complaint should not be dismissed unless there was no set of facts upon which relief could be granted.[12] The Court spoke of "the accepted rule that a complaint should not be dismissed for failure to state a claim unless it appears beyond doubt that the plaintiff can prove no set of facts in support of his claim which would entitle him to relief."[13] The goal was to make sure people with meritorious claims were not thrown out of court just because they had not yet had the opportunity to gather all of the facts. In other words, so long as the law allowed for recovery for those injuries, the claim would not be dismissed on the ground that the plaintiff did not yet have sufficient facts to prove the allegations of wrongdoing.

These standards subjected some defendants to needless litigation. But the philosophy behind notice pleading and the Federal Rules was that people asserting injuries should have a chance at discovery to find the facts to prove their claims. The screening out of nonmeritorious claims would occur only after the parties had the opportunity for discovery, generally through motions for summary judgment. A court could grant summary judgment if it concluded that upon the facts before it, a reasonable jury could only find for one party.

This was the law from the 1930s until 2007, when the Supreme Court dramatically changed the standard for pleading in federal court. The shift came abruptly and without warning, and was done entirely by the Court at its own initiation and based on its own views. There is an elaborate process for changing the Federal Rules of Civil Procedure, but it was not used.

The Court initially signaled a change in the pleading standard in *Bell Atlantic v. Twombly*.[14] *Twombly* was an antitrust case: consumers brought a claim against local exchange carriers claiming that they had illegally acted to limit competition. The defendant filed a motion to dismiss the complaint for failure to state a claim upon which relief can be granted. Justice Souter, writing for the Court, in a 7–2 decision, criticized the *Conley v. Gibson* standard and wrote: "We could go on, but there is no need to pile up further citations to show that *Conley*'s 'no set of facts' language has been questioned, criticized, and explained away long enough. . . . After puzzling the profession for 50 years, this famous observation has earned its retirement. The phrase is best forgotten as an incomplete, negative gloss on an accepted pleading standard: once a claim has been stated adequately, it may be supported by showing any set of facts consistent with the allegations in the complaint."[15] In other words, no longer would the law be that a complaint would be dismissed by a federal court only if there was no set of facts upon which the plaintiff could recover.

None of the parties in *Twombly*, and none of the briefs filed in the case, asked the Court to reconsider *Conley*. It had been accepted as the standard for pleading for over fifty years. I taught Civil Procedure many times and always told my students that it was the classic formulation of the criterion by which a complaint could be dismissed for failure to state a claim.

Justice Stevens, in a dissent joined by Justice Ginsburg, strongly objected to the Court's overruling of a test that had stood for a half century, especially when no party to the litigation requested or even suggested that it be changed. He wrote:

> Consistent with the design of the Federal Rules, *Conley*'s 'no set of facts' formulation permits outright dismissal only when proceeding to discovery or beyond would be futile. Once it is clear that a plaintiff has stated a claim that, if true, would entitle him to relief, matters of proof are appropriately

relegated to other stages of the trial process. Today, however, in its explanation of a decision to dismiss a complaint that it regards as a fishing expedition, the Court scraps *Conley's* "no set of facts" language. . . . That exact language . . . has been cited as authority in a dozen opinions of this Court and four separate writings. In not one of those 16 opinions was the language "questioned," "criticized," or "explained away." Indeed, today's opinion is the first by any Member of this Court to express *any* doubt as to the adequacy of the *Conley* formulation. Taking their cues from the federal courts, 26 States and the District of Columbia utilize as their standard for dismissal of a complaint the very language the majority repudiates: whether it appears "beyond doubt" that "no set of facts" in support of the claim would entitle the plaintiff to relief. Petitioners have not requested that the *Conley* formulation be retired, nor have any of the six *amici* who filed briefs in support of petitioners.[16]

After the *Twombly* decision was announced, it became unclear what standard should be used to decide whether a case should be dismissed for failure to state a claim upon which relief can be granted. In November 2008, I attended a national conference of federal appellate judges in Washington, D.C. There were panels on several topics, each with a Supreme Court justice and two law professors. The panel on civil litigation included Justice Stephen Breyer.

During the question-and-answer period, several federal court of appeals judges, with real frustration and even anger in their voices, asked what is the standard of pleading in federal court after *Twombly*. Finally, Breyer responded, also with frustration and anger in his voice, that *Twombly* is just about pleading in antitrust cases. That was certainly a possible reading of Justice Souter's majority opinion. But six months later, in *Iqbal,* the Court rejected this view and said that the new, more restrictive pleading standard applied to all civil litigation in federal court.

Iqbal sued fifty-three defendants, including Attorney General John Ashcroft, asserting that his detention and treatment violated the United

States Constitution. In a 5–4 decision, the Supreme Court concluded that Iqbal's complaint should be dismissed because he failed to allege sufficient facts for a court to conclude that it was "plausible" he could recover. Justice Kennedy wrote for the Court, joined by Chief Justice Roberts and Justices Scalia, Thomas, and Alito. No longer could plaintiffs go forward with a claim unless there was no set of facts upon which they could recover. No longer did courts have to accept the allegations of the complaint as true; the Court said that federal courts should ignore factual allegations that were just conclusions without evidentiary support. To see how radical this is in changing the law, one need only pick up a copy of the Federal Rules of Civil Procedure, the rules that govern the procedures in all civil cases in federal court. Every sample complaint that it presents as acceptable would have had to be dismissed under the new standard adopted by *Iqbal,* for failing to allege adequate facts.

The new standard is "plausibility." This requires a plaintiff to allege enough facts that a court can find it plausible for the plaintiff to recover. The Supreme Court declared: "To survive a motion to dismiss, a complaint must contain sufficient factual matter, accepted as true, to state a claim to relief that is plausible on its face."[17] It is unclear what this means. Justice Kennedy's majority opinion simply said that courts should decide what is plausible based on the context. "Determining whether a complaint states a plausible claim for relief will . . . be a context-specific task that requires the reviewing court to draw on its judicial experience and common sense."[18]

Obviously, what is plausible to one district court judge might not be plausible to another. By October 2009, just six months after the Supreme Court's decision, there already were over five thousand lower federal court cases citing *Ashcroft v. Iqbal.* Hundreds of cases had been dismissed that previously would have been gone forward.

As of the end of its 2015–16 term in June 2016, the Court has not decided another case clarifying this standard. It will take years and maybe decades for it to clarify what it means by "plausibility." In 2010, Arlen Specter, then a senator from Pennsylvania, introduced a bill into Congress to restore the standard that had been followed for decades.[19] One staff member of the House Judiciary Committee told me at the time that it would be difficult to get the bill enacted because it is hard for members of Congress to understand why pleading rules matter so much. Until there was a parade of injured, sympathetic individuals who had their cases thrown out of court, he said, there was no chance of Congress doing anything. But these rules matter tremendously, because they determine who can get his or her case heard in federal court.

It is striking that the five most conservative justices, on their own, changed the law in a way that greatly protects defendants from lawsuits. Congress could have changed the pleading rules at any time over the last seven decades but did not. The Federal Rules Advisory Committee, which promulgates the Federal Rules of Civil Procedure, also could have changed the pleading rules but did not. No studies showed any problems with the approach, which had been followed for seventy years. But the Supreme Court has now closed the courthouse doors to many plaintiffs with meritorious lawsuits.

I am discussing *Iqbal* because this decision has had its largest effect on civil rights litigation, including constitutional claims. In many cases it has become a serious obstacle to the federal courts' ability to enforce the Constitution. Many studies have confirmed this. A study by Professor Raymond H. Brescia focused especially on the effects of *Bell Atlantic* and *Iqbal* in civil rights cases, and showed that "motions to dismiss challenging the sufficiency of the pleadings are much more common since *Iqbal,* and far more cases are being dismissed after the release of that decision than before."[20] Brescia concluded that "there did appear to be an *Iqbal* effect, both in terms of dismissal rates and in the frequency of motions to dismiss based on challenges to the sufficiency of the pleadings. Not only were cases dismissed at a higher rate since Iqbal, but also, plaintiffs were forced to defend themselves on these grounds far more often than before, meaning significant transactions costs."[21]

Professor Patricia Hatamayr Moore conducted a statistical analysis and came to similar conclusions, specifically with regard to constitutional claims: "In constitutional civil rights cases, even excluding pro se plaintiffs, courts granted 12(b)(6) motions [i.e., motions to dismiss] at a higher-than-average rate under Iqbal.[22] . . . Courts granted 64% of the 12(b)(6) motions in the database in constitutional civil rights cases under Iqbal, even when the plaintiff was represented by counsel. Comparatively, under Conley, courts granted in full 41% of the motions."[23]

Put another way, "constitutional civil rights cases courts were 3.77 times more likely to grant motions to dismiss in full without leave to amend, as compared to deny, under Iqbal than under Conley."[24]

If a case presenting a constitutional complaint is dismissed at the pleading stage, there is no opportunity for the federal court to enforce the Constitution. As I noted above, the chance of a meritorious constitutional case being dismissed is high because many plaintiffs do not have the necessary facts prior to discovery. For example, holding a local government liable requires alleging and proving that there was a policy that caused the constitutional violation. But obtaining the documents or testimony to show the existence of such a policy often requires the discovery process. The approach adopted by the Court means that many plaintiffs, including in constitutional cases, will never get to that point. Simply put, the Court acted to deal with a problem that did not exist and did so in a manner that limits the enforcement of the Constitution and other federal laws.

Abstention Doctrines

The Supreme Court has identified certain circumstances in which the federal courts must refuse to decide cases that are properly within their jurisdiction. The term *abstention* refers to judicially created rules whereby a federal court may not decide a matter before it even though all jurisdictional and justiciability requirements are met.

There is a strong argument that abstention doctrines violate separation of powers. Long ago, Chief Justice John Marshall wrote: "It is most true that this Court will not take jurisdiction if it should not: but it is equally true, that it must take jurisdiction, if it should."[25] Congress created the lower federal courts and specified their jurisdiction. Where Congress desired federal court abstention it enacted particular statutes to prevent federal courts from hearing a matter, such as the Anti-Injunction Act, the Tax Injunction Act, and the Johnson Act. There is thus a strong argument that the Supreme Court acted impermissibly in creating the abstention doctrines and ordering federal courts to not hear cases even though authorized to do so by the Constitution and federal statutes. In an important article, Professor Martin Redish forcefully argued that the doctrines are "a judicial usurpation of legislative authority in violation of separation of powers."[26]

But my focus is on how abstention doctrines keep federal courts from enforcing the Constitution. There are many abstention doctrines, but I will examine just one: what is often called *Younger* abstention, which provides that federal courts cannot hear constitutional claims when the matter is pending in state court. Unlike much of what is discussed in this book, the *Younger* abstention is not a recent development. It has existed since 1971. Yet it is undesirable because it leaves constitutional issues in state court, subject only to the remote chance of review by the Supreme Court.

John Harris, Jr., the plaintiff in *Younger v. Harris,* was indicted in California state court for distributing leaflets alleged to violate the California Criminal Syndicalism Act, a law that prohibited advocacy of the overthrow of the government or of any industrial organization by force or violence. Harris sought a federal court injunction against the state criminal prosecution on the grounds that the existence of the Act and his prosecution under it violated the First and Fourteenth Amendments. Three other persons later intervened as plaintiffs, claiming that Harris's prosecution inhibited their teaching and political activities as members of the Progressive Labor Party. A federal district court granted an injunction on the ground that the California law was unconstitutionally vague and overbroad. There is no doubt that the California law was unconstitutional, as the Supreme Court later made clear in *Brandenburg v. Ohio,* which struck down an Ohio criminal syndicalism law as unconstitutionally vague and overbroad.[27]

In *Younger v. Harris,* the Court ruled that the injunction against the state proceedings "must be reversed as a violation of the national policy forbidding federal courts to stay or enjoin pending state court proceedings except under special circumstances."[28] Justice Black, writing for the Court, first dismissed the intervening plaintiffs' claims as not presenting a ripe controversy. Because the intervenors had not been indicted, arrested, or even threatened with prosecution, Black concluded that "persons having no fears of state prosecution except those that are imaginary or speculative, are not to be accepted as appropriate plaintiffs."[29]

Although Harris presented a live controversy because he was currently being prosecuted in state court, he was nonetheless denied injunctive relief. Black spoke of "the basic doctrine of equity jurisprudence that courts of equity should not act, and particularly should not act to restrain a criminal prosecution, when the moving party has an adequate remedy at law and will not suffer irreparable injury if denied equitable relief."[30] As long as Harris could raise his constitutional claims as a defense in the state court criminal prosecution, there was a preexisting remedy that made the injunction unnecessary.

Black then identified a separate, albeit interrelated, consideration: comity. He wrote that the "underlying reason for restraining courts of equity from interfering with criminal prosecutions is reinforced by an even more vital consideration, the notion of 'comity,' that is, a proper respect for state functions."[31] This idea, he explained, could best be captured in the phrase "Our Federalism"—a belief that "the National Government will fare best if the states and their institutions are left free to perform their separate functions in their separate ways."[32]

Younger thus created a firm bar against federal courts enjoining *pending* state criminal prosecutions. Interestingly, there is a federal statute—the Anti-Injunction Act—that generally bars federal courts from enjoining pending state court proceedings. The *Younger* Court explicitly stated that its decision was based on considerations of equity and comity, not on the Anti-Injunction Act.[33] A year later, in *Mitchum v. Foster,* the Court held that suits under Section 1983 of the Civil Rights Act of 1871—*Younger v. Harris* was such a suit—are not barred by the Anti-Injunction Act.[34] The Anti-Injunction Act prohibits federal courts from enjoining state court proceedings unless one of three specific exceptions is fulfilled. One exception is if injunctions are "expressly authorized by an Act of Congress." In *Mitchum,* the Court held that Section 1983 expressly authorized injunctions, and that federal courts could enjoin state courts pursuant to a Section 1983 suit. "The very purpose of §1983," the Court emphasized, "was to interpose the federal courts between the States and the people, as guardians of the people's federal rights—to protect the people from unconstitutional action under color of state law."[35]

But even though the litigation in *Younger* also was brought under Section 1983, the Court refused to allow the federal courts to enjoin the state court proceedings. This heightens the separation of powers concern: Congress wanted federal courts to hear such constitutional claims, but the Supreme Court ruled that federal courts may not do so.

The Court justified this holding on the grounds of equity and comity. But these arguments are questionable. The traditional principle of equity is that a court should not issue an injunction if an adequate remedy at law exists. This usually means refusing injunctions if money damages are sufficient; it has no direct relevance to one court refusing to hear an issue because another court can do so. Yet in *Younger,* the Supreme Court said that a federal court should not issue an injunction if a state court has proceedings available where it can review the constitutionality of the state statute. In fact, twenty years before *Younger,* in *Alabama Public Service Commission v. Southern Railway,* the Supreme Court declared: "'An adequate remedy at law as a bar to equitable relief in the federal courts refers to a remedy on the law side of federal courts. It was never a doctrine of equity that a federal court should exercise its judicial discretion to dismiss a suit merely because a state court could entertain it.'"[36]

Critics of the equity rationale also question whether the state court remedy is adequate. In part, they disagree with the assumption that there is parity between federal and state courts in deciding constitutional issues.[37] They also argue that if a statute is unconstitutionally broad in violation of the First Amendment, state court invalidation is not an adequate substitute for a federal court injunction because it is not possible to restore the speech that was lost.

Professor Douglas Laycock has persuasively argued that the opportunity to raise constitutional claims in state court is often a poor substitute for federal court review, because many state courts lack the ability to provide relief available in federal courts.[38] Laycock concludes, "even if one accepts the core of *Younger*—that federal relief should be withheld where the pending state remedy is adequate—a pending prosecution should not be a near automatic bar to a federal action. The federal court should consider whether the state remedy is actually adequate on each set of facts and provide supplemental relief where needed."[39]

The comity rationale is also questionable. The claim that injunctions breed friction is based on an assumption about the psychological reactions of state court judges. In most instances, however, the state judges probably will not even know that an injunction has been issued. Professor Wells explains that usually "federal relief will consist of removal of a state case from a list of unheard cases kept in the clerk's office. There will be no more disruption than if the state case had been settled and state judges may scarcely be aware of the insult visited upon them."[40]

Even if state judges are aware of the injunctions, they may welcome the lessening of their caseload and the removal of controversial cases from their dockets. Because most states have some form of electoral review of judges, it is likely that state court judges would rather let federal judges take the heat for declaring state laws unconstitutional.

State judges may believe, moreover, that just as state courts are the preeminent interpreters and enforcers of state laws, federal courts occupy that role for federal law. No insult, other than whatever is inherent to the existence of the federal courts, is implied. Or they might view the jurisdictional statutes as creating a choice of forum for constitutional litigants.[41] From this perspective, permitting federal court relief when there are pending state proceedings is no more an affront to state courts than is the existence of removal jurisdiction.

Finally, we may ask whether avoiding friction between federal and state courts should really be a basis for crafting jurisdictional rules. Critics of *Younger* contend that the Court never explained the value of harmony—a far less important value than protection of constitutional rights. Professors Soifer and Macgill argue, for example, that the Reconstruction-era civil rights laws were based on a distrust of state courts, and considerations of comity do not justify federal courts ignoring this legislative history.[42]

After issuing the *Younger* ruling, the Court immediately extended the decision to require federal courts to abstain in other circumstances. In *Samuels v. Mackell,* a companion case to *Younger,* the Court held that federal courts may not provide a plaintiff with declaratory relief when he or she is subject to a pending state court criminal prosecution.[43] Three years later, in *Steffel v. Thompson,* the Court held that declaratory relief from a federal court is permissible if no state proceedings were pending when the federal suit was initiated.[44] But it then limited this and held that federal courts may not provide declaratory judgments if a state prosecution is commenced before the federal court procedures are substantially completed. In *Hicks v. Miranda,* for example, the state prosecuted an individual the day after he had filed a civil suit for declaratory relief in federal court.[45] Even though the federal suit was filed first, the Court ordered the case dismissed from the federal docket.

In *Hicks,* police in Buena Park, California, seized copies of the film *Deep Throat* from a movie theater and arrested two of the theater's employees. The state also began legal proceedings to have the movie declared obscene, which it succeeded in doing. At that point, the theater owner, who was not a defendant in the state court criminal prosecutions, filed a lawsuit in federal court, which he won, to have the state's obscenity law declared unconstitutional.

The Supreme Court reversed the federal court's ruling, holding that the initiation of state proceedings against the owner provided him a forum to adjudicate his constitutional claims. Because the federal court suit was in its early stages, federal abstention and deference to the state courts was appropriate. Justice White, writing for the majority in a 5–4 decision, observed that "neither *Steffel v. Thompson,* nor any other case in this Court, has held that for *Younger v. Harris* to apply, the state criminal proceedings must be pending on the day the federal case is filed."[46] To the contrary, the Court held that "where state criminal proceedings are begun against the federal plaintiffs after the federal complaint is filed but before any proceedings of substance on the merits have taken place in the federal court, the principles of *Younger v. Harris* should apply in full force."[47]

Hicks gives prosecutors a tool to remove cases from federal court: they can retaliate against federal plaintiffs by initiating state prosecutions.[48] Justice Stewart, in his dissent, warned that the *Hicks* decision "virtually instructs state officials to answer federal complaints with state indictments."[49] Professors Soifer and Macgill contend that *Hicks* "laid waste the century-old canon of federalism that the filing of an action in state court could not oust a federal court first obtaining jurisdiction of the case."[50] In essence, it gave the state district attorney the power to remove a case from federal court to state court.[51] Professor Owen Fiss remarks that "*Hicks* fundamentally altered the structure of the federal jurisdictional scheme: it vested the district attorney—not the aggrieved citizen—with the power to choose the forum, and indeed, the nature of the proceeding in which the federal constitutional claim would be litigated."[52]

And then, in a very troubling series of cases, the Court extended *Younger*. In addition to keeping federal courts from interfering with state criminal prosecutions, it now also prevents federal courts from stopping civil proceedings where constitutional rights are at stake. The Court first considered the application of *Younger* abstention to civil cases in *Huffman v. Pursue, Ltd.*,[53] a decision heralded as "Our Federalism's great leap forward."[54]

In *Huffman*, state officials instituted a civil proceeding against an adult movie theater in Allen County, Ohio, for violating an Ohio statute declaring the exhibition of obscene films to be a nuisance. The state prevailed and obtained a judgment in the county Court of Common Pleas closing the theater for a year. Rather than appeal the judgment within the state court system, the theater management sought injunctive and declaratory relief in federal court under Section 1983 of the Civil Rights Act of 1871, arguing that the state court order to close the theater down violated management's rights under the First Amendment. A three-judge federal court ruled in favor of the plaintiffs.

The Supreme Court reversed this ruling, holding that the district court should have abstained under the principles of *Younger v. Harris*. Justice Rehnquist, writing for the Court, emphasized that the state's nuisance proceeding was "more akin to a criminal prosecution than are most civil cases."[55] Rehnquist noted that the state was a party to the proceeding, which was "both in aid of and closely related to criminal statutes which prohibit the dissemination of obscene materials."[56] Thus federal court injunctive and declaratory relief was "likely to be every bit as great as it would be were this a criminal proceeding."[57]

In dissent, Justices Brennan, Marshall, and Douglas argued that criminal and civil proceedings are very different. Criminal proceedings are not initiated until after "the completion of steps designed to safeguard . . . against spurious prosecution—arrest, charge, information, or indictment."[58] But the state can initiate a civil action simply by filing a complaint. Thus, the dissenters argued, it is too easy for the state to "strip [someone] of a forum and a remedy that federal statutes were enacted to assure him."[59] Although *Huffman* was a limited holding involving quasi-criminal state nuisance proceedings, Brennan correctly predicted that it was "obviously only the first step" in applying *Younger* abstention to all civil cases in state court.[60]

In *Trainor v. Hernandez,* the Supreme Court clarified that *Younger* and *Huffman* apply in all civil proceedings to which the state is a party.[61] In *Trainor,* the Illinois Department of Public Aid instituted a civil fraud proceeding to recover the welfare benefits obtained by Juan Hernandez and his wife, Maria, who allegedly had concealed their personal assets when applying for public assistance. After the department obtained a writ of attachment against the defendants' savings in a credit union, Hernandez brought a federal court action challenging the constitutionality of the state's attachment statute. The district court invalidated the statute.

In reversing the district court's decision, the Court held that *Younger* abstention should apply even though the proceeding was wholly civil. It emphasized that "the State was a party to the suit in its role of administering its public assistance programs. . . . [The state] was vindicat[ing] important state policies such as safeguarding the fiscal integrity of those programs."[62] The case was similar to *Huffman,* the Court reasoned, because in both cases the state might have initiated criminal enforcement actions.[63] But this decision broadened abstention beyond state-initiated civil suits where there are parallel criminal statutes. Justice White, writing for the Court, stated: "the principles of *Younger* and *Huffman* are broad enough to apply to interference by a federal court with an ongoing civil enforcement action such as this, brought by the State in its sovereign capacity."[64]

Another important case applying *Younger* to civil proceedings in which the government was a party was *Moore v. Sims.*[65] In *Moore,* the Texas Department of Human Resources removed children from their parents following an emergency order giving the Department temporary custody, because the parents were suspected of child abuse. The parents filed suit in federal court, challenging the constitutionality of the Texas law concerning the authority of the Department of Human Resources to protect children. A district court held Texas's law unconstitutional be-cause it failed to provide adequate notice to parents and did not ensure a prompt hearing after children were removed from their home.

The Supreme Court concluded that the lower court should have abstained and dismissed the case. Justice Rehnquist, writing for the Court, observed that earlier decisions had established that *Younger* is "fully applicable to civil proceedings in which important state interests are involved."[66] He concluded that a federal court should abstain so long as proceedings exist in the state system to adjudicate the constitutional claim: "abstention is appropriate unless state law clearly bars the inter-position of the constitutional claim."[67]

The Supreme Court has held that parents have a fundamental right to custody of their children. A state could bring a proceeding to terminate parental custody for unconstitutional reasons, such as the parents' speech or sexual orientation. But after the Court's ruling in *Moore*, federal courts are powerless to protect the Constitution and stop the state proceedings. For this reason, four justices—Stevens, Bren-nan, Stewart, and Marshall—filed a vehement dissent. They contended that the parents in *Moore* lacked a state forum in which they could have brought their constitutional challenges, and argued that *Younger* should not apply where "there is no single pending state proceeding in which the constitutional claims may be raised 'as a defense' and effective relief secured."[68] The dissent contended that there was no reason why a court should relinquish jurisdiction over all claims simply because some of the issues are pending in state court.

The extension of *Younger* to civil cases is disturbing because it means that the federal courts can almost never hear the constitutional claims. Criminal cases contain the possibility that a convicted person may come to federal court with a habeas corpus petition (although ex-plained in Chapter 5, this is growing ever more difficult). But in civil cases, the *only* possibility of review in the federal courts is the unlikely chance of Supreme Court review.

Even more troubling has been the extension of *Younger* abstention to keep federal courts from hearing constitutional claims when there are pending state *administrative* proceedings. Making federal courts abstain when a matter is pending in a state administrative proceeding cannot be justified under the rationale of *Younger.*

In *Middlesex County Ethics Commission v. State Bar,*[69] the plaintiffs brought an action in the federal district court contending that their First Amendment rights were violated by ongoing investigations by a state bar ethics committee. A New Jersey attorney, who also was executive director of the National Conference of Black Lawyers, criticized a judge's fairness and referred to proceedings in that judge's courtroom as a "travesty," a "legalized lynching," and a "kangaroo court."[70] The attorney was charged with acting in a manner "prejudicial to the administration of justice" in the New Jersey administrative bar discipline system. He then filed suit in federal court, contending that the pertinent regulations and bar proceedings were unconstitutional.

The Supreme Court, in an opinion by Chief Justice Burger, upheld the federal district court's decision to dismiss the proceedings out of deference to the pending state proceedings. He found the *Younger* decision "fully applicable to noncriminal judicial proceedings when important state interests are involved."[71] The bar disciplinary actions should be considered judicial, Burger wrote, because they were supervised and ultimately reviewed by the State Supreme Court and because they were closely related to the functioning of the state's judicial system. Moreover, the state's interest was deemed "extremely important" because of the need to ensure attorneys' "professional conduct."[72]

These extensions of *Younger* are troubling. In *Younger,* the Court emphasized that federal court relief was unnecessary because constitutional claims could be raised in the pending state judicial proceedings. Yet in *Middlesex County,* there was no indication that the state administrative bodies were empowered to decide the attorney's constitutional claims. In *Younger,* the Court emphasized the need for federal deference to state judicial proceedings; comity is the respect owed to the court system of another sovereign. But the extension of deference to state administrative actions cannot be justified without substantial explanation, which the Court did not provide.

By itself, the *Middlesex County* decision might be viewed as a narrow expansion of *Younger* abstention principles because bar disciplinary proceedings are a part of the state judicial system. One might draw a distinction between administrative matters that are handled under authority delegated by the state judiciary and those that are pending in other state agencies. *Younger* abstention, based on deference to the state judiciary, would apply to the former, because it is part of the court system, but not the latter.

But the Supreme Court rejected that distinction too, in *Ohio Civil Rights Commission v. Dayton Christian Schools, Inc.*[73] After a teacher at a church-run school informed school officials she was pregnant, she was told that her contract would not be renewed. The school principal informed her that the school's religious doctrine held that mothers should stay home with their preschool children.[74] When the teacher contacted an attorney, she was immediately fired for not following the dispute resolution provisions contained in her contract.

The teacher filed a complaint with the Ohio Civil Rights Commission, contending that her nonrenewal was unlawful sex discrimination in violation of Ohio law and that her firing was impermissible retaliation for attempting to exercise her rights. The Commission concluded that there was probable cause to believe that the teacher had been wrongfully terminated and began administrative proceedings. The school raised the First Amendment as a defense to the state proceedings and also filed suit in federal district court seeking to enjoin the administrative action.

The Supreme Court held that the federal court "should have abstained from adjudicating this case under *Younger v. Harris*,"[75] ruling that *Younger* principles apply when there are state administrative proceedings "in which important state interests are vindicated, so long as in the course of those proceedings the federal plaintiff would have a full and fair opportunity to litigate his constitutional claim."[76] Justice Rehnquist's majority opinion concluded that the state's interest in eliminating gender discrimination justified the application of *Younger* and *Middlesex County*. Rehnquist also found that the availability of state judicial review of the commission's decisions assured the school an adequate opportunity to raise constitutional issues.

Four justices—Stevens, Brennan, Marshall, and Blackmun—disagreed with the majority's conclusion that abstention was required under the *Younger* doctrine. "*Younger* abstention has never been applied," they wrote, "to subject a federal court plaintiff to an allegedly unconstitutional state administrative order when the constitutional challenge to that order can be asserted, if at all, only in state court judicial review of the administrative proceeding."[77]

Only in its most recent case about *Younger* abstention has the Court begun to hint at where it might set the doctrine's limits. In *Sprint Communications, Inc. v. Jacobs,* it called *Younger* abstention "exceptional" and limited to three circumstances: "First, *Younger* precluded federal intrusion into ongoing state criminal prosecutions. Second, certain 'civil enforcement proceedings' warranted abstention. Finally, federal courts refrained from interfering with pending 'civil proceedings involving certain orders . . . uniquely in furtherance of the state courts' ability to perform their judicial functions.'"[78] But none of this changes any of the cases described above or any of the situations where the Court has required *Younger* abstention. In *all* of these situations the federal courts cannot hear constitutional claims or enforce the Constitution.

Class Action Suits

Class action suits are an essential procedural device for enforcing the Constitution, enforcing civil rights statutes, and remedying other violations of law. They are especially important as a means for changing the law in a systemic way. When a government institution—prisons, police, schools—violates people's rights, a class action suit offers a way for reform. Furthermore, when a large number of people are each suffering a relatively small injury, a class action is often the only means to a remedy. Most people will not sue for small sums because it is not worth the cost of litigation. Lawyers rarely take such cases. But defendants can be enormously enriched by wrongful conduct that imposes small injuries on large numbers of people.

In recent years, the Roberts Court has imposed significant restrictions on class action suits. None of these cases has arisen in the context of constitutional litigation, though sometimes they have involved statutory civil rights claims. But the rulings unquestionably limit class actions to enforce the Constitution as well.

A key case in this regard was *Wal-Mart Stores, Inc. v. Dukes:* a class action filed in 2011 by 1.5 million women who alleged sex discrimination by Wal-Mart in pay and promotions.[79] It was one of the largest class action suits in history, against the largest corporation in American history. The Court said that their suit could not go forward because the plaintiffs could not show sufficient "commonality" to their claims. Commonality, one of the requirements for a class action suit to proceed, means that there are significant common issues of law or fact such that trying the case as a class action suit makes more sense than adjudicating each claim separately.

In concluding that the women who alleged sex discrimination lacked sufficient commonality, Justice Scalia, who wrote for the majority in a 5–4 decision, explained that because Wal-Mart had an official nondiscrimination policy, the discriminatory actions were actually due to the decisions of many different individuals in stores across the country.

The Court came to this conclusion even though the plaintiffs presented a great deal of evidence to show that company-wide practices and policies had caused the sex discrimination throughout Wal-Mart's large enterprise. Statistical studies showed that nationally the company's female employees were paid less than men and were less likely to be promoted. As Justice Ginsburg noted in her dissent: "Women fill 70 percent of the hourly jobs in the retailer's stores but make up only '33 percent of management employees.' 'The higher one looks in the organization the lower the percentage of women.'"[80]

The plaintiffs brought expert witnesses who testified about how Wal-Mart's practices led to discrimination against women. They presented a large number of affidavits from women employees detailing their experience and the discrimination they suffered while working at Wal-Mart. It is impossible to imagine that the significant differences between men's and women's average pay were just a mass coincidence.

But the Court rejected all of this evidence as insufficient to allow the class action. The issue before the Court was not whether the plaintiffs proved enough to win their case; the only question was whether the facts alleged were enough to show common issues and permit a class action. First, the Court found the plaintiffs' statistical evidence of nationwide gender disparities was "insufficient."[81] Justice Scalia speculated that the pay disparities between men and women "may be attributable to only a small set of Wal-Mart stores."[82] Second, the majority found the plaintiffs' expert witness not worthy of belief and thus "disregard[ed]" his testimony about the ways Wal-Mart's personnel policies and corporate culture allowed gender bias to infect pay and promotion decisions.[83] Scalia's majority opinion rejected the expert's entire testimony, merely because the witness could not determine how often Wal-Mart's individual employment decisions were "determined by stereotyped thinking."[84] Third, the majority dismissed the 120 affidavits recounting discriminatory statements and decisions as insufficient given Wal-Mart's size and the size of the plaintiff class. Having thus brushed aside the evidence of bias, the Court found that the gender disparities were the result of individual supervisors' decisions and had to be litigated individually.

The result is that it will be very difficult to litigate future employment discrimination claims as class actions. Smaller groups face a different hurdle. In a small workplace with a single decision-maker, employees who feel they've suffered discrimination will likely fail to meet a requirement called "numerosity," which demands that there be enough individuals suffering the same injury that it makes sense to try the matter as a class action. In a larger workplace where multiple people make pay and promotion decisions, the Court's decision in *Wal-Mart v. Dukes* will make it difficult to show sufficient commonality. Consider, for example, a university, where hiring, pay, and promotion decisions are made in separate departments and schools across campus. Under the reasoning of *Wal-Mart v. Dukes,* no class action suit would be permitted because the Court has made it next to impossible to link each department's discriminatory practices, even if the school shows a pattern of blatant discrimination based on race or gender.

The remedy, according to the Court, is for each individual to pursue a separate claim. But often, the amount lost by an individual employee does not justify bringing a separate lawsuit. An employee may be reluctant to bring an individual suit against the employer for fear of retaliation and adverse consequences. It is very difficult to find a new job if potential employers know that you've sued your previous employer.

And even employees who want to sue sometimes cannot get lawyers to handle the matter.

Wal-Mart v. Dukes is part of a pattern of Supreme Court decisions restricting class action suits and strongly favoring arbitration over court adjunction, including in civil rights cases. Saint Clair Adams worked for a Circuit City store in southern California.[85] When he applied for the job, he had to sign an application form that said that any grievances against Circuit City, including discrimination claims, would go to arbitration. Two years after his hiring, Adams sued Circuit City for discrimination. His lawyer decided it was best to keep the case in California state courts and sued entirely under California law, eschewing any claims under federal civil rights laws.

Circuit City then filed a separate action in federal district court to compel arbitration under the Federal Arbitration Act.[86] This is a federal law, adopted in 1925, that requires that federal courts enforce clauses in contracts that call for disputes to go to arbitration. The Federal Arbitration Act contains an exception: arbitration is not required for claims by "contracts of employment of seamen, railroad employees, or any other class of workers engaged in foreign or interstate commerce."[87] Under the language of the statute, Adams was an employee in interstate commerce. Many federal laws regulating the workplace, adopted by Congress under its commerce power—such as the Fair Labor Standards Act, which requires a minimum wage, and Title VII of the 1964 Civil Rights Act, which prohibits employment discrimination—explicitly treat people who work for major companies as employees in interstate commerce. The Supreme Court would not even question in these contexts that someone like Adams was an employee in interstate commerce.

Because Adams was an employee in interstate commerce, the Court of Appeals for the Ninth Circuit therefore said that the Federal Arbitration Act did not apply to his claim. Moreover, there are important public policy reasons for wanting civil rights claims to be litigated in court rather than handled before private arbiters.

But the Supreme Court, in a 5–4 decision, reversed the court of appeals and held that the employment discrimination claim had to go to arbitration. Justice Kennedy's opinion, joined by the four most conservative justices then on the Court—Rehnquist, O'Connor, Scalia, and

Thomas—interpreted the statute to say that "employees in interstate commerce" refers only to transportation workers. Under this interpretation, contractual clauses requiring arbitration are unenforceable only for those working in the transportation industry. All other employees must have their employment disputes, including discrimination claims, resolved through arbitration. This is not what the statute says, but it is what the Supreme Court has decreed.

Moreover, it is hard to see there having been a contractual agreement between Adams and Circuit City. A clause on an employment application, where the employee has no choice but to sign in order to be considered for employment, is not a contract in any meaningful sense of the word. The California Supreme Court has described arbitration clauses in consumer contracts as "contracts of adhesion,"[88] meaning that they are not really an agreement at all; they are terms that one party imposes on the other. Contracts connote an agreement. Adams hardly could have realized that in applying for employment he was also forgoing any ability to sue the company in the future.

The Supreme Court's decision, of course, does not apply only to Saint Clair Adams. It means that countless other employees with claims of race, gender, or age discrimination cannot go to court. As Justice Stevens lamented in his dissenting opinion, the Supreme Court has "pushed the pendulum far beyond a neutral attitude and endorsed a policy that strongly favors private arbitration."[89]

AT&T Mobility LLC v. Concepcion is another example of the Supreme Court restricting class action suits in favor of arbitration.[90] Vincent and Liza Concepcion purchased cellular telephones from AT&T Mobility. Like most of us, they had to sign an agreement for their cell phone service. The form contract they signed provided for arbitration of all disputes between the parties. In other words, if they had a legal dispute with AT&T, they could not sue in court; instead, their claim would go before a private arbiter.

Such clauses are increasingly common in consumer contracts, employment contracts, even medical contracts. Businesses would much prefer that complaints from injured consumers or aggrieved employees never go before a jury. Juries are perceived as pro-plaintiff and too likely to be swayed by emotions (whether that perception is accurate is much debated in the scholarly literature). Professional arbiters are considered more likely to rule in favor of business and, when they do rule for plaintiffs, likely to award less in damages.

Scholars such as Yale law professor Judith Resnik have identified another reason businesses prefer arbitration: an institutionalized bias among arbiters in favor of repeat players in the system.[91] Professor Resnik explains that professional arbiters depend for their work on being selected, or at least not rejected, by the parties. Arbiters know that if they develop a reputation for being pro-plaintiff, businesses will not use them in the future. The corollary is that arbiters who develop reputations as pro-business are much more likely to find work.

In *AT&T Mobility LLC v. Concepcion,* AT&T had advertised that the phones were free, but it charged the Concepcions $30.22 in sales taxes. The Concepcions' suit was consolidated with similar claims in a class action suit filed in federal court, alleging that AT&T had engaged in false advertising and fraud by charging sales tax on phones that it had advertised as free.

AT&T moved to compel arbitration under the terms of its contract with the Concepcions. The federal district court and the United States Court of Appeals for the Ninth Circuit rejected this because California law says clearly that such a contractual provision is not enforceable. There was no meaningful waiver of the customers' right to sue, and arbitration of a dispute between two parties is no substitute for a class action remedy. The California Supreme Court said that these clauses were "contracts of adhesion," and that is exactly what they were.[92] AT&T imposed this condition on consumers, and a person who wanted a cell phone had no choice but to sign an agreement mandating arbitration of any dispute. It is a long-standing principle of contract law that contracts of adhesion are not enforceable.

The Federal Arbitration Act, which requires enforcement of arbitration clauses in contracts, specifically says that such clauses are not enforceable where state law provides for the revocation of the contractual provision.[93] Both the federal district court and the federal court of appeals said that this exception to the Federal Arbitration Act meant that the Concepcions did not have to go to arbitration and could sue AT&T. California law was clear, and there was a California Supreme

Court case on point, that such arbitration clauses in consumer contracts are not enforceable.

Nonetheless, Justice Scalia, writing for the Court in a 5–4 decision, ruled that the California law allowing consumer class actions in such circumstances was preempted by federal law and that arbitration was required under the Federal Arbitration Act. The Court stressed the efficiency benefits of arbitration over court litigation and said that it was important to protect defendants, such as corporations, from the "in terrorem" effects of class action, which pressure them into settlements.[94] The Court's desire to protect business and its hostility to class action suits could not have been more clearly stated.

Scalia wrote that the Federal Arbitration Act requires the arbitration of claims on an individual basis and thus prohibits class arbitration. Nowhere, though, does the Federal Arbitration Act say or imply this. It is dubious that arbitration should be required at all, since the Act specifically says that arbitration clauses are not to be enforced when state law would not do so. But even if the matter must go to arbitration, nothing in the text or history of the Federal Arbitration Act implies that it must be individual as opposed to class arbitration.

The effect of this ruling is to keep those injured by an allegedly illegal practice from getting any recovery. Justice Breyer described the practical reality: "What rational lawyer would have signed on to represent the Concepcions in litigation for the possibility of fees stemming from a $30.22 claim? The realistic alternative to a class action is not 17 million individual suits, but zero individual suits, as only a lunatic or a fanatic sues for $30."[95] A federal court of appeals said in another case invalidating class action waivers that, absent unusual circumstances, "only a fanatic or a lunatic" would litigate a case worth just a few hundred dollars.[96] Since the overwhelming majority of lawyers are neither fanatics nor lunatics, the agreement effectively insulates the company from any judicial review or civil liability for its practices. Class actions exist precisely for this situation, where a large number of people each lose a small amount of money and none is likely to bring an individual claim.

In a subsequent case, in 2013, the Court repeated that an arbitration clause is to be enforced, and a class action suit precluded, even when the effect will surely be to immunize a defendant against liability for wrongful conduct. In *American Express v. Italian Colors Restaurant,* the Court said that an arbitration clause in a contract must be enforced even if it means that an antitrust suit realistically has no chance of going forward.[97]

Italian Colors Restaurant, a small business, accepted American Express cards and tried to bring a class action against American Express for antitrust violations. The restaurant alleged that American Express used its monopoly power in the market to force merchants to accept their credit cards at rates approximately 30 percent higher than the fees for competing credit cards. It claimed that this violated federal antitrust law.

American Express sought to prevent this litigation by invoking a clause in its agreement that requires all disputes between the parties to be resolved by arbitration. The agreement also provides that "there shall be no right or authority for any Claims to be arbitrated on a class action basis."[98] In other words, the agreement between American Express and Italian Colors Restaurant required that any dispute between them go to arbitration and be settled by individual, not class, arbitration. American Express, of course, dictated the terms of the agreement.

Italian Colors said that the antitrust suit could not realistically go forward except as a class action. Successfully suing for an antitrust violation can cost hundreds of thousands, even millions of dollars, yet recovery for a claim under the antitrust law is limited to $39,000, including treble damages. No one is going to spend hundreds of thousands of dollars to bring a lawsuit to collect $39,000. In contrast, a class action on behalf of all similarly situated plaintiffs is economically viable. Like *AT&T Mobility v. Concepcion,* this is a situation where a class action is needed because a large number of people each suffer a relatively small injury.

The Court ruled 5–4, in an opinion by Justice Scalia, that the Federal Arbitration Act required that the arbitration clause be strictly enforced, even if it meant that the antitrust claims would not be brought. As in *AT&T Mobility v. Concepcion,* the Court's conservative majority required enforcement of an arbitration clause even though it would effectively immunize the defendant from liability for illegal conduct. As Justice Scalia declared, "Truth to tell, our decision in AT&T Mobility all but resolves this case."[99]

There is a long-standing principle under the Federal Arbitration Act that arbitration clauses are not to be enforced if they prevent "effective vindication" of a claim.[100] This seems obviously to apply to Italian Colors's claim. But the Court refused to allow the exception.

Justice Kagan wrote in dissent: "Here is the nutshell version of this case, unfortunately obscured in the Court's decision. The owner of a small restaurant (Italian Colors) thinks that American Express (Amex) has used its monopoly power to force merchants to accept a form contract violating the antitrust laws. . . . So if the arbitration clause is enforceable, Amex has insulated itself from antitrust liability—even if it has in fact violated the law. The monopolist gets to use its monopoly power to insist on a contract effectively depriving its victims of all legal recourse. And here is the nutshell version of today's opinion, admirably flaunted rather than camouflaged: Too darn bad."[101]

This conclusion, Kagan added, was "a betrayal of our precedents, and of federal statutes like the antitrust laws."[102] Because of these decisions, big businesses have the power to enter into agreements that violate antitrust laws, and then to shield themselves from liability with clauses that require arbitration and preclude class action suits. This was certainly not Congress's intent when it adopted the Federal Arbitration Act or enacted the federal antitrust laws.[103]

These arbitration clauses are increasingly common. When we are injured—whether as consumers, as employees, or as patients—we are increasingly unable to go to court, and often will not be able to get any recovery at all.

In *AT&T Mobility v. Concepcion, American Express v. Italian Colors Restaurant,* and *Circuit City v. Adams,* the Court strictly enforced the Federal Arbitration Act, including to prevent class action suits and to protect business. In *AT&T Mobility v. Concepcion,* Justice Scalia expressed solicitous concern over the terrorizing effect of class actions in forcing businesses to settle meritless suits. He brought forward no evidence to support this assertion, nor did he or the justices who voted with him express concern for the adverse effects on those who never will have their day in court.

The effect of these cases, especially *Wal-Mart v. Dukes,* is to dramatically reduce the ability to bring a class action against a business.

Why does that matter? With the rise of the large business corporation in the early twentieth century, courts and legislatures developed class actions as a procedural device to protect individuals from exploitation by large entities. Courts and legislatures realized that large entities have incentives to engage in small, widespread violations of law because most people cannot afford to sue over a small violation. When individual litigation is not economically rational, the threat of litigation is not an effective deterrent to illegal behavior. Absent a robust government bureaucracy dedicated to enforcing consumer or employee protection laws, class actions are essential to law enforcement. Litigation is needed to deter wrongdoing, and class action suits are necessary when there is a large number of people and each individual has suffered a relatively small injury.

The same logic applies to constitutional violations by governments. When government entities violate people's rights—school systems in their treatment of students, prisons in their treatment of prisoners, police departments in their treatment of suspects—systemic reform is crucial. Class actions are an essential vehicle for this. The Supreme Court's restrictions on class actions thus, again, make it harder for federal courts to enforce the Constitution.

The Way Forward

One obvious way to change the law in these areas would be for the Supreme Court to reverse itself. Each of the decisions discussed in this chapter was a 5–4 decision by a Court split along ideological lines. If a Democratic president replaces even one conservative justice in the next administration, there realistically might be five justices to overturn the decisions about pleading and class actions and restore citizens' access to the courts. Justice Scalia's death makes that a realistic possibility depending on who replaces him. The abstention doctrine has existed for much longer—*Younger v. Harris* was decided in 1971—and is less likely to be changed by a future Court, even though it should be. Perhaps the Court's recent decision in *Sprint Communications, Inc. v. Jacobs* reflects a willingness to reconsider and further limit *Younger* abstention.

Failing Supreme Court action, Congress can cure the problems with pleading and class actions. Everything I have discussed here on those topics is a result of the Supreme Court's interpretation of the Federal Rules of Civil Procedure and a federal law, the Federal Arbitration Act. These can be changed by statute. Proposals to do this have been introduced into Congress but have never gone very far.

Senator Arlen Specter introduced a bill in the Senate in July 2009, the Notice Pleading Restoration Act, that would restore pleading to the standard followed under *Conley v. Gibson,* in which plaintiffs needed only a short statement of facts, sufficient to show a plausible likelihood of recovering damages, in order to file a suit in federal court.[104] The same year, Representative Jerrold Nadler introduced the Open Access to the Courts Act to the same end.[105] Such legislation would return the pleading standard to what it was before *Bell Atlantic v. Twombly* and *Ashcroft v. Iqbal.*

On May 12, 2011, Senators Al Franken and Richard Blumenthal, and U.S. Representative Hank Johnson, introduced the Arbitration Fairness Act of 2011.[106] The passage of this act would invalidate pre-dispute arbitration clauses in employment, consumer, and civil rights contracts. It has been reintroduced into subsequent sessions of Congress but has never gone very far.[107]

Congress could also amend Rule 23 of the Federal Rules of Civil Procedure to be more permissive of class actions than the Supreme Court's interpretation in *Wal-Mart v. Dukes.*

These reforms, of course, would not be limited to constitutional cases; they would affect all civil litigation in federal courts. But they would be vital for ensuring that federal courts can play their crucial role in enforcing the Constitution.

Enforcing the Constitution

K haled el-Masri, a car salesman from Ulm, Germany, was stopped at a border crossing between Serbia and Macedonia.[1] The CIA, which had confused him with someone else of a similar name, took him into custody. As Jane Mayer recounts in her book *The Dark Side,* a CIA official in Langley, Virginia, believed el-Masri had ties to Al Qaeda. On this hunch, he was held for 149 days, without word to his family or anyone else, during which he says he was beaten by unseen assailants, stripped, subjected to a body cavity exam, clothed in a diaper and tracksuit, hooded, shackled to the floor of a plane, and finally knocked out by a pair of injections. When he regained consciousness, he was in Afghanistan.[2]

He was fed putrid food and lost sixty pounds and was regularly "roughed up" during his interrogations. Eventually the CIA officials realized they had the wrong man and decided to release him. As Mayer describes it: "The CIA meanwhile, had flown Masri to Tirana, Albania, driven him blindfolded down a long, winding, potholed road, handed him back his possessions, and dropped him near the border with Serbia and Macedonia, where he was told to start walking and not look back."[3]

El-Masri sued in federal district court for his capture and treatment, which violated countless requirements of international law. The

United States moved to dismiss the case on the grounds that if a court even considered his case, it could reveal "state secrets" about the United States' rendition program. The government's position was that the entire matter had to be thrown out of court at the outset. At no time did the United States dispute the facts given in el-Masri's complaint or his allegations that the U.S. government was responsible for his apprehension and treatment. Its sole argument was that allowing the case to go forward risked revealing "state secrets."

El-Masri opposed the motion to dismiss on the ground that the facts of his case had already been made public, in Mayer's book and elsewhere. His lawyer argued that the entire case could be tried on publicly available information, eliminating the risk of disclosing any state secrets.

The federal courts sided with the United States government, and el-Masri's case was dismissed without being heard. The United States Court of Appeals for the Fourth Circuit, affirming the dismissal,[4] wrote that "those central facts—the CIA means and methods that form the subject matter of El-Masri's claim—remain state secrets. Consequently, pursuant to the standards that El-Masri has acknowledged as controlling, the district court did not err in dismissing his Complaint at the pleading stage."[5]

The Court of Appeals stressed what it saw as the limited role of the federal courts: "El-Masri's position . . . fundamentally misunderstands the nature of our relationship to the executive branch. El-Masri envisions a judiciary that possesses a roving writ to ferret out and strike down executive excess. Article III, however, assigns the courts a more modest role: we simply decide cases and controversies. . . . We would be guilty of excess in our own right if we were to disregard settled legal principles . . . , especially when the challenged action pertains to military or foreign policy. We decline to follow such a course, and thus reject El-Masri's invitation to rule that the state secrets doctrine can be brushed aside on the ground that the President's foreign policy has gotten out of line."[6] Thus, the courts refused to even hear el-Masri's claim that his rights under the Constitution and international law were violated because there was a chance that secrets might be revealed.

Other courts, too, have dismissed lawsuits against those who participated in torture on the ground that it might reveal state secrets. In *Mohammed v. Jeppesen Dataplan, Inc.,* the United States Court of Appeals for the Ninth Circuit dismissed a lawsuit brought by five individuals who claimed, like el-Masri, to have been subjected to rendition and torture.[7] They sued Jeppesen Dataplan, a United States corporation that the plaintiffs said provided flight planning and logistical support services for all of the flights transporting them among the various locations where they were detained and allegedly tortured. The complaint asserted "Jeppesen played an integral role" in the abductions and detentions and "provided direct and substantial services to the United States for its so-called 'extraordinary rendition' program," thereby "enabling the clandestine and forcible transportation of terrorism suspects to secret overseas detention facilities." The complaint also alleged that Jeppesen provided this assistance with "knowledge of the objectives of the rendition program," including knowledge that the plaintiffs "would be subjected to forced disappearance, detention, and torture" by U.S. and foreign officials.[8] The plaintiffs sued Jeppesen because, as I explained in Chapter 2, the United States government has sovereign immunity and cannot be sued, while Jeppesen was a private company that participated in the violation of rights.

The plaintiffs' complaint details egregious violations of the United States Constitution and international law. Binyam Mohamed, the named plaintiff in the lawsuit, was a twenty-eight-year-old Ethiopian citizen and legal resident of the United Kingdom.[9] He was flown to Morocco where he was subjected to "severe physical and psychological torture," including routine beatings that resulted in broken bones. He says that his captors cut him with a scalpel all over his body, including on his penis, and poured "hot stinging liquid" into the open wounds. After eighteen months in a Moroccan prison, Mohamed was transferred back to American custody and flown to Afghanistan. There, he claims, he was detained in a CIA "dark prison" where he was kept in "near permanent darkness" and subjected to loud noise, such as the recorded screams of women and children, twenty-four hours a day. He was fed sparingly and irregularly, and in four months he lost between forty and sixty pounds. Eventually, he was transferred to the United States military prison at

Guantanamo Bay, Cuba, where he remained for nearly five years. He was then released and returned to the United Kingdom.

Plaintiff Ahmed Agiza, an Egyptian national who had been seeking asylum in Sweden, was captured by Swedish authorities, transferred to American custody, and flown to Egypt. There, he claims, he was held for five weeks "in a squalid, windowless, and frigid cell" where he was "severely and repeatedly beaten" and subjected to electric shock through electrodes attached to his ear lobes, nipples, and genitals.[10] Agiza was held in detention for two and a half years, after which he was given a six-hour trial before a military court, convicted, and sentenced to fifteen years in Egyptian prison.

The other plaintiffs—Abou Elkassim Britel, a forty-year-old Italian citizen of Moroccan origin, and Bisher al-Rawi, a thirty-nine-year-old Iraqi citizen and legal resident of the United Kingdom—were subjected to similar treatment.[11] All claimed that Jeppesen Dataplan was liable for its knowing participation in the violations of their rights.

As in el-Masri's case, the United States government moved to dismiss their lawsuit based on the state secrets doctrine. The director of Central Intelligence at the time, General Michael Hayden, filed two declarations in support of the motion to dismiss, one classified, the other redacted and unclassified. The public declaration states that "disclosure of the information covered by this privilege assertion reasonably could be expected to cause serious—and in some instances, exceptionally grave—damage to the national security of the United States and, therefore, the information should be excluded from any use in this case." It further asserts that "because highly classified information is central to the allegations and issues in this case, the risk is great that further litigation will lead to disclosures harmful to U.S. national security and, accordingly, this case should be dismissed."[12]

The federal district court dismissed the case based on the state secrets doctrine. The United States Court of Appeals for the Ninth Circuit reversed and held that the case should go forward. But then the Ninth Circuit, in a 6–5 *en banc* decision, reversed and ordered the case dismissed. It concluded: "we hold that the government's valid assertion of the state secrets privilege warrants dismissal of the litigation."[13] As in el-Masri's case, the court did not question the complaint's allegations,

including that the United States government was responsible for torture. The court accepted all of that as true and said that nonetheless, the
case had to be dismissed because it risked revealing state secrets.

The dissenting judges objected that the plaintiffs' complaint was
based on publicly available information and that there had not been
a showing that litigating the case would require revealing state secrets.
The dissent, expressing great concern that the judiciary was abdicat-
ing its most important role, declared that "the [state secrets] doctrine
is so dangerous as a means of hiding governmental misbehavior under
the guise of national security, and so violative of common rights to due
process, that courts should confine its application to the narrowest circumstances that still protect the government's essential secrets. When,
as here, the doctrine is successfully invoked at the threshold of litigation,
the claims of secret are necessarily broad and hypothetical. The result
is a maximum interference with the due processes of the courts, on the
most general claims of state secret privilege."[14] Judge Michael Hawkins,
the author of the dissent, wrote that the majority opinion "disregards
the concept of checks and balances. Permitting the executive to police
its own errors and determine the remedy dispensed would not only deprive the judiciary of its role, but also deprive Plaintiffs of a fair assessment of their claims by a neutral arbiter."[15]

Torture by agents of the United States in these and other cases has
been documented, including in a report released by the Senate Select
Committee on Intelligence in 2014.[16] Yet those who suffered from these
acts could not even have their complaints heard in federal courts. The
cases were dismissed at the earliest stage of litigation because the courts
held that they failed to state a claim upon which relief could be granted
based on the state secrets doctrine.

This reasoning is deeply flawed. The government made no showing that state secrets would have been revealed during litigation. As the
plaintiffs alleged, and as the dissent pointed out in *Jeppesen Dataplan*,
they sought to rely on information about their abduction, detention,
and treatment that was already widely available. At the very least, the
courts could have allowed the cases to go forward and given the plaintiffs
the opportunity to prove their case with publicly available documents.
Moreover, the courts saw only two choices: allow national security in-

formation to be disclosed, or dismiss the lawsuits. But there was a middle course: try the cases, but do so with safeguards to protect secrecy.

Most important, the federal courts failed at their most basic mission: upholding the Constitution. Any doctrine, like the states secrets doctrine, that renders the federal courts powerless to hear and remedy constitutional violations must be rejected. The plaintiffs in these cases were left with no recourse. They could not sue in federal court and they could not sue in state court. No international tribunal exists to adjudicate their claims or to provide a remedy. No judicial forum was available to them, despite the injuries they suffered. The federal courts had no ability to enforce the Constitution, federal statutes, or international law.

I chose this example for the concluding chapter because I want to emphasize that my thesis is not limited to the areas I discussed in prior chapters. *All* doctrines that keep the federal courts from enforcing the Constitution are unacceptable. The areas I have focused on in this book—immunities for government and government officers, justiciability doctrines, habeas corpus, and procedural limitations on suit in federal court—do not exhaust the subject. All legal rules that keep federal courts from enforcing the Constitution, such as the state secrets doctrine, should be eliminated.

If the government, through the CIA or any other agency, in the name of war can pluck a person off the street and detain and interrogate and torture him or her without charges or due process, then all of us are at risk. The idea of a constitutional democracy is that the government must act within the limits set forth in the Constitution. History teaches that for a constitutional order to be preserved, there must be an institutional mechanism to keep the government from exceeding the limits on its power. Trust in self-restraint by government officials has never been enough. No government—especially a hugely powerful government—has ever been restrained only by voluntary, unenforced limits. My central thesis is that the federal courts must enforce, and must be able to enforce, the limits on government power found in the United States Constitution.

Because some will disagree with this thesis, I want to respond to three possible objections: that my approach would give too much power in the federal judiciary; that I simply want the courts to come to liberal results; and that everything I propose is unrealistic and unlikely to occur.

Too Much Power in the Federal Courts?

The underlying subject of this book is the appropriate role of the federal courts in a democratic society. Federal judges are unelected, and many have argued that there is a tension between judicial review and democracy. Over a half century ago, Professor Alexander Bickel called judicial review a "deviant institution" in American society and that raised a "counter-majoritarian difficulty."[17]

The Supreme Court often has invoked the need to limit the judicial role. As we just saw, the Fourth Circuit did this in justifying the dismissal of el-Masri's case. One of the more famous declarations was the Court's statement in *United Public Workers v. Mitchell*: "Should the courts seek to expand their power so as to bring under their jurisdiction ill-defined controversies over constitutional issues, they would become the organs of political theories. Such abuse of judicial power would properly meet rebuke and restriction from other branches."[18]

I, of course, agree that the federal courts should not expand their power to hear "ill-defined controversies over constitutional issues." The matters that I have described in this book, however, which federal courts cannot hear, do not fit that description. They all involve people whose rights were violated and who had nowhere else to turn for a remedy. The immunity doctrines that keep an injured person from having any recovery, or the limits on habeas corpus relief that keep a wrongly convicted person in prison, are not "ill-defined" controversies. These cases presented constitutional claims that should have been heard.

The Supreme Court has repeatedly declared that limiting the federal courts' role serves the goal of separation of powers.[19] But the assumption behind such statements is that less judicial review means better separation of powers. Such a conclusion begs the question of what is the proper role of the federal judiciary.

I have argued throughout this book that the appropriate, and indeed the most important, role of the federal courts is to enforce the Constitution. When jurisdictional doctrines facilitate that, they give the federal judiciary its proper degree of authority. Doctrines that do more than this would unduly expand the role of the federal courts. But the doctrines I have described throughout this book undermine the courts' authority to enforce the Constitution. Therefore they should be changed.

Phrased slightly differently, doctrines that facilitate the federal courts hearing constitutional cases, by definition, should never be regarded as giving the courts too much power. The content of the constitutional principles, and not jurisdictional doctrines, should determine when courts defer to the government and when they invalidate its actions. Of course there are areas where courts should defer to the choices of elected government officials. But that deference can be reflected in the constitutional doctrines and the merits of the decisions. It should not be the basis for dismissals on jurisdictional grounds that keep the federal courts from hearing the cases at all.

Is It All a Quest for Liberal Results?

Both liberals and conservatives should be able to agree on the changes I propose. Conservatives, who have long professed a desire for less government, should not favor immunity for governments and government officers who exceed constitutional limits. Justiciability rules make the government unaccountable, a result that conservatives and libertarians, as well as liberals, have long abhorred. There is no reason why conservatives would want to keep those who have been brutally tortured, like el-Masri and the plaintiffs in *Jeppeson Dataplan*, from being heard in federal court. I believe the desire to ensure enforcement of the Constitution is nonpartisan.

Perhaps that is naïve. The reality is that the vast majority of cases I have discussed in this book were decided by a 5–4 margin, with the justices split exactly along ideological lines. To pick just a few examples, the Court's decisions about sovereign immunity, standing, and habeas corpus almost all were decided this way. *Jeppesen Dataplan* fits this pattern as well. Of the six appellate judges in the majority voting to dismiss that case, five were appointed by Republican presidents; all five of the dissenters were appointed by Democratic presidents. The restrictions on the federal courts' authority that I discuss in this book are almost entirely the result of decisions by a conservative majority of the Supreme Court.

Why have conservative justices so embraced limiting the power of the federal courts to enforce the Constitution? I believe it is a way to achieve the substantive results they desire. They think many constitutional rights have been broadened beyond their desirable scope, and one way to limit them is through procedural doctrines that prevent people from being heard in court. Again, to select just a few examples, one way to allow more government aid to religion—which conservatives favor—is to restrict who has standing to challenge it. One way to limit the rights of criminal defendants is to deny review on habeas corpus. Businesses can be protected from lawsuits by imposing heightened pleading standards and restricting class action suits. In other words, the restrictions on jurisdiction I have described often reflect a desire for a particular outcome.

That, of course, is true across the political spectrum. Everyone, including me, looks to jurisdictional doctrines as a way to facilitate their views about constitutional law. But to be clear, I favor federal courts having the authority to enforce all aspects of the Constitution, even where I am skeptical of the Supreme Court's interpretations, such as its finding that individuals have a Second Amendment right to possess handguns.[20] The content of substantive rights should be decided in the definition of those rights, not through restrictive doctrines that keep them from being enforced in federal court. It is wrong to use procedural devices to achieve substantive results. It prevents proper analysis of issues and undermines accountability, as the actual basis for the decision is not revealed and discussed. Also, decisions based on the procedure and jurisdiction rarely receive public scrutiny.

The federal courts doctrines that have evolved over the past forty years have often come about when conservative justices were confronted with claims brought by liberal civil rights lawyers challenging the actions of those in the military, the conduct of the police, or racial discrimination by the government. Between 1969 and 2016, Republican presidents have been able to appoint ten justices to the Court, while Democratic presidents have appointed only four. But there is no reason why federal court jurisdiction must have the political valence it has had for the past forty years. Conservatives as well as liberals should be concerned about the need to limit government power.

Why Bother?

For me, the hardest question to answer is whether I realistically believe the reforms I have proposed can come about. This question often plagued me as I was writing this book. I was determined not just to criticize current doctrines but to propose reforms in every area I discuss. Do these reforms have any chance of being adopted?

The most obvious answer is that there is no way to know. We cannot know what the composition of the Supreme Court will be in even a few years. It is easy to envision a Court with five justices who are committed to what I have proposed in this book, and equally easy to imagine an even more conservative court in years ahead. I continue to hope that new justices, whether appointed by Democrats or Republicans, will share the vision for the federal courts that I have described in this book.

There is no way to know the future political composition of Congress or the White House. The Court could effectuate almost all of the reforms I propose, or Congress could bring them about by statutory changes. Most important, it must be remembered that a great many of the changes I advocate would only restore the law to what it was a few years ago, before restrictive doctrines were adopted.

What I do know is that change will not happen unless people advocate for it, and what seems unlikely today might be very realistic a short time from now. I know, too, that the course of American history overall has been an expansion of freedom and equality. It is what Dr. Martin Luther King, Jr. conveyed so well when he declared: "The arc of the moral universe is long, but it bends towards justice."

That is what I have argued: for the federal courts to provide justice to those whose constitutional rights have been violated. This book is not a prediction of the likelihood of reform, but is written out of a conviction that change can occur. Federal courts can do a much better job of enforcing the Constitution. I hope I have helped to point the way.

Notes

ONE Why Do We Have Federal Courts?

1. *Klay v. Panetta*, 758 F.3d 369 (D.C. Cir. 2014).

2. *Id.* at 379.

3. *See* Rep. Jackie Speier, *A Woman Who Channels Pain into Solutions,* Politico (December 10, 2013), http://www.politico.com/story/2013/12/women-rule-jackie-speier-ariana-klay-100898.html.

4. *Id.*

5. *Id.*

6. 758 F.3d. at 371.

7. Brief for Appellants at 3, *Klay v. Panetta*, 758 F.3d 369 (D.C. Cir. 2014) (No. 13–5081).

8. *Id.* at 3–4.

9. *Id.* at 3.

10. *Klay v. Panetta*, 924 F. Supp. 2d 8, 9 (D.D.C. 2013).

11. *Id.*

12. *Id.*

13. Brief for Appellants at 4, *Klay v. Panetta*, 758 F.3d 369 (D.C. Cir. 2014) (No. 13–5081).

14. *Klay v. Panetta*, 758 F.3d 369, 372 (D.C. Cir. 2014).

15. *Id.* at 379.

16. *See, e.g., United States v. Stanley*, 483 U.S. 669 (1987) (no suits can be brought against military officers for harms suffered in the military). These cases are discussed in detail in Chapter 3.

17. 5 U.S. (1 Cranch) 137 (1803).

18. *Id.* at 163.

19. *Id.*

20. For a persuasive criticism of this conclusion, and other aspects of the Court's reasoning in *Marbury v. Madison, see* Burt Neuborne, MADISON'S MUSIC 146–194 (2015); William Van Alstyne, *A Critical Guide to Marbury v. Madison,* DUKE L.J. 1 (1969).

21. 5 U.S. at 176.

22. 5 U.S. at 176. *See* THE FEDERALIST No. 78, at 446–469 (A. Hamilton) (Clinton Rossiter ed. 1961).

23. 5 U.S. at 177.

24. *Tarble's Case,* 80 U.S. 397, 411 (1871).

25. *Zivotofsky v. Kerry,* 135 S.Ct. 2076 (2015) (because the power to recognize foreign states resides in the President alone, Section 214(d) of the Foreign Relations Authorization Act of 2003—which directs the Secretary of State, upon request, to designate "Israel" as the place of birth on the passport of a U.S. citizen who is born in Jerusalem—infringes on the executive's consistent decision to withhold recognition with respect to Jerusalem).

26. *See, e.g., Alden v. Maine,* 527 U.S. 706 (1999) (state governments have sovereign immunity and cannot be sued in state court, including on federal claims). The limits on suing government entities are discussed in Chapter 2 and the restrictions on suing government officers are considered in Chapter 3.

27. There is an endless debate among academics, and even justices, as to whether there is parity between federal courts and state courts. *See, e.g.,* Burt Neuborne, *The Myth of Parity,* 90 HARV. L. REV. 1105 (1977); for a review of the literature in the debate over parity, *see* Erwin Chemerinsky, *Parity Reconsidered: Defining a Role for the Federal Judiciary,* 36 UCLA L. REV. 233 (1988). I do not need to take a position on this debate for purposes of this book. The choice to create federal courts in 1789 reflected a view that some matters should not be left exclusively to state courts with federal court review only in the United States Supreme Court.

28. There are those who argue that this is sufficient and that judicial review should be eliminated. *See, e.g.,* James MacGregor Burns, PACKING THE COURT (2009); Mark Tushnet, TAKING THE CONSTITUTION AWAY FROM THE COURTS (1999).

29. Erwin Chemerinsky and Larry Kramer, *Defining the Role of the Federal Courts,* 1990 BYU L. REV. 67.

30. *Id.* at 77.

31. *Id.* at 77–88.

32. *Cohens v. Virginia,* 19 U.S. (6 Wheat.) 264, 404 (1824).

33. See *Richardson v. Ramirez,* 418 U.S. 24 (1974).

34. Alexis de Toqueville, DEMOCRACY IN AMERICA, ed. Bradley 103 (1945).

35. Owen Fiss, *Foreword: The Forms of Justice,* 93 HARV. L. REV. 1, 10 (1979).

36. Harry Wellington, *Common Law Rules and Constitutional Double Standards: Some Notes on Adjudication,* 83 YALE L.J. 221, 246–247 (1973).

37. Alexander Bickel, THE LEAST DANGEROUS BRANCH: THE SUPREME COURT AND THE BAR OF POLITICS (1962), 26.

38. G. Edward White, *The Evolution of Reasoned Elaboration: Jurisprudential Criticism and Social Change,* 59 VA. L. REV. 279, 299 (1973).

39. Abram Chayes, *The Role of the Judge in Public Law Litigation,* 89 HARV. L. REV. 1281 (1976).

40. *Id.* at 1282–1283.

41. *Arizona State Legislature v. Arizona Independent Redistricting Comn,* 135 S.Ct. 2652, 2695 (2015) (Scalia, J., dissenting), quoting *Allen v. Wright,* 468 U.S. 737, 752 (1984).

42. These cases are described in detail in Chapter 4.

43. *See* Bickel, THE LEAST DANGEROUS BRANCH; *Baker v. Carr,* 369 U.S., 186, 267 (Frankfurter, J., dissenting).

44. John Hart Ely, DEMOCRACY AND DISTRUST 47–48 (1980).

45. Laurence H. Tribe, AMERICAN CONSTITUTIONAL LAW viii (2d ed. 1988).

46. *Id.* at 163.

TWO Suing the Government

1. Brief for Respondents at 10, *Bd. of Trs. of the Univ. of Ala. v. Garrett,* 531 U.S. 356 (2001) (No. 99–1240), 2000 U.S. S.Ct. Briefs LEXIS 563.

2. *Id.*

3. *Id.*

4. *Id.*

5. *Plaintiff in Supreme Court ADA Case Loses Under Rehab Act Too, Eleventh Circuit Says,* GOV'T EMP. REL. REP. (BNA) 00:49:50 (November 27, 2007).

6. *Id.*; Lehr Middlebrooks & Vreeland, P.C., *Courts Limit Duty to Accommodate Disability, in* 18 ALA. EMP'T LAW LETTER (M. Lee Smith Pub. & Print.) (December 31, 2007).

7. *Plaintiff in Supreme Court ADA Case Loses Under Rehab Act Too, Eleventh Circuit Says,* GOV'T EMP. REL. REP. (BNA) 00:49:50 (November 27, 2007); Lehr Middlebrooks & Vreeland, P.C., *Courts Limit Duty to Accommodate Disability, in* 18 ALA. EMP'T LAW LETTER (M. Lee Smith Pub. & Print.) (December 31, 2007).

8. Lehr Middlebrooks & Vreeland, P.C., *Courts Limit Duty to Accommodate Disability, in* 18 ALA. EMP'T LAW LETTER (M. Lee Smith Pub. & Print.) (December 31, 2007).

9. Brief for Respondents at 11, *Garrett,* 531 U.S. 356 (2001) (No. 99–1240); Richard Carelli, *Court to Clarify Disabilities Act,* ASSOCIATED PRESS, Apr. 17, 2000, *available at* Bloomberg Law 06:13:58.

10. Brief for Respondents at 11, *Garrett,* 531 U.S. 356 (2001) (No. 99–1240).

11. *Id.*

12. *Id.*

13. *Id.*

14. *Id.*; Lehr Middlebrooks & Vreeland, P.C., *Courts Limit Duty to Accommodate Disability, in* 18 ALA. EMP'T LAW LETTER (M. Lee Smith Pub. & Print.) (December 31, 2007).

15. Lehr Middlebrooks & Vreeland, P.C., *Courts Limit Duty to Accommodate Disability, in* 18 ALA. EMP'T LAW LETTER (M. Lee Smith Pub. & Print.) (December 31, 2007); *Plaintiff in Supreme Court ADA Case Loses Under Rehab Act Too, Eleventh Circuit Says,* GOV'T EMP. REL. REP. (BNA) 00:49:50 (November 27, 2007).

16. Brief for Respondents at 12, *Garrett,* 531 U.S. 356 (2001) (No. 99–1240).

17. Laurie Asseo, *Justices Limit Disability Law,* ASSOCIATED PRESS, Feb. 21, 2001, *available at* Bloomberg Law 07:29:03; Lehr Middlebrooks & Vreeland, P.C., *Courts Limit Duty to Accommodate Disability, in* 18 ALA. EMP'T LAW LETTER (M. Lee Smith Pub. & Print.) (December 31, 2007).

18. Brief for Respondents at 12, *Garrett,* 531 U.S. 356 (2001) (No. 99–1240).

19. *Id.*

20. *Id.*

21. *Id.*

22. 104 Stat. 327 (1990).

23. The Americans with Disabilities Act defines disability as: "(A) a physical or mental impairment that substantially limits one or more of the major life activities of such individual; (B) a record of such an impairment; or (C) being regarded as having such an impairment." Americans with Disabilities Act of 1990, 104 Stat. 327, 330 (1990).

24. *University of Alabama at Birmingham v. Garrett,* 531 U.S. 356 (2001).

25. *See* 5 Kenneth Culp Davis, ADMINISTRATIVE LAW TREATISE 6–7 (2d ed. 1984) (quoting Blackstone); 2 Charles H. Koch, Jr., ADMINISTRATIVE LAW AND PRACTICE 210 (1985). Actually, as John Orth pointed out to me, the phrase "the King can do no wrong" has many possible meanings. It might simply mean that when a wrong occurs, someone else must have done it, because the King can do no wrong. Alternatively, it might mean that a remedy must exist, because the King cannot do a wrong, as would occur if harm went without a remedy.

26. *United States v. Lee,* 106 U.S. 196, 205 (1882).

27. *Id.* at 207 ("The principle has never been discussed or the reasons for it given, but it has always been treated as an established doctrine") (citations omitted).

28. *See, e.g.,* U.S. CONST. art. I, §9 ("No Title of Nobility shall be granted by the United States").

29. U.S. CONST. art. VI.

30. John E. H. Sherry, *The Myth That the King Can Do No Wrong: A Comparative Study of the Sovereign Immunity Doctrine in the United States and New York Courts of Claims,* 22 ADMIN. L. REV. 39, 58 (1969).

31. *Marbury v. Madison,* 5 U.S. (1 Cranch) 137, 163 (1803).

32. 527 U.S. 706 (1999).

33. 517 U.S. 44 (1996). Congress may authorize suits against states only when acting pursuant to Section 5 of the Fourteenth Amendment and not pursuant to any other federal power. *See id.* at 59.

34. *Florida Prepaid Postsecondary Educ. Expense Bd. v. College Sav. Bank,* 527 U.S. 627 (1999).

35. *Kimel v. Florida Bd. of Regents,* 528 U.S. 62 (2000).

36. 527 U.S. 706, 712 (1999).

37. 517 U.S. 44, 59 (1996).

38. *Cohens v. Virginia,* 19 U.S. (6 Wheat.) 264, 411–412 (1821).

39. *United States v. Lee,* 106 U.S. 196, 204 (1882); *see also Kennecott Copper Corp. v. State Tax Commn.,* 327 U.S. 573, 580 (1946) (Frankfurter, J., dissenting); *Hill v. United States,* 50 U.S. (9 How.) 386, 389 (1850); *United States v. Clarke,* 33 U.S. (8 Pet.) 436, 444 (1834) (noting the same).

40. John Hart Ely, DEMOCRACY AND DISTRUST 3 (1980).

41. *Id.*

42. *Seminole Tribe of Florida v. Florida,* 517 U.S. 44 (1996), held that Congress cannot authorize suits against state governments except when acting under Section 5 of the Fourteenth Amendment and that state governments therefore could not be sued to enforce the federal Indian Gaming Act. *Alden v. Maine,* 527 U.S. 706 (1999), held that sovereign immunity bars suits against state governments in state courts even on federal claims. *Florida Prepaid v. College Savings Bank,* 527 U.S. 627 (1999), held that state governments cannot be sued for patent infringement, even though a federal statute expressly authorized this. *College Savings Bank v. Florida Prepaid,* 527 U.S. 666 (1999), ruled that there is no implied waiver of sovereign immunity by a state government. *Kimel v. Florida Board of Regents,* 528 U.S. 62 (2000), held that state governments cannot be sued for violating the Age Discrimination in Employment Act. *Coleman v. Maryland Court of Appeals,* 132 S.Ct. 1327 (2012), ruled that state governments cannot be sued for violating the medical leave provisions of the Family and Medical Leave Act.

43. *See, e.g.,* Antonin Scalia, A MATTER OF INTERPRETATION 23–25 (1998) (expressing adherence to a philosophy of original meaning).

44. 527 U.S. 706, 728 (1999).

45. 134 U.S. 1 (1890).

46. 527 U.S. at 713 (citations omitted).

47. *See, e.g.,* Joseph D. Grano, *Judicial Review and a Written Constitution in a Democratic Society,* 28 WAYNE L. REV. 1, 7 (1981) (articulating the originalist philosophy); *see also* Robert H. Bork, THE TEMPTING OF AMERICA (1990) (defending originalist constitutional interpretation).

48. *Seminole Tribe of Florida v. Florida,* 517 U.S. 44, 104 (1996) (Souter, J., dissenting).

49. *See, e.g.,* John J. Gibbons, *The Eleventh Amendment and State Sovereign Immunity: A Reinterpretation,* 83 COLUM. L. REV. 1889, 1902–1914 (1983) (recounting the debate).

50. THE DEBATES IN THE SEVERAL STATES CONVENTIONS ON THE ADOPTION OF THE FEDERAL CONSTITUTION, 526–527 (Jonathan Elliot ed., 1937).

51. *Atascadero State Hosp. v. Scanlon,* 473 U.S. 234, 265 (1985) (Brennan, J., dissenting) (describing Mason's opposition to Article III).

52. THE DEBATES IN THE SEVERAL STATES CONVENTIONS ON THE ADOPTION OF THE FEDERAL CONSTITUTION, ed. Elliot, at 543.

53. *Id.*

54. Gibbons, *The Eleventh Amendment and State Sovereign Immunity,* at 1902–1914.

55. The Debates in the Several States Conventions on the Adoption of the Federal Constitution, ed. Elliot, at 575.

56. 14 John P. Kaminski and Gaspare J. Saladino, The Documentary History of the Ratification of the Constitution 204 (1983).

57. The Federalist No. 81, at 487–488 (Alexander Hamilton) (Clinton Rossiter ed., 1961) (emphasis in original).

58. The Debates in the Several States Conventions on the Adoption of the Federal Constitution, ed. Elliot, at 533.

59. *Id.*

60. *Seminole Tribe of Florida v. Florida,* 517 U.S. 44, 142–143 (1996) (Souter, J., dissenting).

61. 527 U.S. 706, 764 (1999) (Souter, J., dissenting).

62. Elsewhere, I have questioned whether contemporary practices from the time the Constitution was adopted should matter in constitutional interpretation. *See* Erwin Chemerinsky, *The Jurisprudence of Antonin Scalia: A Critical Appraisal,* U. Haw. L. Rev. (2000).

63. 527 U.S. at 764 (Souter, J., dissenting) (quoting 1 J. Story, Commentaries on the Constitution 149 (5th ed. 1891)).

64. William A. Fletcher, *A Historical Interpretation of the Eleventh Amendment: A Narrow Construction of an Affirmative Grant of Jurisdiction Rather Than a Prohibition Against Jurisdiction,* 35 Stan. L. Rev. 1033 (1983); Gibbons, *The Eleventh Amendment and State Sovereign Immunity.*

65. 2 U.S. (Dall.) 419 (1793).

66. *Alden v. Maine,* 527 U.S. at 741.

67. Indeed, before joining the Supreme Court, Antonin Scalia expressed the view that sovereign immunity is not based on historical understanding. He wrote that "at the time of *Marbury v. Madison* there was no doctrine of domestic sovereign immunity, as there never had been in English law." Antonin Scalia, *Historical Anomalies in Administrative Law, in* 1985 Yearbook 103, 104 (Supreme Court Historical Soc'y). I am grateful to Jay Bybee for bringing this to my attention.

68. U.S. Const. art. VI.

69. 5 U.S. (1 Cranch) 137, 180 (1803).

70. 17 U.S. (4 Wheat.) 316, 426 (1819).

71. *Id.* at 405–406.

72. 527 U.S. 706, 754–755 (1999).

73. The Federalist No. 51, at 322 (James Madison) (Clinton Rossiter ed., 1961).

74. 5 U.S. (1 Cranch) 137, 176–177 (1803).

75. *Id.* at 163.

76. 483 U.S. 669 (1987).

77. *Id.* at 683.

78. *Id.* at 709 (O'Connor, J., concurring and dissenting).

79. *Id.* at 710–711 (Brennan, J., dissenting).

80. Akhil Amar, *Of Sovereignty and Federalism,* 96 YALE L.J. 1425 (1987).

81. *See* Calvin R. Massey, *State Sovereignty and the Tenth and Eleventh Amendments,* 56 U. CHI. L. REV. 61 (1989).

82. James E. Pfander, *Sovereign Immunity and the Right to Petition: Toward a First Amendment Right to Pursue Judicial Claims Against the Government,* 91 Nw. U.L. REV. 899 (1997).

83. *Id.* at 906.

84. *Id.* at 980.

85. *See, e.g., Oestereich v. Selective Serv. Sys. Local Bd.,* 393 U.S. 233, 243 n.6 (1968) (Harlan, J., concurring) (noting that a person should not be deprived of personal liberty without a tribunal hearing); *see also* Richard H. Fallon, Jr., *Some Confusions About Due Process, Judicial Review, and Constitutional Remedies,* 93 COLUM. L. REV. 309 (1993) (arguing that the issue of whether there is a constitutional right to judicial review depends on the underlying substantive law).

86. *Johnson v. Robison,* 415 U.S. 361, 368–370 (1974); *see also Webster v. Doe,* 486 U.S. 592, 599–600 (1988) (refusing to find statute to preclude review of a claim by an employee of the CIA who alleged that he was fired because he was a homosexual).

87. *See, e.g., McNary v. Haitian Refugee Ctr., Inc.,* 498 U.S. 479, 491–495 (1991) (noting this point); *United States v. Mendoza-Lopez,* 481 U.S. 828, 835 (1987) (noting this point).

88. *See Roth v. Bd. of Regents,* 408 U.S. 564, 576–578 (1972) (finding existing property interest if law creates a reasonable expectation to a benefit).

89. Joseph W. Little, TORTS: THE CIVIL LAW OF REPARATION FOR HARM DONE BY WRONGFUL ACT 2–7 (1985) (describing changing conceptions of tort law).

90. 445 U.S. 622 (1980).

91. *Id.* at 651–652.

92. *See* Noel P. Fox, *The King Must Do No Wrong: A Critique of the Current Status of Sovereign and Official Immunity,* 25 WAYNE L. REV. 177, 187 (1979); Clark Byse, *Proposed Reforms in Federal "Nonstatutory" Judicial Review: Sovereign Immunity, Indispensable Parties, Mandamus,* 75 HARV. L. REV. 1479, 1526 (1962).

93. *See, e.g., Ex parte Young,* 209 U.S. 123 (1908) (ability to sue state officers for injunctive relief not barred by the Eleventh Amendment).

94. *Alden,* 527 U.S. 706, 749 (1999).

95. *See The Siren,* 74 U.S. (7 Wall.) 152, 154 (1868) ("The public service would be hindered, and the public safety endangered, if the supreme authority could be subjected to suit at the instance of every citizen").

96. *Littell v. Morton,* 445 F.2d 1207, 1214 (4th Cir. 1971) ("The rationale for sovereign immunity essentially boils down to substantial bothersome interference with the operation of government"); James Samuel Sable, *Sovereign Immunity: A Battleground of Competing Considerations,* 12 Sw. U.L. REV. 457, 465 (1981).

97. *Larson v. Domestic & Foreign Commerce Corp.,* 337 U.S. 682, 704 (1949).

98. *See, e.g., Lincoln County v. Luning*, 133 U.S. 529 (1890) (showing this point); *Mt. Healthy City School Dist. Bd. of Educ. v. Doyle*, 429 U.S. 274 (1977). Some criticize these decisions on the ground that states should be able to transfer their immunity to local governments, which are created by the state and through which the states govern. *See, e.g.,* Margreth Barrett, Comment, *The Denial of Eleventh Amendment Immunity to Political Subdivisions of the States: An Unjustified Strain on Federalism*, 1979 DUKE L.J. 1042 (making this criticism).

99. *Monell v. Department of Soc. Serv.*, 436 U.S. 658 (1978) (holding that local governments are persons within the meaning of Section 1983).

100. Pamela S. Karlan, *The Irony of Immunity: The Eleventh Amendment, Irreparable Injury, and Section 1983*, 53 STAN. L. REV. 1311 (2001).

101. *Schneider v. Smith*, 390 U.S. 17 (1968); *Larson*, 337 U.S. 682 (1949); *Land v. Dollar*, 330 U.S. 731 (1947); *see also Ex parte Young*, 209 U.S. 123 (1908).

102. If the monetary relief, in reality, would be against the government, the suit is barred, even though the individual officer is named as the defendant. *Larson*, 337 U.S. at 687 ("The crucial question is whether the relief sought in a suit nominally addressed to the officer is relief against the sovereign"); see also *Hawaii v. Gordon*, 373 U.S. 57, 98 (1963) (noting the same).

103. *See* Davis, ADMINISTRATIVE LAW TREATISE, at 22–24; Peter H. Schuck, SUING GOVERNMENT 90–91 (1983).

104. Joanna Schwartz, *Police Indemnification*, 89 N.Y.U. L.R. 885 (2014) (describing practices of the government indemnifying police officers and the consequences of this).

105. *Kawananakoa v. Polyblank*, 205 U.S. 349, 353 (1907).

106. *Letter from Justice Oliver W. Holmes to Harold J. Laski* 2 (January 29, 1926) (quoted in HOLMES-LASKI LETTERS 822 (Mark De Wolfe Howe ed., 1953)).

107. 491 U.S. 1 (1989) (holding that Congress could override the Eleventh Amendment if the statute was explicit in its text in doing so).

108. *See Mitchum v. Foster*, 407 U.S. 225, 241–242 (1972) and *Monroe v. Pape*, 365 U.S. 167, 173 (1961). Although the Court in *Monroe* held that local governments could not be sued, it allowed local government officials to be sued for monetary and injunctive relief.

109. 440 U.S. 332 (1979).

110. 491 U.S. 58 (1989).

111. *See* text accompanying notes 76–79 supra.

112. Absolute immunity for these officers is discussed in Chapter 3.

113. *O'Shea v. Littleton*, 414 U.S. 488 (1974) (declaring nonjusticiable a suit contending that the defendants, a magistrate and a judge, discriminated against blacks in setting bail and imposing sentences).

114. Federal Courts Improvement Act of 1996, Pub. L. No. 104–317, §309 (a)–(b), 110 Stat. 3847 (1956).

115. *Harlow v. Fitzgerald*, 457 U.S. 800 (1982).

116. 17 U.S. (4 Wheat.) 316, 427 (1819).

117. *Alden,* 527 U.S. 706, 762–803 (1999) (Souter, J., dissenting).

118. 478 U.S. 186, 199 (1986) (quoting O. W. Holmes, *The Path of the Law,* 10 HARV. L. REV. 457, 469 (1897)).

119. *Lincoln Cnty v. Luning,* 133 U.S. 529 (1890); *Mt. Healthy City Sch. Dist. Bd. of Educ. v. Doyle,* 429 U.S. 274 (1977).

120. 365 U.S. 167 (1961).

121. *Id.* at 187.

122. *Id.* at 188.

123. Act of Feb. 25, 1871, §2, 16 Stat. 431. The Dictionary Act was enacted a few months before the Civil Rights Act of 1871, which contained §1983.

124. 365 U.S. at 191.

125. *See City of Kenosha v. Bruno,* 412 U.S. 507 (1973) (equitable relief not allowed); *Moor v. County of Alameda,* 411 U.S. 693 (1973) (monetary relief not allowed). *See also Aldinger v. Howard,* 427 U.S. 1 (1976) (pendent party jurisdiction could not be the basis for §1983 suits in federal court against municipalities).

126. *See, e.g.,* Ronald M. Levin, *The Section 1983 Municipal Immunity Doctrine,* 65 GEO. L.J. 1483 (1977); Don B. Kates and J. Anthony Kouba, *Liability of Public Entities Under Section 1983 of the Civil Rights Act,* 45 S. CAL. L. REV. 131 (1972).

127. *See, e.g., Mahone v. Waddle,* 564 F.2d 1018 (3d Cir. 1977), *cert. denied,* 438 U.S. 904 (1978) (using §1981 to create liability for racial discrimination by police officers).

128. *See, e.g., Hanna v. Drobnick,* 514 F.2d 393 (6th Cir. 1975); *but see Cale v. City of Covington,* 586 F.2d 311 (4th Cir. 1978).

129. 436 U.S 658 (1978).

130. *Id.* at 683.

131. *Id.* at 688–689.

132. *Id.* at 690 (emphasis included).

133. *Id.* at 694.

134. *See, e.g.,* David Jacks Achtenberg, *Taking History Seriously: Municipal Liability Under 42 U.S.C. §1983 and the Debate over Respondeat Superior,* 73 FORDHAM L. REV. 2183 (2005); Karen M. Blum, *From Monroe to Monell: Defining the Scope of Municipal Liability in Federal Courts,* 51 TEMP. L.Q. 409 (1978); Christina B. Whitman, *Government Responsibility for Constitutional Torts,* 85 MICH. L. REV. 225, 236 n.43 (1986).

135. *Owen v. City of Independence,* 445 U.S. 622 (1980); *see* discussion in §8.5.3, *infra.* For a criticism of the argument that liability of local governments deters misconduct, *see* Daryl Levinson, *In Making Government Pay: Markets, Politics, and the Allocation of Constitutional Costs,* 67 U. CHI. L. REV. 345 (2000); *but see* Myriam E. Gilles, *In Defense of Making Government Pay: The Deterrent Effect of Constitutional Tort Remedies,* 35 GA. L. REV. 845 (2001).

136. *Bd. of the Cnty. Comm'rs v. Brown,* 520 U.S. 397, 437 (1997) (Breyer, J., dissenting).

137. *Id.* at 431–433.

138. *Id.* at 433.

139. *Id.* at 436.

140. Id.

141. *Id.* at 400–401.

142. *Id.* at 412.

143. *Connick v. Thompson,* 131 S.Ct. 1350 (2011).

144. *See Id. at* 1356 at n.1, citing *In re Riehlmann,* 04–0680, 891 So.2d 1239 (2005).

145. 373 U.S. 83 (1963).

146. 131 S.Ct. at 1370.

147. *Truvia v. Connick,* 577 F. App'x 317 (5th Cir. 2014).

148. Earl Truvia, Greg Bright, Dan Bright, *State v. Bright,* 875 So.2d 37 (La. 2004); Shareef Cousin, *State v. Cousin,* 710 So.2d 1065 (La. 1998); Roland Gibson, *Gibson v. State,* Case No. 203–904, Orleans Parish Crim. Dist. Ct.; Isaac Knapper, *State v. Knapper,* 579 So.2d 956 (La. 1991), Curtis Lee Kyles, *Kyles v. Whitley,* 514 U.S. 419, 441 (1995), Dwight Labran, *Labran v. State,* Case No. 388–287, Orleans Parish Crim. Dist. Ct.; John Thompson, *State v. Thompson,* 825 So. 2d 552 (La. App. 4 Cir. 2002); Hayes Williams, *Williams v. State,* Case No. 199–523, Orleans Parish Crim. Dist. Ct.; Calvin Williams, *In re Calvin Williams,* 984 So.2d 789 (La. App. 1 Cir. 2008); and Juan Smith, *Smith v. Cain,* 132 S.Ct. 627 (2012).

149. 6 James D. Richardson, A Compilation of the Messages and Papers of the Presidents, 51 (1898), (quoted in *Kennecott Copper Corp. v. State Tax Comm'n.,* 327 U.S. 573, 580 (1946) (Frankfurter, J., dissenting)).

150. 440 U.S. 332 (1979).

151. *City of Boerne v. Flores,* 521 U.S. 507 (1997).

THREE Suing Government Officers

1. *Stump v. Sparkman,* 435 U.S. 349, 351 n. 1 (1978) (the petition and Judge Stump's order was reproduced in its entirety in the first footnote of the Supreme Court's opinion).

2. *See* Ind. Code Ann. §§16–13–13–1 through 16–13–13–4.

3. *See* John Rutherford, *Secret Court Order,* Indianapolis News, Jan. 18, 1978.

4. *See* Jamie Renae Coleman and Paula Bateman Headley, The Blanket She Carried 1, 5, 9, 15–18, 27–29 (2003) (this book is a first-person narrative of Linda Sparkman's life, which she wrote with the assistance of her friend, Paula Headley. Later in her life, Linda changed her name to Jamie Renae Coleman).

5. *Id.* at 34.

6. *Id.* at 20, 31, 35.

7. *Id.* at 1.

8. *Stump v. Sparkman,* 435 U.S. at 362–363 (1978).

9. *See Wheedlin v. Wheeler,* 373 U.S. 647 (1963) (federal officers are not liable under §1983).

10. *See, e.g., Larson v. Domestic & Foreign Commerce Corp.,* 337 U.S. 682 (1949) (federal officers may be enjoined).

11. 5 U.S.C. §702, 90 Stat. 2721 (1976).

12. 403 U.S. 388 (1971).

13. *See Carlson v. Green,* 446 U.S. 14 (1980); *Davis v. Passman,* 442 U.S. 228 (1979) (discussed below).

14. *See, e.g., Hui v. Castaneda,* 130 S.Ct. 1845 (2010); *Wilkie v. Robbins,* 551 U.S. 537 (2007); *Correctional Services Corp. v. Malesko,* 534 U.S. 61 (2001) (all discussed below).

15. *Wilkie v. Robbins,* 551 U.S. 537, 568 (2007) (Scalia, J., concurring) (citations omitted).

16. *See, e.g., Ali v. Rumsfeld,* 649 F.3d 762 (D.C. Cir. 2011) (individuals who claimed that they were tortured while in United States custody could not bring a *Bivens* claim because it might obstruct United States foreign policy and military objectives); *Wilson v. Libby,* 535 F.3d 697 (D.C. Cir. 2008) (no *Bivens* cause of action by former secret operative, Valerie Plame Wilson, whose name was wrongly revealed in retaliation for her husband's revealing an inaccuracy in the President's State of the Union Address because other federal laws exist and because the suit might disclose national security information).

17. 403 U.S. 388 (1971).

18. 327 U.S. 678 (1946).

19. *Id.* at 684 (on remand, the district court found that there was no cause of action for money damages under the Constitution). *Bell v. Hood,* 71 F. Supp. 813 (S.D. Cal. 1947).

20. 409 F.2d 718, 719 (2d Cir. 1969), *rev'd,* 403 U.S. 388 (1971).

21. 403 U.S. at 394–395.

22. *Id.* at 392.

23. *Id.*

24. *Id.* at 396.

25. *Id.* at 397.

26. *Id.* at 402–403 (Harlan, J., concurring).

27. *Id.* at 403.

28. *Id.* at 409–410.

29. *Id.* at 410–411.

30. *Id.* at 412 (Burger, C.J., dissenting).

31. *Id.* at 427–428 (Black, J., dissenting).

32. *Id.* at 429 (Black, J., dissenting).

33. *Id.* at 430 (Blackmun, J., dissenting).

34. For an excellent defense of the *Bivens* cause of action, *see* Susan Bandes, *Reinventing Bivens: The Self-Executing Constitution,* 68 S. Cal. L. Rev. 289 (1995); Walter Dellinger, *Of Rights and Remedies: The Constitution as a Sword,* 85 Harv. L. Rev. 1532 (1972).

35. 534 U.S. 61 (2001).

36. *Id.* at 69.

37. *Id.* at 70.

38. *Id.* at 75 (Scalia, J., concurring).

39. *Id.* at 82 (Stevens, J., dissenting).

40. *Carlson v. Green*, 446 U.S. at 18–19 (emphasis in original); *see also Bivens v. Six Unknown Named Agents of Fed. Bureau of Narcotics*, 403 U.S. at 397.

41. 446 U.S. at 18.

42. 442 U.S. 228 (1979).

43. 42 U.S.C. §2000e-16(a).

44. 442 U.S. at 247.

45. *Id.* at 242.

46. 446 U.S. at 14.

47. 28 U.S.C. §2680. The Federal Tort Claims Act was amended in 1974 to permit suits against law enforcement officers for intentional torts. Pub. L. No. 93–253, §1, 88 Stat. 50, 28 U.S.C. §2680(h).

48. 446 U.S. at 20.

49. *Id.* at 22.

50. *Id.* at 21.

51. 462 U.S. 367 (1983).

52. *Id.* at 378.

53. *Id.* at 388.

54. *See, e.g., Grisham v. United States*, 103 F.3d 24 (5th Cir. 1997) (precluding *Bivens* claims for improper termination because there is a comprehensive remedial scheme under the Civil Service Reform Act); *Rollins v. Marsh*, 937 F.2d 134 (5th Cir. 1991) (no *Bivens* suit for improper suspension because the Civil Service Reform Act provides adequate remedies); *Jones v. Tennessee Valley Auth.*, 948 F.2d 258 (6th Cir. 1991) (even if remedies are inadequate under the Civil Service Reform Act, no *Bivens* suit exists).

55. *Jones v. Tennessee Valley Auth.*, 948 F.2d at 264.

56. 487 U.S. 412 (1988). For an excellent discussion of *Chilicky, see* Gene R. Nichol, Bivens, Chilicky, *and Constitutional Damage Claims*, 75 VA. L. REV. 1117 (1989).

57. *Id.* at 416.

58. *Id.* at 423.

59. *Id.* at 425.

60. *Id.* at 432 (Brennan, J., dissenting).

61. S.Ct. 1845 (2010).

62. *Id.* at 1849.

63. *Id.* at 1855.

64. For an argument that *Bush* represents a retreat from the principles of *Bivens, see* George Brown, *Letting Statutory Tails Wag Constitutional Dogs—Have the Bivens Dissenters Prevailed*, 64 IND. L.J. 263 (1989); Joan Steinman, *Backing Off Bivens and the Ramifications of This Retreat for the Vindication of First Amendment Rights*, 83 MICH. L. REV. 269 (1984).

65. 462 U.S. 296 (1983).

66. *Id.* at 300.

67. *See, e.g., Mollnow v. Carlton*, 716 F.2d 627, 629–630 (9th Cir. 1984), *cert. denied*, 465 U.S. 1100 (1984) (*Chappell* precludes all suits arising from military service);

Stanley v. United States, 786 F.2d 1490 (11th Cir. 1986), *rev'd*, 483 U.S. 669 (1987) (*Chappell* does not preclude all suits arising from military service).

68. 483 U.S. 669 (1987).

69. 483 U.S. at 683.

70. *Id.* at 709 (O'Connor, J., concurring and dissenting).

71. *Id.* at 710–711 (Brennan, J., dissenting).

72. Scholars are virtually unanimous in strongly criticizing *Chappell* and *Stanley. See, e.g.,* Bruce Beach, *The Death of Wilkes v. Dinsman: Special Factors Counseling Hesitation in Abandoning a Common Law Doctrine,* 41 BAYLOR U.L. REV. 179 (1989); Barry Kellman, *Judicial Abdication of Military Tort Accountability: But Who Is to Guard the Guards Themselves,* 1989 DUKE L.J. 1597; Jonathan Tomes, *Feres to Chappell to Stanley: Three Strikes and Service Members Are Out,* 25 U. RICH. L. REV. 93 (1990).

73. 551 U.S. 537 (2007).

74. *Id.* at 568–569 (Ginsburg, J., dissenting).

75. 551 U.S. at 550.

76. *Id.* at 554.

77. *Id.* at 560.

78. *See* Mary Sigler, *Private Prisons, Public Functions, and the Meaning of Punishment,* 28 FLA. ST. U.L. REV. 149 (2010); Alexander Volokh, *Developments in the Law: The Law of Prisons: III. A Tale of Two Systems: Cost, Quality, and Accountability in Private Prisons,* 115 HARV. L. REV. 1868, 1870 (2002).

79. 534 U.S. 61 (2001).

80. *Id.* at 69.

81. 132 S.Ct. 617 (2012).

82. *Wilson v. Seiter,* 501 U.S. 294, 297 (1991).

83. 132 S.Ct. at 626.

84. *Monroe v. Pape,* 365 U.S. 167, 174 (1961).

85. *Mitchum v. Foster,* 407 U.S. 225, 242 (1972).

86. *Id.* at 242.

87. *Scheuer v. Rhodes,* 416 U.S. 232, 239–240 (1974).

88. 502 U.S. 9 (1991).

89. *Id.* at 11.

90. *Capra v. Cook County Board of Review,* 733 F.3d 705 (7th Cir. 2013). (Taxpayers brought separate §1983 actions against county board of review and its members, alleging that the revocation of their property tax reduction violated their rights under the Equal Protection Clause, the Due Process Clause, and the First Amendment. Board members were entitled to absolute immunity. County board of review was not entitled to absolute immunity, but the principle of comity barred a §1983 claim for damages against county board.)

91. *See also Heyde v. Pittenger,* 633 F.3d 512 (7th Cir. 2011). (Property taxpayer brought a §1983 action against members of county board of review, county assessors, and others, alleging defendants violated his equal protection rights, conspired to violate

his equal protection rights, and retaliated against him for previously challenging assessments by setting property's total taxable assessment value at levels grossly disproportionate to property's fair market value. Board members' actions during review of taxpayer's property assessment claim were quasi-judicial in nature, and thus members were entitled to absolute immunity.)

92. *Keystone Redevelopment Partners, LLC v. Decker,* 631 F.3d 89 (3rd Cir. 2011).

93. *See, e.g., Guzman-Rivera v. Lucena-Zabala,* 642 F.3d 92 (1st Cir. 2011). (Accountant brought §1983 action against members of the Puerto Rico Examining Board of Accountants (PREBA), alleging that they violated accountant's due process rights when they suspended and revoked his certified public accountant (CPA) license. PREBA members performed traditional adjudicatory functions. Deficient manner in which PREBA members presided over revocation hearings did not deprive them of absolute quasi-judicial immunity.)

94. 424 U.S. 409 (1976).

95. *Id.* at 423.

96. 555 U.S. 335 (2009).

97. *Goldstein v. City of Long Beach,* 715 F.3d 750, 751 (9th Cir. 2013).

98. 373 U.S. 83 (1963). *See also Giglio v. United States,* 405 U.S. 150 (1972) (impeachment evidence must be disclosed by prosecutors to defendants).

99. 523 U.S. 44 (1998).

100. 460 U.S. 325 (1983).

101. *Id.* at 343.

102. *Rehberg v. Paulk,* 132 S.Ct. 1497 (2012).

103. *Id.* at 1506.

104. *Id.* at 1506–1507.

105. *Nixon v. Fitzgerald,* 457 U.S. 731 (1982).

106. *Marbury v. Madison,* 5 U.S. (1 Cranch) 103, 163 (1803).

107. 416 U.S. 232 (1974).

108. *Id.* at 247–248.

109. 420 U.S. 308 (1975).

110. *Id.* at 321–322.

111. *Id.* at 329 (Powell, J., dissenting; Justices Burger, Blackmun, and Rehnquist concurred in Powell's dissent).

112. 457 U.S. 800 (1982).

113. *Nixon v. Fitzgerald,* 457 U.S. 731 (1982).

114. 457 U.S. at 818.

115. *Id.* at 816–817.

116. Peter W. Low and John C. Jeffries, Federal Courts and the Law of Federal State Relations 8th (4th ed. 1998) at 871.

117. 131 S.Ct. 2074 (2011).

118. *Al-Kidd v. Ashcroft,* 580 F.3d 949, 973 (9th Cir. 2009).

119. 131 S.Ct. at 2083.

120. *Id.* at 2086.

121. *Safford Unified School Dist. No. 1 v. Redding,* 557 U.S. 364 (2009).

122. 134 S.Ct. 2369, 2381 (2014).

123. 536 U.S. 730 (2002).

124. 134 S.Ct. 2012 (2014).

125. 134 S.Ct. 2056 (2014).

FOUR An Alleged Constitutional Violation
Always Should Be Adjudicated

1. *See* Petitioner's Brief at 12–16, *City of Los Angeles v. Lyons,* 461 U.S. 95 (1983) (No. 81–1064), 1982 U.S. S. Ct. Briefs LEXIS 1458; *see also* Justice Thurgood Marshall's dissent for a thorough description of the traffic stop in *Lyons,* 461 U.S. 95, 114–115 (1983).

2. "Lyons feared for his life, gasped for air, choked, spit up blood, urinated and defecated on himself (symptoms of impending death, A.329) and almost died." Respondent's Brief at 8, *Lyons,* 461 U.S. 95 (No. 81–1064).

3. Erwin Chemerinsky, *The Story of City of Los Angeles v. Lyons: Closing Federal Courthouse Doors, in* CIVIL RIGHTS STORIES 131, 137 (Myriam E. Gilles and Risa L. Goluboff eds., 2008).

4. *See* Petitioner's Brief at 17–19, *Lyons,* 461 U.S. 95 (1983) (No. 81–1064).

5. *See Id.*

6. *See Id.*

7. Chemerinsky, *The Story of City of Los Angeles v. Lyons,* at 135 (citing 461 U.S. 98 n.1).

8. *See* 461 U.S. at 115–116 (Marshall, J., dissenting).

9. *See Id.*

10. "The complaint maintained that the stranglehold violated the First Amendment (prior restraint on speech), the Fourth Amendment (unreasonable search and seizure), the Eighth Amendment (cruel and unusual punishment), and the Fourteenth Amendment (due process)." Chemerinsky. *The Story of City of Los Angeles v. Lyons,* at 137.

11. "The consensus of the experts in this case is that the strangleholds are extremely dangerous." Respondent's Brief at 24, *Lyons,* 461 U.S. 95 (1983) (No. 81–1064).

12. "'This transmission immediately sets up a 'fight or flee' syndrome wherein the body reacts violently to save itself or escape. Adrenalin output increases enormously; blood oxygen is switched to muscles and strong, violent struggle ensues which is to a great extent involuntary. From a medical point of view, there would be no way to distinguish this involuntary death struggle from a wilful, voluntary resistance. Thus an instruction to cease applying the hold when 'resistance ceases' is meaningless. [P]ressure on both carotid sheaths also result in pressure, if inadvertent or unintended, on both vagus nerves . . . [s]timulation of these nerves can activate reflexes . . . that can result in immediate heart stoppage (cardiac arrest).' Declaration of Alex Griswold, M.D., A.365, 367. In a manual criminal strangulation, 'strangulation may be quickened by the

struggling of the victim, the inhalation of vomitus or by shock triggering a vagal nerve mechanism.' Moenssens and Ibau, Scientific Evidence in Criminal Cases 2d Ed. (Foundation Press, 1978) pp. 228–229." Respondent's Brief at 22, *Lyons,* 461 U.S. 95 (1983) (No. 81–1064).

13. "Los Angeles police officers generally and callously refer to applying the stranglehold as causing the victim to 'do the chicken.' Deposition of City's expert Jarvis Ex 44:93." Respondent's Brief at 23, *Lyons,* 461 U.S. 95 (1983) (No. 81–1064).

14. Respondent's Brief at 15–21, *Lyons,* 461 U.S. 95 (1983) (No. 81–1064).

15. Respondent's Brief at 15, *Lyons,* 461 U.S. 95 (1983) (No. 81–1064).

16. Respondent's Brief at 25–27, *Lyons,* 461 U.S. 95 (1983) (No. 81–1064).

17. Respondent's Brief at 26, *Lyons,* 461 U.S. 95 (1983) (No. 81–1064).

18. *Lyons,* 461 U.S. at 105.

19. *Id.* at 111.

20. Gene Nichol, Jr., *Rethinking Standing,* 72 CAL. L. REV. 68, 100–101 (1982).

21. For an excellent development of this and other criticisms, *see* Richard H. Fallon, Jr., *Some Confusions About Due Process, Judicial Review, and Constitutional Remedies,* 93 COLUM. L. REV. 309 (1993).

22. *See* 461 U.S. at 137 (Marshall, J., dissenting).

23. *Warth v. Seldin,* 422 U.S. 490, 498 (1975).

24. *See* Antonin Scalia, *The Doctrine of Standing as an Essential Element of the Separation of Powers,* 17 SUFFOLK L. REV. 881 (1983) (describing standing as a function of separation of powers).

25. 422 U.S. at 498.

26. 133 S.Ct. 1138, 1146 (2013).

27. *Raines v. Byrd,* 521 U.S. 811, 819 (1997).

28. *See also* Susan Bandes, *The Idea of a Case,* 42 STAN. L. REV. 227 (1990).

29. *Schlesinger v. Reservists Comm. to Stop the War,* 418 U.S. 208, 227 (1974).

30. "To establish Article III standing, an injury must be 'concrete, particularized, and actual or imminent; fairly traceable to the challenged action; and redressable by a favorable ruling.'" *Clapper v. Amnesty Int'l USA,* 133 S.Ct. at 1147.

31. *Curtis v. New Haven,* 726 F.2d 65 (2d Cir. 1984) (no standing to challenge police use of mace); *Brown v. Edwards,* 721 F.2d 1442 (5th Cir. 1984) (no standing to challenge state policy awarding money to constables for each arrest they made that led to a conviction); *Jones v. Bowman,* 664 F. Supp. 433 (N.D. Ind. 1987) (no standing to challenge strip searches of women performed by county jail); *John Does 1–100 v. Boyd,* 613 F. Supp. 1514 (D. Minn. 1985) (no standing to challenge strip searches of people brought to the city jail for minor offenses).

32. *Clapper,* 133 S.Ct. 1138 (2013).

33. 50 U.S.C. §1881a.

34. 133 S.Ct. at 1159–1160.

35. *Id.* at 1160 (Breyer, J., dissenting).

36. *Id.* at 1150.

37. *Id.* at 1165 (Breyer, J., dissenting).

38. *Allen v. Wright*, 468 U.S. 737 (1984).

39. *Allen* 468 U.S. at 755–756. *Allen* also denied standing based on failure to meet the causation requirement.

40. *Id.* at 757 (citations omitted).

41. *Id.* at 753 n.19.

42. 422 U.S. 490, 499 (1975) (emphasis added) (citations omitted); *Gladstone, Realtors v. Bellwood*, 441 U.S. 91, 99–100 (1979). However, in a subsequent decision the Supreme Court indicated that the ban on citizen standing is constitutional not prudential. *Lujan v. Defenders of Wildlife*, 504 U.S. 555 (1992). *Lujan* is discussed below.

43. *United States v. Students Challenging Regulatory Agency Procedures*, 412 U.S. 669, 686–688 (1973).

44. *FEC v. Akins*, 524 U.S. 11, 24 (1998).

45. 262 U.S. 447 (1923). In a companion case, *Massachusetts v. Mellon*, 262 U.S. 447 (1923), the Supreme Court denied the state of Massachusetts standing to attack the constitutionality of the Maternity Act.

46. *Frothingham*, 262 U.S. at 487.

47. *Id.* at 488.

48. 302 U.S. 633 (1937).

49. *Id.* at 634.

50. 392 U.S. 83 (1968).

51. *Id.* at 101; at 119–120 (Harlan, J., dissenting).

52. *Id.* at 102.

53. *Id.*

54. *Id.*

55. *Id.*

56. *Id.* at 105.

57. *See* Kenneth Davis, *The Liberalized Law of Standing*, 37 U. Chi. L. Rev. 450 (1970). Kenneth Davis, *Standing: Taxpayers and Others*, 35 U. Chi. L. Rev. 601 (1968).

58. 418 U.S. 166 (1974).

59. *Id.* at 175 (citations omitted).

60. *Id.* at 179.

61. *Id.* at 208 (1974).

62. *Id.* at 227.

63. 454 U.S. 464 (1982).

64. *Id.* at 485–486.

65. *Id.* at 479.

66. *Id.* at 480.

67. Subsequent to *Valley Forge*, the Court reaffirmed *Flast v. Cohen* in *Bowen v. Kendrick*, 487 U.S. 589 (1988). The Court allowed taxpayer standing to challenge the constitutionality of the Adolescent Family Life Act, which provided grants that required specific types of counseling to prevent teenage pregnancy. The Court explained that it had continually adhered to *Flast* and the narrow exception it had created for taxpayer standing to challenge government expenditures that violate the Establishment Clause.

68. 551 U.S. 587 (2007).

69. *Id.* at 605.

70. *Id.* at 618 (Scalia, J., dissenting).

71. The Court also rejected taxpayer standing in *DaimlerChrysler Corp. v. Cuno,* 547 U.S. 332 (2006), where it rejected the argument that *Flast* should be extended to allow taxpayer standing to challenge government actions which allegedly violate the dormant Commerce Clause. The Court dismissed a challenge to a state program to give tax benefits to businesses relocating from out of state.

72. 131 S.Ct. 1436 (2011).

73. *Id.* at 1147.

74. *Id.* at 1450 (Scalia, J., concurring).

75. *Id.* at 1450 (Kagan, J., dissenting).

76. *See, e.g., United States v. Richardson,* 418 U.S. 166, 192 (1974) (Powell, J., concurring).

77. *United Pub. Workers v. Mitchell,* 330 U.S. 75, 90–91 (1947).

78. 369 U.S. 186, 204 (1962).

79. *Singleton v. Wulff,* 428 U.S. 106, 113–114 (1976). For an excellent explanation of this fairness argument, *see* Lea Brilmayer, *The Jurisprudence of Article III: Perspectives on the "Case or Controversy" Requirement,* 93 HARV. L. REV. 297, 306–310 (1979).

80. Ideological plaintiffs are sometimes referred to as non-Hohfeldian plaintiffs. *See, e.g.,* Richard Fallon, *Of Justiciability, Remedies and Public Law Litigation: Notes on the Jurisprudence of Lyons,* 59 N.Y.U. L. REV. 1, 3 n.12 (1984). The term originates from the scholar Wesley Newcomb Hohfeld, who devised a taxonomy of legal rights. *See* Wesley Hohfeld, *Some Fundamental Legal Conceptions as Applied in Judicial Reasoning,* 23 YALE L.J. 16 (1913). Because the claims of ideological plaintiffs do not fit into any of Hohfeld's categories of legal rights, such plaintiffs are termed "non-Hohfeldian."

81. Martin Redish, *Judicial Review and the Political Question,* 79 Nw. U.L. REV. 1033 (1985).

82. *Id.* at 1045–1046.

83. 369 U.S. 186 (1962).

84. *Id.* at 217.

85. Bickel, THE LEAST DANGEROUS BRANCH at 184.

86. 418 U.S. 683 (1974).

87. *See, e.g.,* Erwin Chemerinsky, *Cases Under the Guarantee Clause Should Be Justiciable,* 65 U. COLO. L. REV. 849 (1994); Deborah Merritt, *The Guarantee Clause and State Autonomy: Federalism for a Third Century,* 88 COLUM. L. REV. 1 (1988) (arguing that the Guarantee Clause should be seen as a basis for protecting federalism and states' rights from congressional interference); *but see* Ann Althouse, *Time for Federal Courts to Enforce the Guarantee Clause?—A Response to Professor Chemerinsky,* 65 U. COLO. L. REV. 881 (1994); Louise Weinberg, *Political Questions and the Guarantee Clause,* 65 U. COLO. L. REV. 887 (1994).

88. *New York v. United States,* 505 U.S. 144 (1992).

89. 48 U.S. (7 How.) 1 (1849).

90. *Id.* at 10.

91. *Id.* at 13–14.

92. There are instances in which the Supreme Court decided cases on the merits under the republican form of government clause, upholding the challenged government action. *See, e.g., Forsyth v. Hammond,* 166 U.S. 506 (1897); Foster v. Kansas ex rel. Johnson, 112 U.S. 201 (1884); Kennard v. Louisiana ex rel. Morgan, 92 U.S. 480 (1875).

93. 178 U.S. 548 (1900).

94. 223 U.S. 118 (1912).

95. *Id.* at 151.

96. 328 U.S. 549 (1946).

97. *Id.* at 552–554.

98. *Id.* at 556.

99. 339 U.S. 276, 277 (1950).

100. *See, e.g., Gomillion v. Lightfoot,* 364 U.S. 339 (1960) (redrawing of Tuskegee, Alabama, districts to disenfranchise blacks); *Terry v. Adams,* 345 U.S. 461 (1953); *Smith v. Allwright,* 321 U.S. 649 (1944) (discrimination against blacks in political parties).

101. 369 U.S. 186 (1962).

102. *Id.* at 223–226.

103. *See Reynolds v. Sims,* 377 U.S. 533 (1964) (articulating the one-person one-vote standard).

104. Chief Justice Earl Warren remarked that the most important decisions during his tenure on the Court were those ordering reapportionment. *The Warren Court: An Editorial Preface,* 67 MICH. L. REV. 219, 220 (1968).

105. *See, e.g.,* Louis Pollak, *Judicial Power and the Politics of the People,* 72 YALE L.J. 81, 88 (1962).

106. 541 U.S. 267 (2004).

107. 478 U.S. 109 (1986).

108. 548 U.S. 399 (2006).

109. *Id.* at 414.

110. *Id.* at 493 (Roberts, C.J., concurring in part, concurring in the judgment in part, and dissenting in part).

111. For a defense of this use of the political question doctrine, *see* Theodore Blumoff, *Judicial Review, Foreign Affairs, and Legislative Standing,* 25 GA. L. REV. 227 (1991).

112. 246 U.S. 297, 302 (1918). *See also Chi. & S. Air Lines, Inc. v. Waterman S.S. Corp.,* 333 U.S. 103, 111 (1948).

113. 369 U.S. at 211.

114. *See, e.g., Dames & Moore v. Regan,* 453 U.S. 654 (1981); *United States v. Pink,* 315 U.S. 203, 229 (1942); *Belmont,* 301 U.S. at 330.

115. *See, e.g., Missouri v. Holland,* 252 U.S. 416, 433 (1920) (approving the constitutionality of a treaty with Great Britain concerning migratory birds).

116. 132 S.Ct. 1421 (2012).

117. *Id.* at 1430.

118. *Zivotofsky v. Kerry*, 135 S.Ct. 2076 (2015).

119. 262 U.S. 51 (1923).

120. *Id.* at 57.

121. *See, e.g., Martin v. Mott*, 25 U.S. (12 Wheat.) 19, 30 (1827).

122. *See, e.g., Belmont*, 301 U.S. at 330 (Court confirmed President's power to recognize and assume diplomatic relations with the Soviet Union); *Oetjen v. Cent. Leather Co.*, 246 U.S. 297 (1918). The Court also has held that the recognition of Indian tribes is left to the political process. *See, e.g., United States v. Sandoval*, 231 U.S. 28, 45–46 (1913).

123. *See, e.g., In re* Baiz, 135 U.S. 403 (1890).

124. 184 U.S. 270 (1902).

125. 444 U.S. 996 (1979).

126. *Id.* at 1004. Justice Powell concurred in the result, arguing that the matter was not yet ripe because Congress had not taken a position on the issue. *Id.* at 997 (Powell, J., concurring in the judgment).

127. *See, e.g., Holtzman v. Schlesinger*, 484 F.2d 1307, 1309 (3d Cir.), *cert. denied*, 416 U.S. 936 (1973); *Da Casta v. Laird*, 471 F.2d 1146, 1147 (2d Cir. 1973); *Sarnoff v. Connally*, 457 F.2d 809, 810 (9th Cir. 1972), *cert. denied*, 409 U.S. 929 (1972); *Orlando v. Laird*, 443 F.2d 1039, 1043 (2d Cir.), *cert. denied*, 404 U.S. 869 (1971); *Simmons v. United States*, 406 F.2d 456, 460 (5th Cir.), *cert. denied*, 395 U.S. 982 (1969); *see also* Anthony D'Amato and Robert O'Neil, THE JUDICIARY AND VIETNAM 51–58 (1972) (description of cases concerning the Vietnam War as a political question); Louis Henkin, *Vietnam in the Courts of the United States: Political Questions*, 63 AM. J. INTL. L. 284 (1969).

128. *See, e.g., Crockett v. Reagan*, 720 F.2d 1355 (D.C. Cir. 1983), *cert. denied*, 467 U.S. 1251 (1984); *Sanchez-Espinoza v. Reagan*, 770 F.2d 202 (D.C. Cir. 1985); *Lowry v. Reagan*, 676 F. Supp. 333 (D.D.C. 1987); *but cf. Ramirez de Arellano v. Weinberger*, 745 F.2d 1500 (D.C. Cir. 1984) (holding justiciable a claim by a United States citizen that the federal government had taken his property in Honduras for the purpose of using it as a military training site; no challenge to the legality of the military activities was present).

129. *See Doe v. Bush*, 322 F.3d 109 (1st Cir. 2003).

130. 413 U.S. 1 (1973).

131. *Id.* at 8.

132. 143 U.S. 649 (1892).

133. 395 U.S. 486 (1969).

134. *Id.* at 506–512.

135. The Court relied on *Powell* to declare unconstitutional a state law that limited access to the ballot for candidates for the United States House of Representatives or the United States Senate after they had served a specified number of terms. *United States Term Limits v. Thornton*, 514 U.S. 779 (1995). The Court again emphasized that Article I sets the only permissible qualifications for a member of Congress.

136. 395 U.S. at 548.

137. *Id.* at 549.

138. 506 U.S. 224 (1993).

139. *Id.* at 234.

140. *Id.* at 233–237.

141. 5 U.S. (1 Cranch) 103 (1803).

142. A similar position is advocated in Redish, *Judicial Review and the Political Question.* For a defense of the political question doctrine, see Rachel E. Barkow, *More Supreme Than Court?: The Fall of the Political Question Doctrine and the Rise of Judicial Supremacy,* 102 COLUM. L. REV. 237 (2002).

143. Arthur S. Miller, *An Inquiry into the Relevance of the Intentions of the Founding Fathers, with Special Emphasis Upon the Doctrine of Separation of Powers,* 27 ARK. L. REV. 583, 600 (1973).

144. Paul Gewirtz, *The Courts, Congress, and Executive Policy-Making: Notes on Three Doctrines,* 40 LAW AND CONTEMP. PROBLEMS 46, 79 (1976).

145. 369 U.S. 186, 211 (1962).

146. *Goldwater v. Carter,* 444 U.S. 999, 1007 (1979) (Brennan, J., dissenting).

147. *Chi. & S. Air Lines,* 333 U.S. 103, 111 (1948).

148. 444 U.S. 996 (1979).

149. 533 U.S. 98 (2000).

150. *Id.* at 128–129 (Stevens, J., dissenting).

151. *See* Jeffrey M. Jones, *Hispanics, Whites Rate Bush Positively, While Blacks Are Much More Negative,* GALLUP NEWS SERVICE, June 21, 2001.

152. 422 U.S. 490 (1975).

153. 504 U.S. 555 (1992).

154. 16 U.S.C. §1540(g).

155. For a discussion of these implications, *see* Cass Sunstein, *What's Standing After Lujan? Of Citizen Suits, "Injuries," and Article III,* 91 MICH. L. REV. 163 (1992).

156. 33 U.S.C. §1365(e).

157. 30 U.S.C. §1270.

158. 42 U.S.C. §300j-8.

159. 42 U.S.C. §6972.

160. 42 U.S.C. §7604.

161. 42 U.S.C. §4911.

162. 42 U.S.C. §6305.

163. 524 U.S. 11 (1998).

164. *Id.* at 30.

165. *Id.* at 22.

FIVE The Great Writ

1. Cal. Penal Code §488 (West 1990).

2. *Id.* at §490.

3. *Id.* at §666 (West 1999 and Supp. 2003).

4. *Andrade v. Attorney Gen. of Cal.,* 270 F.3d 742, 746 (9th Cir. 2001) (citing Cal. Penal Code §§18, 666).

5. Cal Penal Code §1170.1 (a) (West 1999).

6. Career Criminal Punishment Act, ch. 12, 1994 State. 71 (codified at Cal. Penal Code §667 (West 1999)). California's "Three Strikes" law was initially adopted by the California Legislature as a statute, *see id.,* and then approved by the voters as an initiative, Proposition 184, approved by voters, Gen. Elec. (Nov. 8, 1994) (codified at Cal. Penal Code §1170.12 (West Supp. 2003)).

7. Cal. Penal Code §667 (e)(2)(A) (West 1999); *id.* §1170.12 (c)(2)(a) (West Supp. 2003).

8. *Id.* §§667 (d), 1170.12 (b) (defining "prior conviction of a felony").

9. *See id.* §§667 (e)(2)(A), 1170.12 (c)(2)(A) (subjecting defendants to a possible sentence of life imprisonment upon their third "felony" conviction, without qualifying the term felony); *see also Lockyer v. Andrade,* 123 S.Ct. 1166, 1170 (2003) ("Under California's three strikes law, any felony can constitute the third strike, and can thus subject a defendant to a term of 25 years to life in prison").

10. *Andrade,* 270 F.3d at 749 (9th Cir. 2001).

11. *Id.* at 750.

12. *Id.*

13. Erwin Chemerinsky, *The Supreme Court's Blockbuster Term,* 39 TRIAL 72 (2003).

14. *Andrade v. Roe,* No. CV 98–6776-CAS, 1999 U.S. Dist. LEXIS 23176, at *2 (C.D. Cal. Jan. 11, 1999) (noting the judgment in the California Court of Appeal).

15. *People v. Andrade,* No. S062030, 1997 Cal. LEXIS 4637, at *1 (Cal. July 23, 1997).

16. *Andrade v. Roe,* 1999 U.S. Dist. LEXIS 23176, at *2.

17. *Id.* at *1.

18. *Andrade,* 270 F.3d at 746 (9th Cir. 2001).

19. *Id.* at 767.

20. *Lockyer v. Andrade,* 535 U.S. 969 (2002).

21. *Ewing v. California,* 123 S. Ct. 1179 (2003).

22. *Solem v. Helm,* 463 U.S. 277 (1983).

23. *Id.* at 288.

24. *Id.* at 292.

25. *Harmelin v. Mich.,* 501 U.S. 957 (1991).

26. *Id.* at 996–997 (Kennedy, O'Connor, and Souter, J.J., concurring in part and concurring in the judgment); *id.* at 1009 (White, Blackmun, and Stevens, J.J., dissenting); *id.* at 1027–1028 (Marshall, J., dissenting).

27. *Id.* at 996 (Kennedy, J., concurring in part and concurring in the judgment).

28. *Id.* at 1018–1019 (White, J., dissenting); *id.* at 1027 (Marshall, J., dissenting); *id.* at 1028 (Stevens, J., dissenting).

29. *Id.* at 1002 (Kennedy, J., concurring).

30. *Id.* at 1004 (Kennedy, J., concurring).

31. 270 F.3d 743, 762 (9th Cir. 2001).

32. *See United States v. Bajakajian,* 524 U.S. 321, 336 (1998); *Pulley v. Harris,* 465 U.S. 37, 42–43 (1984); *Stanford v. Ky.,* 492 U.S. 361, 371 (1989); *Txo Prod. Corp. v. Alliance Res. Corp.,* 509 U.S. 443, 457 (1993).

33. *Lockyer v. Andrade,* 538 U.S. 63, 72 (2003).

34. *Bell v. Cone,* 535 U.S. 685, 694 (2002).

35. *Lockyer,* 538 U.S. at 74.

36. *Rummel v. Estelle,* 445 U.S. 263 (1980).

37. Pub. L. No. 104–132, April 24, 1996.

38. Stephen Reinhardt, *The Demise of Habeas Corpus and the Rise of Qualified Immunity: The Court's Ever Increasing Limitations on the Development and Enforcement of Constitutional Rights and Some Particularly Unfortunate Consequences,* 113 MICH. L. REV. 1219 (2015).

39. W. Duker, A CONSTITUTIONAL HISTORY OF HABEAS CORPUS (1980) at 3.

40. For an excellent history of habeas corpus, *see id.*

41. 3 BLACKSTONE'S COMMENTARIES 129 (1791).

42. U.S. CONST. art. I, §9, cl. 2.

43. Judiciary Act of 1789, ch. 20, 1 Stat. 73.

44. 28 U.S.C. §2254.

45. Reinhardt, *The Demise of Habeas Corpus,* at 1223.

46. I summarize this debate in Erwin Chemerinsky, ENHANCING GOVERNMENT: FEDERALISM FOR THE 21ST CENTURY 171–177 (2008).

47. *See, e.g.,* Paul Carrington, *Judicial Independence and Democratic Accountability in Highest State Courts,* 61 LAW & CONTEMP. PROBS. 79 (1998); Burt Neuborne, *The Myth of Parity,* 90 HARV. L. REV. 1105, 1115–1130 (1977); Gary Peller, *In Defense of Federal Habeas Corpus Relitigation,* 16 HARV. C.R.-C.L. L. REV. 579, 677–685 (1982); Donald A. Ziegler, *Federal Court Reform of State Criminal Justice Systems: A Reassessment of the Younger Doctrine from a Modern Perspective,* 19 U.C. DAVIS L. REV. 31, 46–48 (1985).

48. See, e.g., John Blume and Theodore Eisenberg, *Judicial Politics, Death Penalty Appeals, and Case Selection: An Empirical Study,* 72 S. CAL. L. REV. 465, 498–499 (1999); see also Richard W. Brooks and Steven Raphael, *Criminal Law: Life Terms or Death Sentences: The Uneasy Relationship Between Judicial Elections and Capital Punishment,* 92 J. CRIM. L. & CRIMINOLOGY 609, 610 (2002) ("conditional on being found guilty of murder, criminal defendants were approximately 15% more likely to be sentenced to death when the sentence was issued during the judge's election year"); Amanda Frost and Stefanie A. Lindquist, *Countering the Majoritarian Difficulty,* 96 VA. L. REV. 719, 750, 793–795 (2010) ("elected state supreme court justices are more likely to affirm jury verdicts in favor of the death penalty during the two years prior to their reelections than at other times during their terms in office").

49. *See, e.g.,* Richard A. Posner, THE FEDERAL COURTS: CRISIS AND REFORM 144 (1985) ("It is widely believed that federal judges are, on average (an important qualifier), of higher quality than their state counterparts."); Neuborne, *The Myth of Parity,* at 1121–1125; Martin H. Redish, *Judicial Parity, Litigant Choice, and Democratic Theory: A Comment on Federal Jurisdiction and Constitutional Rights,* 36 UCLA L. REV. 329 (1988) (arguing that institutional differences make federal courts superior for constitutional adjudication).

50. Erwin Chemerinsky, *Parity Reconsidered: Redefining a Role for the Federal Judiciary*, 36 UCLA L. Rev. 233 (1988).

51. Habeas corpus also is available to federal prisoners under 28 U.S.C. §2255. My focus in this chapter is on the availability of habeas corpus for state prisoners, though many of the same restrictions apply to both state and federal prisoners bringing habeas corpus petitions.

52. 428 U.S. 465 (1976).

53. *Id.* at 494.

54. *Id.* at 495.

55. *Id.* at 490–491.

56. 344 U.S. 443 (1953).

57. 428 U.S. at 493–494 n.35.

58. *Id.*

59. For an excellent article criticizing *Stone v. Powell* and arguing in favor of allowing relitigation of issues on habeas corpus, *see* Peller, *In Defense of Federal Habeas Corpus Relitigation*.

60. *See* 28 U.S.C. §§2241, 2254.

61. *See Stone v. Powell*, 428 U.S. at 535–536 (Brennan, J., dissenting). For a development of the separation of powers criticism of Stone v. Powell, *see* Mark Tushnet, *Constitutional and Statutory Analysis in the Law of Federal Jurisdiction*, 25 UCLA L. Rev. 1301 (1978).

62. *See, e.g.,* Neuborne *The Myth of Parity*; Peller, *In Defense of Federal Habeas Corpus Relitigation*, at 665–669.

63. *Schneckloth v. Bustamonte*, 412 U.S. 218, 257–258 (1973). *See generally* Henry Friendly, *Is Innocence Irrelevant? Collateral Attack on Criminal Judgments*, 38 U. Chi. L. Rev. 142 (1970) (arguing for a limit of habeas corpus to cases where there is a colorable showing of innocence).

64. *Stone v. Powell*, 428 U.S. at 524 (Brennan, J., dissenting); *see also* Robbins and Sanders, *Judicial Integrity, the Appearance of Justice, and the Great Writ of Habeas Corpus: How to Kill Two Thirds (or More) with One Stone*, 15 Am. Crim. L. Rev. 63 (1977).

65. 372 U.S. 391 (1963).

66. *Id.* at 428.

67. *Id.* at 438.

68. 411 U.S. 233 (1973).

69. 425 U.S. 536 (1976).

70. 433 U.S. 72 (1977).

71. *Id.* at 88–91.

72. *Id.* at 89.

73. *Id.* at 90.

74. *Id.* at 104 (Brennan, J., dissenting).

75. Judith Resnik, *Tiers*, 57 S. Cal. L. Rev. 837, 897 (1984) (The sandbagging argument "assumes a fantastically risk-prone pool of defendants and attorneys. Given that the success rate at trial and on appeal, while low, is greater than the success rate on ha-

beas corpus, the odds are against being able to 'sandbag' in a first procedure and emerge victorious in a second").

76. *Wainwright v. Sykes*, 433 U.S. at 105 (Brennan, J., dissenting). *See also* Robert Cover and Alexander Aleinikoff, *Dialectical Federalism: Habeas Corpus and the Court*, 86 YALE L.J. 1035, 1069–1086 (1977) (analyzing binding defendants to attorneys' errors).

77. 501 U.S. 722 (1991).

78. *Id.* at 750.

79. *See* Jill Smolowe, *Must This Man Die? (Convicted Killer Roger Keith Coleman)* TIME MAGAZINE, May 18, 1992 at 40.

80. 477 U.S. 478 (1986).

81. *Id.* at 527.

82. 506 U.S. 390, 404 (1993).

83. *Id.* at 417.

84. *Id.* at 419 (O'Connor, J., concurring).

85. *Id.* at 427.

86. *Id.* at 419.

87. *Id.* at 427 (Scalia, J., dissenting).

88. *Id.* at 427–428.

89. 489 U.S. 288 (1989). For a discussion of the impact of *Teague, see* Marc Arkin, *The Prisoner's Dilemma: Life in the Lower Federal Courts After Teague v. Lane,* 69 N.C. L. REV. 371 (1991); Vivian Berger, *Justice Delayed or Justice Denied: A Comment on Recent Proposals to Reform Death Penalty Habeas Corpus,* 90 COLUM. L. REV. 1665 (1990); David R. Dow, *Teague and Death: The Impact of Current Retroactivity Doctrine on Criminal Defendants,* 19 HASTINGS CONSTIT. L.Q. 23 (1991); Barry Friedman, *Habeas and Hubris,* 45 VAND. L. REV. 797 (1992); Joseph Hoffmann, *Retroactivity and the Great Writ: How Congress Should Respond to Teague v. Lane,* B.Y.U. L. REV. 183 (1990); Mary C. Hutton, *Retroactivity in the States: The Impact of Teague v. Lane on State Postconviction Remedies,* 44 ALA. L. REV. 421 (1993).

90. 489 U.S. at 300.

91. As described below, this also is the effect of 28 U.S.C. §2254(d), which says that a federal court can grant relief only if the state court decision is contrary to or an unreasonable application of clearly established law as articulated by the Supreme Court.

92. 536 U.S. 584 (2002).

93. In *Schriro v. Summerlin,* 542 U.S. 348 (2004), the Court held that the requirement that a death sentence be imposed by a jury does not apply retroactively.

94. *Id.* at 301.

95. The test for retroactivity used by the Court is found in Justice Harlan's opinion in *Mackey v. United States,* 401 U.S. 667, 675 (1971). The Court in *Teague* recognized that retroactivity is rare. 489 U.S. 288, 304.

96. 489 U.S. 288, 307.

97. *Id.*

98. *Id.* at 311.

99. In his dissenting opinion, Justice Brennan offers a long list of criminal proce-dure rights that were recognized for the first time on habeas corpus. *See id.* at 334–335 (Brennan, J., dissenting).

100. *See* Larry W. Yackle, *The Habeas Hagioscope,* 66 S. CAL. L. REV. 2331 (1993); Susan Bandes, *Taking Justice To Its Logical Extreme: A Comment on Teague v. Lane,* 66 S. CAL. L. REV. 2453 (1993); Barry Friedman, *Pas De Deux: The Supreme Court and Ha-beas Corpus,* 66 S. CAL. L. REV. 2467 (1993).

101. *Id.* at 341 (Brennan, J., concurring in part and dissenting in part).

102. 494 U.S. 484 (1990).

103. 497 U.S. 227 (1990).

104. 472 U.S. 320 (1985).

105. *Id.* at 236.

106. *Id.* at 231.

107. *Cullen v. Pinholster,* 131 S.Ct. 1388, 1395 (2011).

108. *Id.* at 1395.

109. *See Id.*

110. *Id.* at 1396.

111. *People v. Pinholster,* 1 Cal. 4th 865, 909–911, 942–945 (1992).

112. *Pinholster v. Ayers,* 590 F.3d 651, 659 (9th Cir. 2009).

113. *See Pinholster v. Ayers,* 590 F.3d at 660.

114. *See Id.* at 658.

115. *See Id.* at 659–662 for a full description of the evidence presented during the hearing.

116. *See Cullen v. Pinholster,* 131 S.Ct. at 1397.

117. *See Id.*

118. *See Id.* at 1411.

119. *See Id.* at 1398.

120. Erwin Chemerinsky, *Closing the Courthouse Doors,* NATIONAL LAW JOURNAL (June 21, 2011).

121. Reinhardt, *The Demise of Habeas Corpus,* at 1238.

122. *Id.* at 1239.

123. *Id.*

124. 499 U.S. 467 (1991).

125. 377 U.S. 201 (1964).

126. 499 U.S. at 490–491.

127. *Id.* at 493.

128. *Id.* at 506 (Marshall, J., dissenting).

129. Antiterrorism and Effective Death Penalty Act of 1996, §106(b), 28 U.S.C. §2244(3)(A).

130. *Id.* The Supreme Court ruled that a habeas petition filed after an earlier peti-tion was dismissed for failure to exhaust is not barred as a second or successive petition. *Slack v. McDaniel,* 529 U.S. 473 (2000).

131. 533 U.S. 656 (2001), at 656.

132. 533 U.S. 656 (2001).

133. 498 U.S. 39 (1990).

134. 28 U.S.C. §2244 (b)(2)(A).

135. 533 U.S. at 657.

136. 28 U.S.C. §2244 (d)(1).

137. *Rose v. Lundy*, 455 U.S. 509, 522 (1982).

138. 529 U.S. 362 (2000).

139. *Id.* at 377–378.

140. *Id.* at 405.

141. *Id.* at 409.

142. *Id.* at 410.

143. 538 U.S. 63 (2003).

144. *Id.* at 73.

145. 463 U.S. 277 (1983).

146. *See also Yarborough v. Alvarado*, 541 U.S. 652 (2004) (finding that the standard under §2254(d) was not met).

147. S.Ct. 770 (2011).

148. *Id.* at 784.

149. *Id.* at 787 (emphasis added).

150. Reinhardt, *The Demise of Habeas Corpus*, at 1229.

151. Fred L. Cheesman II, Nancy J. King, and Brian J. Ostrom, Final Technical Report: Habeas Litigation in U.S. District Courts: An Empirical Study of Habeas Corpus Cases Filed by State Prisoners Under the Antiterrorism and Effective Death Penalty Act of 1996 51–52 (2007).

152. *Brown v. Allen*, 344 U.S. 443, 456–457 (1953).

153. *Gibbs v. Frank*, 387 F.3d 268, 278 (3d Cir. 2004) (Nygaard, J., concurring) ("To the extent AEDPA was actually intended by Congress to deny access by habeas petitioners to the protections of the Bill of Rights subject to a condition precedent, in my view this preclusion should be considered a suspension of the writ"); *Irons v. Carey*, 479 F.3d 658, 665–670 (9th Cir. 2007) (Noonan, J., concurring) (summarizing the problematic nature of post-AEDPA review).

154. Alex Kozinski, *Criminal Law 2.0*, 44 Geo. L.J. Ann. Rev. Crim. Proc. iii, xlii (2015).

155. Friendly, *Is Innocence Irrelevant?*; Nancy J. King and Joseph Hoffmann, Habeas for the 21st Century: Uses, Abuses, and the Future of the Great Writ (2011).

156. *See, e.g.*, Richard Broughton, *Habeas Corpus and the Safeguards of Federalism*, 2 Geo. J.L. & Pub. Pol'y 109 (2004).

six Opening the Federal Courthouse Doors

1. *Ashcroft v. Iqbal*, 556 U.S. 662, 668 (2009).

2. *Id.* at 668.

3. *Id.*

4. Dept. of Justice, Office of Inspector General, *The September 11 Detainees: A Review of the Treatment of Aliens Held on Immigration Charges in Connection with the Investigation of the September 11 Attacks* 1, 142 (Apr. 2003).

5. *Id.* at 143.

6. *Id.* at 144.

7. *Id.*

8. *Id.* at 146.

9. *Id.* at 1.

10. *Id.* at 111.

11. *Iqbal,* 556 U.S. at 662.

12. *Conley v. Gibson,* 355 U.S. 41 (1957).

13. *Id.* at 45–46.

14. 550 U.S. 544 (2007).

15. *Id.* at 563.

16. *Id.* at 577–578 (Stevens, J., dissenting).

17. 556 U.S. at 678.

18. *Id.*

19. Notice Pleading Restoration Act, S. 4054, 111th Cong. (2010).

20. Raymond H. Brescia, *The Iqbal Effect: The Impact of New Pleading Standards in Employment and Housing Discrimination Litigation,* 100 Ky. L.J. 235, 241 (2012).

21. *Id.* at 284. He wrote: In conclusion, "this study reveals that two things appear to be happening. First, these types of [housing and employment] discrimination cases are being dismissed at a higher rate since Iqbal. Second at the same time, judges appear to be mostly ignoring the text of Iqbal and the instructions the Court gave for how district courts should apply the plausibility standard. Thus, courts are using Iqbal, but not its plausibility standard, to dismiss certain classes of cases at a higher rate." *Id.* at 286.

22. Patricia Hatamyar Moore, *An Updated Quantitative Study of Iqbal's Impact on 12(B)(6) Motions,* 46 Rich. L. Rev. 603, 618 (2012).

23. *Id.* at 619.

24. *Id.* at 623. A study by the Federal Judicial Center came to an opposite conclusion and did not find this effect of *Twombly* and *Iqbal. See* Joe S. Cecil, George W. Cort, Margaret S. Williams, and Jared J. Bataillon, *Motions to Dismiss for Failure to State a Claim After Iqbal: Report to the Judicial Conference Advisory Committee on Civil Rules,* Federal Judicial Center (March 2011). Professor Moore, however, pointed out significant methodological problems with this study. Overall, the article finds that the FJC's study was underinclusive in its methods for collecting cases for its database. *Id.* at 633. "Most critically, the FJC excluded all cases brought by pro se plaintiffs (which constitute 29% of my database and 26% of all civil cases in federal district court). The FJC also excluded all cases in which the 12(b)(6) motion was granted on the basis of sovereign or qualified immunity (as in Iqbal itself)." *Id.* at 634. "Further, the FJC database is limited to orders entered in two six-month periods from twenty-three of the ninety-four district courts." *Id.* at 634–635.

25. *Cohens v. Virginia,* 19 U.S. (6 Wheat.) 264, 404 (1821). *Accord* Bacon v. Rutland R.R., 232 U.S. 134, 137 (1914); Ex parte Young, 209 U.S. 123, 143 (1908).

26. Martin H. Redish, *Abstention, Separation of Powers and the Limits of the Judicial Function,* 94 YALE L.J. 71, 76 (1984).

27. U.S. 444 (1969).

28. *Younger v. Harris,* 401 U.S. 37, 41 (1971).

29. *Id.* at 42.

30. *Id.* at 43–44.

31. *Id.* at 44.

32. *Id.*

33. *Id.* at 54. Justice Black stated: "Because our holding rests on the absence of the factors necessary under equitable principles to justify federal intervention, we have no occasion to consider whether 28 U.S.C. §2283 . . . would in and of itself be controlling under the circumstances of this case."

34. 407 U.S. 225 (1972).

35. *Id.* at 242.

36. 341 U.S. 341 (1951).

37. Donald H. Zeigler, *Federal Court Reform of State Criminal Justice Systems: A Reassessment of the* Younger *Doctrine from a Modern Perspective,* 19 U.C. DAVIS L. REV. 31 (1985).

38. Douglas Laycock, *Federal Interference with State Prosecutions: The Need for Prospective Relief,* 1977 SUP. CT. REV. 193.

39. *Id.* at 194.

40. Michael Wells, *The Role of Comity in the Law of Federal Courts,* 60 N.C. L. REV. 59, 70 n.65 (1981).

41. Redish, *Abstention, Separation of Powers and the Limits of the Judicial Function,* at 345.

42. Aviam Soifer and H. C. Macgill, *The* Younger *Doctrine: Reconstructing Reconstruction,* 55 TEX. L. REV. 1141 (1977).

43. 401 U.S. 66 (1971).

44. 415 U.S. 452 (1974).

45. 422 U.S. 332 (1975).

46. *Id.* (citations omitted).

47. *Id.*

48. *Id.* at 357 (Stewart, J., dissenting).

49. *Id.*

50. Soifer and Macgill, *The* Younger *Doctrine* at 1141, 1192.

51. Owen M. Fiss, *Dombrowski,* 86 YALE L.J. 1103, 1135–1136 (1977).

52. *Id.* at 1135.

53. 420 U.S. 592 (1975).

54. Soifer and Macgill, *The* Younger *Doctrine,* at 1173. *See also* Jeffrey M. Shaman and Richard C. Turkington, Huffman v. Pursue, Ltd.*: The Federal Courthouse Door Closes Further,* 56 B.U. L. REV. 907 (1976).

55. 420 U.S. at 604.

56. *Id.*

57. *Id.*

58. *Id.* at 615 (Brennan, J., dissenting).

59. *Id.*

60. *Id.* at 613.

61. 431 U.S. 434 (1977).

62. *Id.* at 444.

63. *Id.*

64. *Id.*

65. 442 U.S. 415 (1979).

66. *Id.* at 423.

67. *Id.* at 425–426.

68. *Id.* at 436–437 (Stevens, J., dissenting).

69. 457 U.S. 423 (1982).

70. *Id.* at 428.

71. *Id.* at 432.

72. *Id.* at 434.

73. 477 U.S. 619 (1986).

74. *Id.* at 623.

75. *Id.* at 625 (citation omitted).

76. *Id.* at 627.

77. *Id.*

78. 134 S.Ct. 584, 591 (2013).

79. *Wal-Mart Stores, Inc. v. Dukes,* 131 S.Ct. 2541 (2011).

80. *Id.* at 2563 (2011) (Ginsburg, R., dissenting) (internal citations to record omitted).

81. *Id.* at 2555.

82. *Id.*

83. *Id.* at 2554.

84. *Id.*

85. *Circuit City Stores v. Adams,* 532 U.S. 105 (2001).

86. 9 U.S.C. §2.

87. Section 1 of the Federal Arbitration Act exempts "coverage all seamen, as well as all railroad employees, by virtue of fact that all seamen and all railroad employees are directly involved in the transport of goods in interstate commerce." 9 U.S.C. §1.

88. *Discover Bank v. Superior Court,* 36 Cal.4th 148, 30 Cal.Rptr.3d 76, 113 P.3d 1100 (2005).

89. 532 U.S. at 131–132 (Stevens, J., dissenting).

90. *AT&T Mobility LLC v. Concepcion,* 131 S.Ct. 1740 (2011).

91. Judith Resnik, *Failing Faith: Adjudicatory Procedure in Decline,* 53 U. CHI. L. REV. 494 (1986); Judith Resnik, *Managerial Judges,* 96 HARV. L. REV. 374 (1982).

92. *Discover Bank v. Superior Court,* 36 Cal. 4th 148, 160, 30 Cal. Rptr. 3d 76, 85, 113 P.3d 1100, 1108 (2005).

93. Section 2 of the Federal Arbitration Act (FAA) makes agreements to arbitrate "valid, irrevocable, and enforceable, save upon such grounds as exist at law or in equity for the revocation of any contract." 9 U.S.C. §2.

94. *AT&T Mobility,* 131 S.Ct. at 1752.

95. *Id.* at 1761 (Breyer, J., dissenting).

96. "The realistic alternative to a class action is not 17 million individual suits, but zero individual suits, as only a lunatic or a fanatic sues for $30." *Carnegie v. Household Int'l, Inc.,* 376 F.3d 656, 661 (7th Cir. 2004).

97. *Am. Express Co. v. Italian Colors Rest.,* 133 S.Ct. 2304 (2013).

98. *Id.* at 2308.

99. *Id.* at 2312.

100. *See Mitsubishi Motors Corp. v. Soler Chrysler-Plymouth, Inc.,* 473 U.S. 614 (1985).

101. S.Ct. 2313 (2013) (Kagan, J., dissenting).

102. *Id.*

103. *See* 473 U.S. at 637 n.19.

104. Notice Pleading Restoration Act of 2010, S. 4504, 111th Cong. (2010).

105. Open Access to the Courts Act of 2009, H.R. 4115, 111th Cong. (2009).

106. Arbitration Fairness Act of 2011, S. 987, 112th Cong. (2011) (as reported by S. Comm. on the Judiciary, May 12, 2011); Arbitration Fairness Act of 2011, H.R. 1873, 112th Cong. (2011) (as reviewed H. Comm. on the Judiciary and referred to the Sub-comm. on the Courts, the Commercial, and the Admin. law, June 1, 2011). Senator Al Franken is the Senator for Minnesota, Senator Richard Blumenthal is the Senator for Connecticut, and U.S Representative Hank Johnson is the Representative for Georgia. S. 987; see also H.R. 1873.

107. Arbitration Fairness Act of 2013, H.R. 1844, 113th Cong.; Arbitration Fairness Act of 2013, S. 878, 113th Cong. In 2012, Senators and House Representatives introduced a bill called the "Equal Employment Opportunity Restoration Act of 2012" (112 H.R. 5978; 112 H.R. 5978), which would "restore the effective use of group actions for claims arising under title VII of the Civil Rights Act of 1964, title I of the Americans with Dis-abilities Act of 1990, title V of the Rehabilitation Act of 1973, section 1977 of the Revised Statutes, and the Genetic Information Nondiscrimination Act of 2008, and for other purposes." Senators Blumenthal, Boxer, and Kerry are just a few of the many senators who introduced the bill. The bill was read twice in the Senate and referred to the House Judicial Committee.

SEVEN Enforcing the Constitution

1. The facts of this case are recited in Jane Mayer, THE DARK SIDE 282–287 (2008).

2. Complaint, *Khaled El-Masri v. Tenet*, 437 F. Supp. 2d 530 (E.D. Va. 2005) (No. 1:05cv1417), available at http:// www.aclu.org/safefree/extraordinaryrendition/222 11lgl20051206.html.

3. Mayer, The Dark Side, at 286–287.

4. *El-Masri v. United States*, 479 F.3d 296 (4th Cir. 2007).

5. *Id.* at 311.

6. *Id.* at 312–313.

7. 614 F.3d 1070 (9th Cir. 2010).

8. *Id.* at 1075.

9. These facts are taken directly from the Ninth Circuit's decision, which is based on the complaint. *Id.* at 1074.

10. *Id.*

11. *Id.*

12. *Id.* at 1076.

13. *Id.* at 1092.

14. *Id.* at 1094 (Hawkins, J., dissenting).

15. *Id.* at 1101.

16. S. Select Comm. on Intelligence, Committee Study of the Central Intelligence Agency's Detention and Interrogation Program Executive Summary (2014).

17. Alexander M. Bickel, The Least Dangerous Branch 18 (1962).

18. *United Pub. Workers v. Mitchell*, 330 U.S. 75, 90–91 (1947).

19. *Ariz. State Legis. v. Ariz. Indep. Redistricting Comm'n*, 135 S.Ct. 2652, 2695 (2015) (Scalia, J., dissenting), (quoting, *Allen v. Wright*, 468 U.S. 737, 752 (1984): "That doctrine of standing, that jurisdictional limitation upon our powers, does not have as its purpose (as the majority assumes) merely to assure that we will decide disputes in concrete factual contexts that enable 'realistic appreciation of the consequences of judicial action.' To the contrary. '[T]he law of Art. III standing is built on a single basic idea—the idea of separation of powers.' It keeps us minding our own business").

20. *See District of Columbia v. Heller*, 540 U.S. 570 (2008) (declaring unconstitutional a District of Columbia ordinance that prohibited ownership and possession of handguns).

Acknowledgments

This is a book that I have wanted to write for a long time. I have taught and written about these issues since 1980 and have litigated many cases about them. I have written about the topics in this book separately over the years in law review articles and essays and op-eds. But I wanted to write a book that looks at the doctrines from a unified perspective and that argues that the legal rules governing federal jurisdiction are inconsistent with the most important purpose of the federal courts: enforcing the Constitution.

I was thrilled when William Frucht, at Yale University Press, reacted with great enthusiasm to the idea of the book. He was wonderfully encouraging throughout my work on the book and then provided me a terrific edit of the manuscript, making it clearer and more accessible. Once more, my wonderful literary agent, Bonnie Nadell, handled all of the details.

I am very grateful to my research assistants—Gillian Kuhlmann, Jordan Liebman, and Laura Lively—who provided invaluable assistance. As always, I am tremendously appreciative to my administrative assistant, Brandy Stewart, who makes it possible for me to get this and everything else done.

I want to thank Joan Biskupic, Seth Davis, Catherine Fisk, Evan Lee, Bill Marshall, and Stephen Reinhardt for reading a draft manuscript and for their enormously helpful comments and suggestions. Each took time from a very busy schedule to offer me great ideas for revisions. I tried to implement all of their suggestions, but the book unquestionably would have been much better if I had followed their advice even more closely.

No book I write would be complete without acknowledging my family and how much their love and support means to me—Adam, Alex, Andrew, Catherine, Jeff, Kim, and Mara. They are truly the best part of my very blessed life.

This book is dedicated to my wife, Catherine Fisk. She helped me formulate the thesis for this book and encouraged me to write it. At times when I was pessimistic about it, she pushed me to keep going. She read every page and offered incisive comments that immeasurably improved my writing and my arguments. This book is dedicated to her with thanks and love more than words ever can express.

Index